PATHWAYS

Listening, Speaking, and Critical Thinking

1

Becky Tarver Chase

NATIONAL GEOGRAPHIC LEARNING | HEINLE CENGAGE Learning

Australia • Brazil • Japan • Korea • Singapore • Spain • United Kingdom • United States

Pathways 1
Listening, Speaking, and Critical Thinking
Becky Tarver Chase

Publisher: Sherrise Roehr

Executive Editor: Laura Le Dréan

Acquisitions Editor: Tom Jefferies

Senior Development Editor: Mary Whittemore

Development Editor: Paul Carne

Director of Global Marketing: Ian Martin

Marketing Manager: Caitlin Thomas

Marketing Manager: Katie Kelley

Marketing Manager: Emily Stewart

Director of Content and Media Production:
Michael Burggren

Content Project Manager: Daisy Sosa

Manufacturing Manager: Marcia Locke

Manufacturing Buyer: Marybeth Hennebury

Cover Design: Page 2 LLC

Cover Image: RAUL TOUZON/National
Geographic Image Collection

Interior Design: Page 2 LLC

Composition: Cenveo Publisher Services/
Nesbitt Graphics, Inc.

Library of Congress Control Number: 2011946077

International Student Edition:

ISBN-13: 978-1-111-35034-5

ISBN-10: 1-111-35034-5

U.S. Edition:

ISBN-13: 978-1-111-35036-9

ISBN-10: 1-111-35036-1

National Geographic Learning
20 Channel Center St.
Boston, MA 02210
USA

Cengage Learning is a leading provider of customized learning solutions with office locations around the globe, including Singapore, the United Kingdom, Australia, Mexico, Brazil, and Japan. Locate your local office at:
international.cengage.com/region

Cengage Learning products are represented in Canada by Nelson Education, Ltd.

Visit Heinle online at **elt.heinle.com**
Visit our corporate website at **www.cengage.com**

Printed in the United States of America
3 4 5 6 7 8 15 14 13

ACKNOWLEDGEMENTS

The author and publisher would like to thank the following reviewers:

UNITED STATES Adrianne Aiko Thompson, Miami Dade College, Miami, Florida; **Gokhan Alkanat**, Auburn University at Montgomery, Alabama; **Nikki Ashcraft**, Shenandoah University, VA; **Karin Avila-John**, University of Dayton, Ohio; **Shirley Baker**, Alliant International University, California; **John Baker**, Oakland Community College, Michigan; **Evina Baquiran Torres**, Zoni Language Centers, New York; **Michelle Bell**, University of South Florida, Florida; **Nancy Boyer**, Golden West College, California; **Carol Brutza**, Gateway Community College, Connecticut; **Sarah Camp**, University of Kentucky, Center for ESL, Kentucky; **Maria Caratini**, Eastfield College, Texas; **Ana Maria Cepero**, Miami Dade College, Miami, Florida; **Daniel Chaboya**, Tulsa Community College, Oklahoma; **Patricia Chukwueke**, English Language Institute – UCSD Extension, California; **Julia A. Correia**, Henderson State University, Connecticut; **Suzanne Crisci**, Bunker Hill Community College, Massachusetts; **Katie Crowder**, University of North Texas, Texas; **Lynda Dalgish**, Concordia College, New York; **Jeffrey Diluglio**, Center for English Language and Orientation Programs: Boston University, Massachusetts; **Tim DiMatteo**, Southern New Hampshire University, New Hampshire; **Scott Dirks**, Kaplan International Center at Harvard Square, Massachusetts; **Margo Downey**, Center for English Language and Orientation Programs: Boston University, Massachusetts; **John Drezek**, Richland College, Texas; **Anwar El-Issa**, Antelope Valley College, California; **Anrisa Fannin**, The International Education Center at Diablo Valley College, California; **Jennie Farnell**, University of Connecticut, American Language Program, Connecticut; **Mark Fisher**, Lone Star College, Texas; **Celeste Flowers**, University of Central Arkansas, Arkansas; **John Fox**, English Language Institute, Georgia; **Pradel R. Frank**, Miami Dade College, Florida; **Sally Gearheart**, Santa Rosa Jr. College, California; **Karen Grubbs**, ELS Language Centers, Florida; **Joni Hagigeorges**, Salem State University, Massachusetts; **Valerie Heming**, University of Central Missouri, Missouri; **Mary Hill**, North Shore Community College, Massachusetts; **Harry L. Holden**, North Lake College, Texas; **Ingrid Holm**, University of Massachusetts Amherst, Massachusetts; **Marianne Hsu Santelli**, Middlesex County College, New Jersey; **Katie Hurter**, Lone Star College – North Harris, Texas; **Justin Jernigan**, Georgia Gwinnett College, Georgia; **Barbara A. Jonckheere**, American Language Institute at California State University, Long Beach, California; **Susan Jordan**, Fisher College, Massachusetts; **Maria Kasparova**, Bergen Community College, New Jersey; **Gail Kellersberger**, University of Houston-Downtown, Texas; **Christina Kelso**, Austin Peay State University, Tennessee; **Daryl Kinney**, Los Angeles City College, California; **Leslie Kosel Eckstein**, Hillsborough Community College, Florida; **Beth Kozbial Ernst**, University of Wisconsin-Eau Claire, Wisconsin; **Jennifer Lacroix**, Center for English Language and Orientation Programs: Boston University, Massachusetts; **Stuart Landers**, Missouri State University, Missouri; **Margaret V. Layton**, University of Nevada, Reno Intensive English Language Center, Nevada; **Heidi Lieb**, Bergen Community College, New Jersey; **Kerry Linder**, Language Studies International New York, New York; **Jenifer Lucas-Uygun**, Passaic County Community College, New Jersey; **Alison MacAdams**, Approach International Student Center, Massachusetts; **Craig Machado**, Norwalk Community College, Connecticut; **Andrew J. MacNeill**, Southwestern College, California; **Melanie A. Majeski**, Naugatuck Valley Community College, Connecticut; **Wendy Maloney**, College of DuPage, Illinois; **Chris Mares**, University of Maine – Intensive English Institute, Maine; **Josefina Mark**, Union County College, New Jersey; **Connie Mathews**, Nashville State Community College, Tennessee; **Bette Matthews**, Mid-Pacific Institute, Hawaii; **Marla McDaniels Heath**, Norwalk Community College, Connecticut; **Kimberly McGrath Moreira**, University of Miami, Florida; **Sara McKinnon**, College of Marin, California; **Christine Mekkaoui**, Pittsburg State University, Kansas; **Holly A. Milkowart**, Johnson County Community College, Kansas; **Warren Mosher**, University of Miami, Florida; **Lukas Murphy**, Westchester Community College, New York; **Elena Nehrebecki**, Hudson Community College, New Jersey; **Bjarne Nielsen**, Central Piedmont Community College, North Carolina; **David Nippoldt**, Reedley College, California; **Lucia Parsley**, Virginia Commonwealth University, Virginia; **Wendy Patriquin**, Parkland College, Illinois; **Marion Piccolomini**, Communicate With Ease, LTD, Pennsylvania; **Carolyn Prager**, Spanish-American Institute, New York; **Eileen Prince**, Prince Language Associates Incorporated, Massachusetts; **Sema Pulak**, Texas A & M University, Texas; **James T. Raby**, Clark University, Massachusetts; **Anouchka Rachelson**, Miami-Dade College, Florida; **Lynn Ramage Schaefer**, University of Central Arkansas, Arkansas; **Sherry Rasmussen**, DePaul University, Illinois; **Amy Renehan**, University of Washington, Washington; **Esther Robbins**, Prince George's Community College, Pennsylvania; **Helen Roland**, Miami Dade College, Florida; **Linda Roth**, Vanderbilt University English Language Center, Tennessee; **Janine Rudnick**, El Paso Community College, Texas; **Rita Rutkowski Weber**, University of Wisconsin – Milwaukee, Wisconsin; **Elena Sapp**, INTO Oregon State University, Oregon; **Margaret Shippey**, Miami Dade College, Florida; **Lisa Sieg**, Murray State University, Kentucky; **Alison Stamps**, ESL Center at Mississippi State University, Mississippi; **Peggy Street**, ELS Language Centers, Miami, Florida; **Lydia Streiter**, York College Adult Learning Center, New York; **Nicholas Taggart**, Arkansas State University, Arkansas; **Marcia Takacs**, Coastline Community College, California; **Tamara Teffeteller**, University of California Los Angeles, American Language Center, California; **Rebecca Toner**, English Language Programs, University of Pennsylvania, Pennsylvania; **William G. Trudeau**, Missouri Southern State University, Missouri; **Troy Tucker**, Edison State College, Florida; **Maria Vargas-O'Neel**, Miami Dade College, Florida; **Amerca Vazquez**, Miami Dade College, Florida; **Alison Vinande**, Modesto Junior College, California; **Christie Ward**, Intensive English Language Program, Central Connecticut State University, Connecticut; **Colin S. Ward**, Lone Star College-North Harris, Texas; **Denise L. Warner**, Lansing Community College, Michigan; **Wendy Wish-Bogue**, Valencia Community College, Florida; **Cissy Wong**, Sacramento City College, California; **Kimberly Yoder**, Kent State University, ESL Center, Ohio.

ASIA Teoh Swee Ai, Universiti Teknologi Mara, Malaysia; **Nor Azni Abdullah**, Universiti Teknologi Mara, Malaysia; **Thomas E. Bieri**, Nagoya College, Japan;

Paul Bournhonesque, Seoul National University of Technology, Korea; **Michael C. Cheng**, National Chengchi University, Taiwan; **Fu-Dong Chiou**, National Taiwan University, Taiwan; **Derek Currie**, Korea University, Sejong Institute of Foreign Language Studies, Korea; **Christoph A. Hafner**, City University of Hong Kong, Hong Kong; **Wenhua Hsu**, I-Shou University, Taiwan; **Helen Huntley**, Hanoi University, Vietnam; **Rob Higgens**, Ritsumeikan University, Japan; **Shih Fan Kao**, JinWen University of Science and Technology, Taiwan; **Ikuko Kashiwabara**, Osaka Electro-Communication University, Japan; **Richard S. Lavin**, Prefecturla University of Kumamoto, Japan;

Mike Lay, American Institute, Cambodia; **Byoung-Kyo Lee**, Yonsei University, Korea; **Lin Li**, Capital Normal University, China; **Hudson Murrell**, Baiko Gakuin University, Japan; **Keiichi Narita**, Niigata University, Japan; **Huynh Thi Ai Nguyen**, Vietnam USA Society, Vietnam; **James Pham**, IDP Phnom Penh, Cambodia; **Duncan Rose**, British Council, Singapore; **Simone Samuels**, The Indonesia Australia Language Foundation Jakarta, Indonesia; **Wang Songmei**, Beijing Institute of Education Faculty, China; **Chien-Wen Jenny Tseng**, National Sun Yat-Sen University, Taiwan; **Hajime Uematsu**, Hirosaki University, Japan **AUSTRALIA Susan Austin**, University of South Australia, **Joanne Cummins**, Swinburne College; **Pamela Humphreys**, Griffith University **LATIN AMERICA AND THE CARIBBEAN Ramon Aguilar**, Universidad Tecnológica de Hermosillo, México; **Livia de Araujo Donnini Rodrigues**, University of São Paolo, Brazil; **Cecilia Avila**, Universidad de Xapala, México; **Beth Bartlett**, Centro Cultural Colombo Americano, Cali, Colombia; **Raúl Billini**, Colegio Loyola, Dominican Republic; **Nohora Edith Bryan**, Universidad de La Sabana, Colombia;

Raquel Hernández Cantú, Instituto Tecnológico de Monterrey, Mexico; **Millie Commander**, Inter American University of Puerto Rico, Puerto Rico; **Edwin Marín-Arroyo**, Instituto Tecnológico de Costa Rica; **Rosario Mena**, Instituto Cultural Dominico-Americano, Dominican Republic; **Elizabeth Ortiz Lozada**, COPEI-COPOL English Institute, Ecuador; **Gilberto Rios Zamora**, Sinaloa State Language Center, Mexico; **Patricia Veciños**, El Instituto Cultural Argentino Norteamericano, Argentina **MIDDLE EAST AND NORTH AFRICA Tom Farkas**, American University of Cairo, Egypt; **Ghada Hozayen**, Arab Academy for Science, Technology and Maritime Transport, Egypt; **Jodi Lefort**, Sultan Qaboos University, Muscat, Oman; **Barbara R. Reimer**, CERTESL, UAE University, UAE

Scope and Sequence

Unit	Academic Pathways	Vocabulary	Listening Skills
1 **Living for Work** *Page 1* **Academic Track:** Interdisciplinary	**Lesson A:** Listening to an Interview Doing an Interview **Lesson B:** Listening to an Informal Conversation Giving a Short Presentation about Yourself	Using a dictionary to understand new words Using new vocabulary in a conversation Understanding meaning from context	Listening for main ideas Listening for details Making inferences **Pronunciation:** Syllable stress
2 **Good Times, Good Feelings** *Page 21* **Academic Track:** Psychology/ Sociology	**Lesson A:** Listening to a Lecture Discussing Celebrations and Holidays **Lesson B:** Listening to a Talk with Questions and Answers Giving a Presentation for a Small Group	Understanding meaning from context Using new vocabulary in a conversation Using new vocabulary to complete a text	Understanding the speaker's purpose Listening for main ideas Listening for details Checking predictions **Pronunciation:** The intonation of *yes/no* questions The intonation of *wh-* questions
3 **Treasures from the Past** *Page 41* **Academic Track:** History/ Archaeology	**Lesson A:** Listening to a Talk about an Ancient City Talking About the Past **Lesson B:** Listening to a Conversation Using Notes in a Presentation	Understanding meaning from context Using new vocabulary to discuss the unit theme Using new vocabulary to complete a text	Listening for main ideas Taking notes on specific information Making inferences **Pronunciation:** The simple past tense *–ed* word endings
4 **Weather and Climate** *Page 61* **Academic Track:** Natural Science/ Environmental Science	**Lesson A:** Listening to a Radio Show Planning an Itinerary **Lesson B:** Listening to a Conversation among Friends Discussing Ways to Reduce Greenhouse Gases	Using a dictionary to understand new vocabulary Understanding meaning from context Using new vocabulary to discuss the unit theme Using new vocabulary to complete a text	Listening for main ideas Listening for details Activating prior knowledge Taking notes to complete a T-chart **Pronunciation:** Reduced *of*
5 **Focus on Food** *Page 81* **Academic Track:** Interdisciplinary	**Lesson A:** Listening to a Talk by an Anthropology Professor Conducting a Survey **Lesson B:** Listening to a Conversation between Students Creating a Description with Interesting Details	Understanding meaning from context Using new vocabulary to complete a text Using new vocabulary to give opinions	Listening for main ideas Listening for details Activating prior knowledge **Pronunciation:** *Can* and *can't*

Grammar	Speaking Skills	Viewing	Critical Thinking Skills
The simple present tense vs. the present continuous Adverbs of frequency	Communicating that you don't understand Doing a career-aptitude interview Using adverbs of frequency to discuss a work schedule **Student to Student:** Giving feedback while listening **Presentation Skills:** Introducing yourself	**Video:** *Butler School* Activating prior knowledge Viewing for general understanding Relating the video to career choices	Making inferences Evaluating career options Explaining a job's impact on the world Reflecting on the content of an interview Using a chart to organize notes for a presentation **Critical Thinking Focus:** Identifying main ideas
The simple present tense: *Yes/No* questions The simple present tense: *Wh-* questions Recognizing past tense signal words	Asking questions to show interest Making small talk **Student to Student:** Asking for repetition **Presentation Skills:** Speaking to a group	**Video:** *Nubian Wedding* Using a map to learn background information Viewing for specific information Discussing the video in the context of one's own experience	Identifying what makes us laugh Judging the appropriateness of laughter Considering benefits and drawbacks Ranking the importance of benefits Generating questions about a presentation **Critical Thinking Focus:** Understanding the speaker's purpose
The simple past tense *Yes/No* questions in the simple past tense *Wh-* questions in the simple past tense	Expressing agreement informally Asking questions about past events **Student to Student:** Making informal suggestions **Presentation Skills:** Speaking from notes	**Video:** *Treasures in Old San Juan* Viewing to confirm predictions Note-taking while viewing Understanding sound bites from the video	Recognizing the value of the past Understanding information on a timeline Recalling information about a classmate Ranking ways to improve one's memory Evaluating one's own methods for remembering information **Critical Thinking Focus:** Recalling facts
Count and noncount nouns *A/n*, *any*, and *some*	Expressing likes and dislikes Expressing quantity with noncount nouns Comparing quantities or amounts **Student to Student:** Showing thanks and appreciation **Presentation Skills:** Making eye contact	**Video:** *Tornado Chase* Using a dictionary Viewing for specific information Discussing the video in the context of the unit theme	Reflecting on ideas about the weather Using prior knowledge in a group discussion Choosing appropriate activities for different types of weather Categorizing information from a map Discussing climate change **Critical Thinking Focus:** Making a list
Can and *can't* Descriptive adjectives	Expressing opinions Conducting a survey about eating habits Describing a favorite food **Student to Student:** Showing agreement **Presentation Skills:** Giving interesting details	**Video:** *Forbidden Fruit* Viewing for general understanding Understanding vocabulary from the video Expressing opinions	Discussing food and culture Selecting interesting information from survey results Categorizing new vocabulary Ranking important aspects of a restaurant or cafeteria Assessing a conversation **Critical Thinking Focus:** Distinguishing between main ideas and details

Scope and Sequence

Grammar	Speaking Skills	Viewing	Critical Thinking Skills
Coordinating conjunctions Time relationships in the simple present tense	Talking about architecture Agreeing and disagreeing Expressing preferences **Student to Student:** Expressing disagreement to a friend **Presentation Skills:** Role-playing	**Video:** *Don't Believe Your Eyes!* Predicting content Checking predictions Viewing for specific information	Drawing conclusions following a talk Choosing the best option Responding to a quotation Explaining a process Describing a government plan in one's own words **Critical Thinking Focus:** Evaluating options
Future time: *will* and *be going to* Future time: The present continuous and the simple present forms	Making predictions Discussing pros and cons **Student to Student:** Asking for another person's opinion **Presentation Skills:** Using signal words	**Video:** *Exploration of the Solar System* Listing advantages and disadvantages Viewing for specific information Speculating on topics related to video content	Making inferences from information in an interview Comparing and evaluating schedules Explaining future plans Discussing a tour of an observatory Choosing a destination for a trip **Critical Thinking Focus:** Discussing pros and cons
Modals of possibility and probability Modals of necessity	Speculating about a situation Giving possible explanations Discussing ideas about photographs **Student to Student:** Responding to invitations **Presentation Skills:** Speaking at an appropriate speed	**Video:** *Urban Art* Discussing the video topic Understanding key vocabulary Using a chart to make comparisons Agreeing and disagreeing with statements	Identifying visuals Speculating on topics related to unit content Making comparisons Explaining ideas and opinions Generating a list of necessities **Critical Thinking Focus:** Supporting an argument
The comparative and superlative forms of adjectives Spelling changes and the irregular forms of the comparative and superlative Comparisons with *as…as*	Making comparisons Giving reasons **Student to Student:** Ending a conversation **Presentation Skills:** Ending a presentation	**Video:** *Horses* Activating prior knowledge Using a time line to preview video content Viewing for general understanding Viewing for specific information	Reflecting on one's own culture Drawing conclusions following a talk Evaluating two studies Forming judgments Using a graphic organizer to plan a presentation **Critical Thinking Focus:** Making comparisons
The present perfect tense The present perfect tense with *ever, already,* and *yet*	Talking about duration Discussing conclusions **Student to Student:** Having a telephone conversation **Presentation Skills:** Inviting and answering questions from the audience	**Video:** *Touching the Stars* Using unit grammar with video content Viewing for general understanding Viewing for specific information	Identifying visuals Making inferences Ranking means of communication Reflecting on one's own use of technology for communication Organizing a group presentation **Critical Thinking Focus:** Drawing conclusions

Each unit consists of two lessons which include the following sections:

- Building Vocabulary
- Using Vocabulary
- Developing Listening Skills
- Exploring Spoken English
- Speaking (called "Engage" in Lesson B)

An **academic pathway** is clearly labeled for learners, starting with formal listening (e.g., lectures) and moving to a more informal context (e.g., a conversation between students in a study group).

The **"Exploring the Theme"** section provides a visual introduction to the unit and encourages learners to think critically and share ideas about the unit topic.

UNIT 9

Our Relationship with Nature

ACADEMIC PATHWAYS
Lesson A: Listening to a Lecture
Comparing Three Natural Attractions
Lesson B: Listening to a Conversation
Giving an Individual Presentation

Think and Discuss

1. Look at the photo. What is this man doing?
2. Is this something you might like to do? Explain.
3. What do you think you will learn about in this unit?

Alvaro del Campo feeds hungry macaws,
Tambopata National Reserve, Peru.

161

Exploring the Theme:
Our Relationship with Nature

Look at the photos and read the captions. Then discuss the questions.

1. What do you see on these pages that represents the natural world?
2. Which of the photos on these pages show a good relationship between people and nature? Which photos show a bad relationship? Explain.
3. What can people do in order to have a positive effect on the natural world?

Sharing Land with Animals

When people and animals have to share the same land, it sometimes causes conflicts, or problems. This polar bear is looking through a cabin window in Svalbard, Norway.

Hunting and Fishing

These Senegalese fishermen are pulling in nets filled with fish. People fish and hunt animals for food. Fishing is the main reason there are fewer large fish in the oceans today than in the past.

Scientific Research

Biologists are scientists who study living things. The information biologists collect can help the animals they study. This biologist is studying Macaroni penguins on Bird Island, South Georgia.

The top of the volcano Santa Maria appears through the clouds in the western highlands of Guatemala.

162 | UNIT 9

OUR RELATIONSHIP WITH NATURE | 163

Key academic and high-frequency vocabulary is introduced, practiced, and expanded throughout each unit. Lessons A and B each present and practice 10 terms.

A **"Developing Listening Skills"** section follows a before, during, and after listening approach to give learners the tools necessary to master listening skills for a variety of contexts.

Listening activities encourage learners to listen for and consolidate key information, reinforcing the language, and allowing learners to think critically about the information they hear.

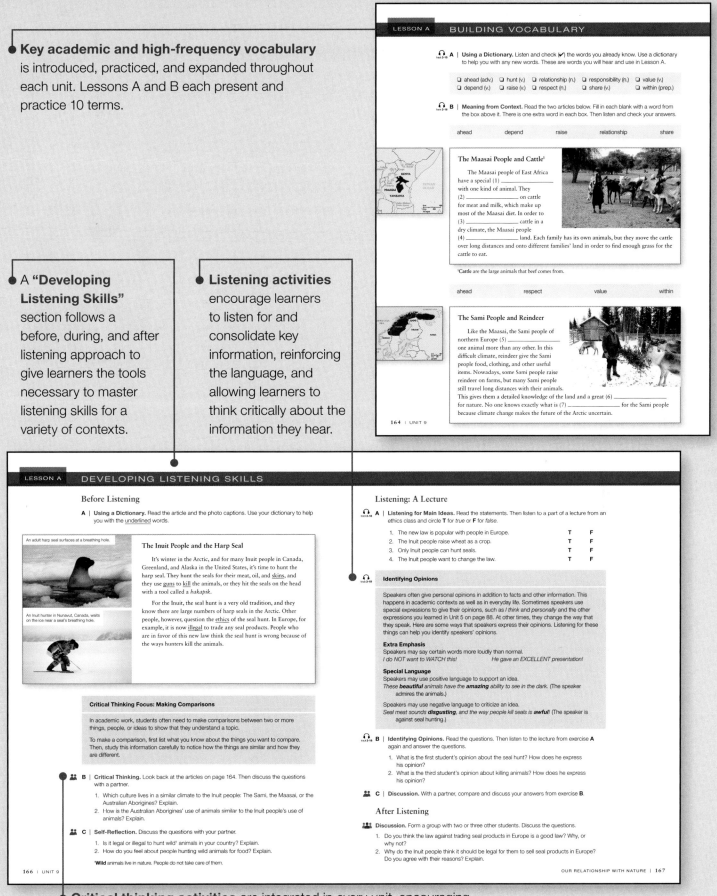

LESSON A   BUILDING VOCABULARY

A | Using a Dictionary. Listen and check (✔) the words you already know. Use a dictionary to help you with any new words. These are words you will hear and use in Lesson A.

- ❏ ahead (adv.)   ❏ hunt (v.)   ❏ relationship (n.)   ❏ responsibility (n.)   ❏ value (v.)
- ❏ depend (v.)   ❏ raise (v.)   ❏ respect (n.)   ❏ share (v.)   ❏ within (prep.)

B | Meaning from Context. Read the two articles below. Fill in each blank with a word from the box above it. There is one extra word in each box. Then listen and check your answers.

| ahead | depend | raise | relationship | share |

The Maasai People and Cattle[1]

The Maasai people of East Africa have a special (1) _____ with one kind of animal. They (2) _____ on cattle for meat and milk, which make up most of the Maasai diet. In order to (3) _____ cattle in a dry climate, the Maasai people (4) _____ land. Each family has its own animals, but they move the cattle over long distances and onto different families' land in order to find enough grass for the cattle to eat.

[1]**Cattle** are the large animals that beef comes from.

| ahead | respect | value | within |

The Sami People and Reindeer

Like the Maasai, the Sami people of northern Europe (5) _____ one animal more than any other. In this difficult climate, reindeer give the Sami people food, clothing, and other useful items. Nowadays, some Sami people raise reindeer on farms, but many Sami people still travel long distances with their animals. This gives them a detailed knowledge of the land and a great (6) _____ for nature. No one knows exactly what is (7) _____ for the Sami people because climate change makes the future of the Arctic uncertain.

164 | UNIT 9

LESSON A   DEVELOPING LISTENING SKILLS

Before Listening

A | Using a Dictionary. Read the article and the photo captions. Use your dictionary to help you with the underlined words.

An adult harp seal surfaces at a breathing hole.

The Inuit People and the Harp Seal

It's winter in the Arctic, and for many Inuit people in Canada, Greenland, and Alaska in the United States, it's time to hunt the harp seal. They hunt the seals for their meat, oil, and skins, and they use guns to kill the animals, or they hit the seals on the head with a tool called a *hakapik*.

For the Inuit, the seal hunt is a very old tradition, and they know there are large numbers of harp seals in the Arctic. Other people, however, question the ethics of the seal hunt. In Europe, for example, it is now illegal to trade any seal products. People who are in favor of this new law think the seal hunt is wrong because of the ways hunters kill the animals.

An Inuit hunter in Nunavut, Canada, waits on the ice near a seal's breathing hole.

Critical Thinking Focus: Making Comparisons

In academic work, students often need to make comparisons between two or more things, people, or ideas to show that they understand a topic.

To make a comparison, first list what you know about the things you want to compare. Then, study this information carefully to notice how the things are similar and how they are different.

B | Critical Thinking. Look back at the articles on page 164. Then discuss the questions with a partner.

1. Which culture lives in a similar climate to the Inuit people: The Sami, the Maasai, or the Australian Aborigines? Explain.
2. How is the Australian Aborigines' use of animals similar to the Inuit people's use of animals? Explain.

C | Self-Reflection. Discuss the questions with your partner.

1. Is it legal or illegal to hunt wild[1] animals in your country? Explain.
2. How do you feel about people hunting wild animals for food? Explain.

[1]**Wild** animals live in nature. People do not take care of them.

166 | UNIT 9

Listening: A Lecture

A | Listening for Main Ideas. Read the statements. Then listen to a part of a lecture from an ethics class and circle **T** for *true* or **F** for *false*.

1. The new law is popular with people in Europe.   T   F
2. The Inuit people raise wheat as a crop.   T   F
3. Only Inuit people can hunt seals.   T   F
4. The Inuit people want to change the law.   T   F

Identifying Opinions

Speakers often give personal opinions in addition to facts and other information. This happens in academic contexts as well as in everyday life. Sometimes speakers use special expressions to give their opinions, such as *I think* and *personally* and the other expressions you learned in Unit 5 on page 88. At other times, they change the way that they speak. Here are some ways that speakers express their opinions. Listening for these things can help you identify speakers' opinions.

Extra Emphasis
Speakers may say certain words more loudly than normal.
I do NOT want to WATCH this!   *He gave an EXCELLENT presentation!*

Special Language
Speakers may use positive language to support an idea.
*These **beautiful** animals have the **amazing** ability to see in the dark.* (The speaker admires the animals.)

Speakers may use negative language to criticize an idea.
*Seal meat sounds **disgusting**, and the way people kill seals is **awful!*** (The speaker is against seal hunting.)

B | Identifying Opinions. Read the questions. Then listen to the lecture from exercise **A** again and answer the questions.

1. What is the first student's opinion about the seal hunt? How does he express his opinion?
2. What is the third student's opinion about killing animals? How does he express his opinion?

C | Discussion. With a partner, compare and discuss your answers from exercise **B**.

After Listening

Discussion. Form a group with two or three other students. Discuss the questions.

1. Do you think the law against trading seal products in Europe is a good law? Why, or why not?
2. Why do the Inuit people think it should be legal for them to sell seal products in Europe? Do you agree with their reasons? Explain.

OUR RELATIONSHIP WITH NATURE | 167

Critical thinking activities are integrated in every unit, encouraging continuous engagement in developing academic skills.

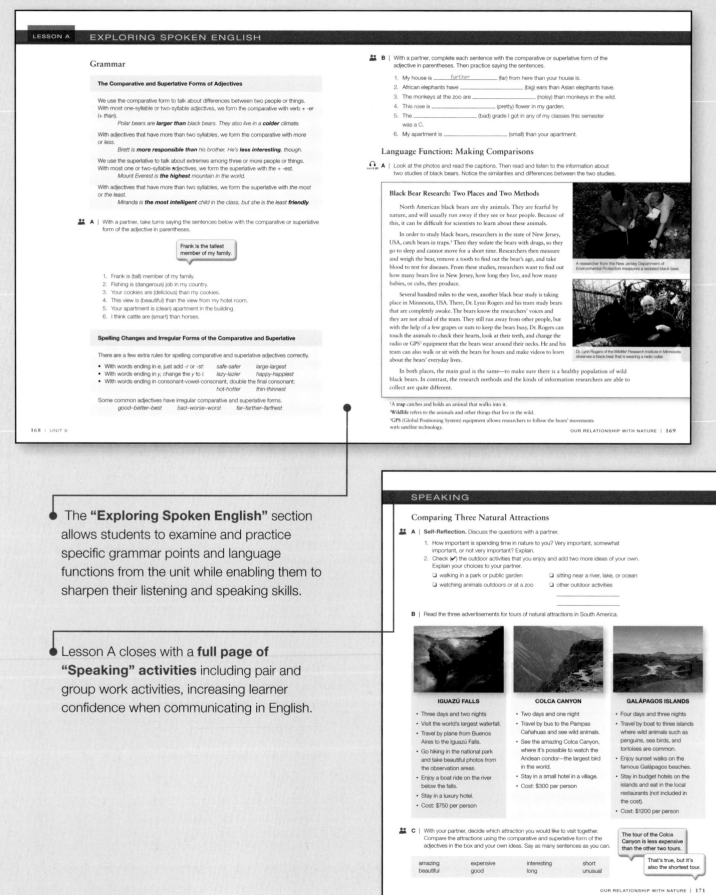

LESSON A EXPLORING SPOKEN ENGLISH

Grammar

The Comparative and Superlative Forms of Adjectives

We use the comparative form to talk about differences between two people or things. With most one-syllable or two-syllable adjectives, we form the comparative with verb + -er (+ than).

*Polar bears are **larger than** black bears. They also live in a **colder** climate.*

With adjectives that have more than two syllables, we form the comparative with *more* or *less*.

*Brett is **more responsible than** his brother. He's **less interesting**, though.*

We use the superlative to talk about extremes among three or more people or things. With most one or two-syllable adjectives, we form the superlative with *the* + -est.

*Mount Everest is **the highest** mountain in the world.*

With adjectives that have more than two syllables, we form the superlative with *the most* or *the least*.

*Miranda is **the most intelligent** child in the class, but she is the least **friendly**.*

A | With a partner, take turns saying the sentences below with the comparative or superlative form of the adjective in parentheses.

> Frank is the tallest member of my family.

1. Frank is (tall) member of my family.
2. Fishing is (dangerous) job in my country.
3. Your cookies are (delicious) than my cookies.
4. This view is (beautiful) than the view from my hotel room.
5. Your apartment is (clean) apartment in the building.
6. I think cattle are (smart) than horses.

Spelling Changes and Irregular Forms of the Comparative and Superlative

There are a few extra rules for spelling comparative and superlative adjectives correctly.

- With words ending in e, just add -r or -st: safe-safer   large-largest
- With words ending in y, change the y to i: lazy-lazier   happy-happiest
- With words ending in consonant-vowel-consonant, double the final consonant: hot-hotter   thin-thinnest

Some common adjectives have irregular comparative and superlative forms.

good–better–best   bad–worse–worst   far–farther–farthest

168 | UNIT 9

B | With a partner, complete each sentence with the comparative or superlative form of the adjective in parentheses. Then practice saying the sentences.

1. My house is ___farther___ (far) from here than your house is.
2. African elephants have _____ (big) ears than Asian elephants have.
3. The monkeys at the zoo are _____ (noisy) than monkeys in the wild.
4. This rose is _____ (pretty) flower in my garden.
5. The _____ (bad) grade I got in any of my classes this semester was a C.
6. My apartment is _____ (small) than your apartment.

Language Function: Making Comparisons

A | Look at the photos and read the captions. Then read and listen to the information about two studies of black bears. Notice the similarities and differences between the two studies.

Black Bear Research: Two Places and Two Methods

North American black bears are shy animals. They are fearful by nature, and will usually run away if they see or hear people. Because of this, it can be difficult for scientists to learn about these animals.

In order to study black bears, researchers in the state of New Jersey, USA, catch bears in traps.[1] Then they sedate the bears with drugs, so they go to sleep and cannot move for a short time. Researchers then measure and weigh the bear, remove a tooth to find out the bear's age, and take blood to test for diseases. From these studies, researchers want to find out how many bears live in New Jersey, how long they live, and how many babies, or cubs, they produce.

Several hundred miles to the west, another black bear study is taking place in Minnesota, USA. There, Dr. Lynn Rogers and his team study bears that are completely awake. The bears know the researchers' voices and they are not afraid of the team. They still run away from other people, but with the help of a few grapes or nuts to keep the bears busy, Dr. Rogers can touch the animals to check their hearts, look at their teeth, and change the radio or GPS[3] equipment that the bears wear around their necks. He and his team can also walk or sit with the bears for hours and make videos to learn about the bears' everyday lives.

In both places, the main goal is the same—to make sure there is a healthy population of wild black bears. In contrast, the research methods and the kinds of information researchers are able to collect are quite different.

A researcher from the New Jersey Department of Environmental Protection measures a sedated black bear.

Dr. Lynn Rogers of the Wildlife[2] Research Institute in Minnesota observes a black bear that is wearing a radio collar.

[1] A **trap** catches and holds an animal that walks into it.
[2] **Wildlife** refers to the animals and other things that live in the wild.
[3] **GPS** (Global Positioning System) equipment allows researchers to follow the bears' movements with satellite technology.

OUR RELATIONSHIP WITH NATURE | 169

The **"Exploring Spoken English"** section allows students to examine and practice specific grammar points and language functions from the unit while enabling them to sharpen their listening and speaking skills.

Lesson A closes with a **full page of "Speaking" activities** including pair and group work activities, increasing learner confidence when communicating in English.

SPEAKING

Comparing Three Natural Attractions

A | Self-Reflection. Discuss the questions with a partner.

1. How important is spending time in nature to you? Very important, somewhat important, or not very important? Explain.
2. Check (✔) the outdoor activities that you enjoy and add two more ideas of your own. Explain your choices to your partner.
   - ☐ walking in a park or public garden
   - ☐ watching animals outdoors or at a zoo
   - ☐ sitting near a river, lake, or ocean
   - ☐ other outdoor activities
   - _____
   - _____

B | Read the three advertisements for tours of natural attractions in South America.

IGUAZÚ FALLS
- Three days and two nights
- Visit the world's largest waterfall.
- Travel by plane from Buenos Aires to the Iguazú Falls.
- Go hiking in the national park and take beautiful photos from the observation areas.
- Enjoy a boat ride on the river below the falls.
- Stay in a luxury hotel.
- Cost: $750 per person

COLCA CANYON
- Two days and one night
- Travel by bus to the Pampas Cañahuas and see wild animals.
- See the amazing Colca Canyon, where it's possible to watch the Andean condor—the largest bird in the world.
- Stay in a small hotel in a village.
- Cost: $300 per person

GALÁPAGOS ISLANDS
- Four days and three nights
- Travel by boat to three islands where wild animals such as penguins, sea birds, and tortoises are common.
- Enjoy sunset walks on the famous Galápagos beaches.
- Stay in budget hotels on the islands and eat in the local restaurants (not included in the cost).
- Cost: $1200 per person

C | With your partner, decide which attraction you would like to visit together. Compare the attractions using the comparative and superlative form of the adjectives in the box and your own ideas. Say as many sentences as you can.

> The tour of the Colca Canyon is less expensive than the other two tours.
>
> That's true, but it's also the shortest tour.

amazing	expensive	interesting	short
beautiful	good	long	unusual

OUR RELATIONSHIP WITH NATURE | 171

The **"Viewing" section** works as a content-bridge between Lesson A and Lesson B and includes two pages of activities based on a fascinating video from National Geographic.

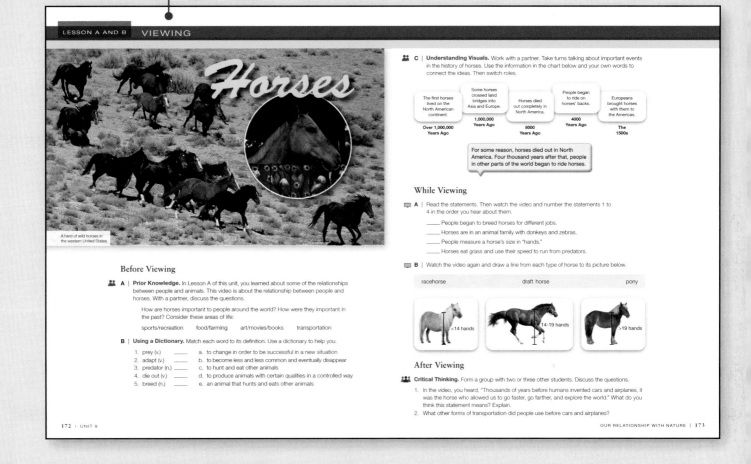

LESSON A AND B — VIEWING

A herd of wild horses in the western United States

Before Viewing

A | Prior Knowledge. In Lesson A of this unit, you learned about some of the relationships between people and animals. This video is about the relationship between people and horses. With a partner, discuss the questions.

How are horses important to people around the world? How were they important in the past? Consider these areas of life:

sports/recreation   food/farming   art/movies/books   transportation

B | Using a Dictionary. Match each word to its definition. Use a dictionary to help you.

1. prey (v.)   _____   a. to change in order to be successful in a new situation
2. adapt (v.)   _____   b. to become less and less common and eventually disappear
3. predator (n.) _____   c. to hunt and eat other animals
4. die out (v.)   _____   d. to produce animals with certain qualities in a controlled way
5. breed (n.)   _____   e. an animal that hunts and eats other animals

C | Understanding Visuals. Work with a partner. Take turns talking about important events in the history of horses. Use the information in the chart below and your own words to connect the ideas. Then switch roles.

The first horses lived on the North American continent.	Some horses crossed land bridges into Asia and Europe.	Horses died out completely in North America.	People began to ride on horses' backs.	Europeans brought horses with them to the Americas.
Over 1,000,000 Years Ago	1,000,000 Years Ago	8000 Years Ago	4000 Years Ago	The 1500s

For some reason, horses died out in North America. Four thousand years after that, people in other parts of the world began to ride horses.

While Viewing

A | Read the statements. Then watch the video and number the statements 1 to 4 in the order you hear about them.

_____ People began to breed horses for different jobs.

_____ Horses are in an animal family with donkeys and zebras.

_____ People measure a horse's size in "hands."

_____ Horses eat grass and use their speed to run from predators.

B | Watch the video again and draw a line from each type of horse to its picture below.

racehorse   draft horse   pony

<14 hands   14-19 hands   >19 hands

After Viewing

Critical Thinking. Form a group with two or three other students. Discuss the questions.

1. In the video, you heard, "Thousands of years before humans invented cars and airplanes, it was the horse who allowed us to go faster, go farther, and explore the world." What do you think this statement means? Explain.
2. What other forms of transportation did people use before cars and airplanes?

A DVD for each level contains 10 authentic videos from National Geographic specially adapted for English language learners.

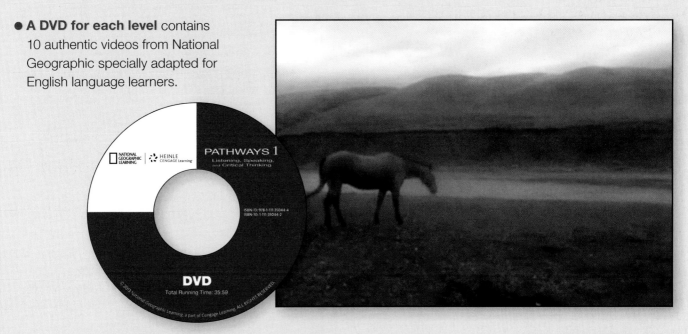

NATIONAL GEOGRAPHIC LEARNING · HEINLE CENGAGE Learning

PATHWAYS 1
Listening, Speaking, and Critical Thinking

ISBN-13: 978-1-111-35044-4
ISBN-10: 1-111-35044-2

DVD
Total Running Time: 35:59

© 2011 National Geographic Learning, a part of Cengage Learning. ALL RIGHTS RESERVED.

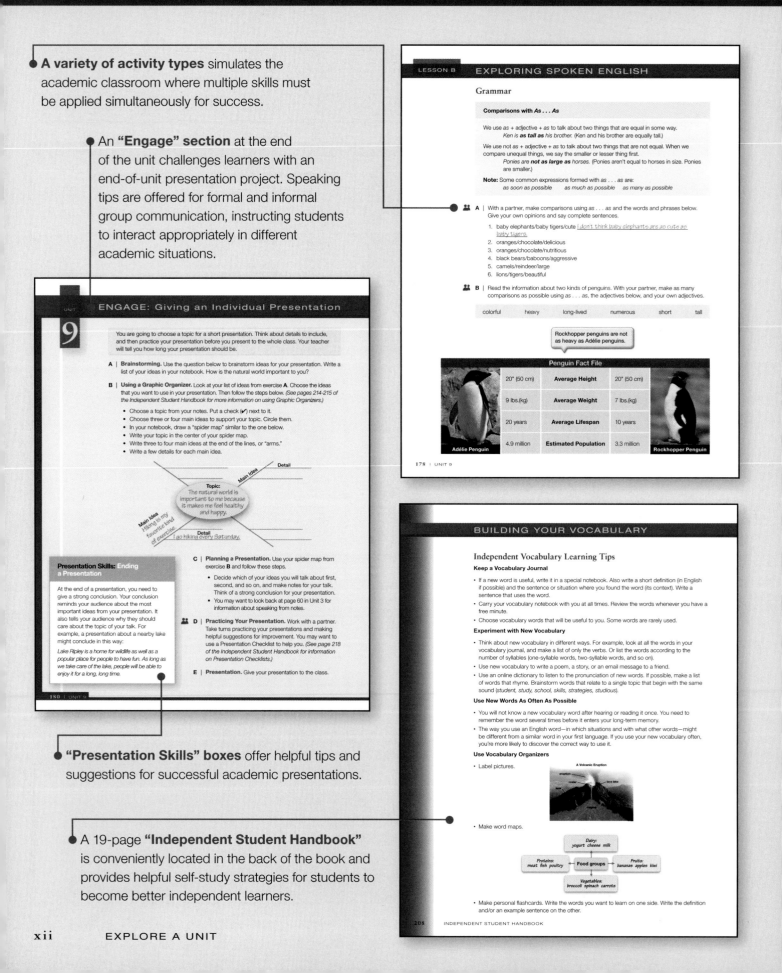

A variety of activity types simulates the academic classroom where multiple skills must be applied simultaneously for success.

An **"Engage" section** at the end of the unit challenges learners with an end-of-unit presentation project. Speaking tips are offered for formal and informal group communication, instructing students to interact appropriately in different academic situations.

"Presentation Skills" boxes offer helpful tips and suggestions for successful academic presentations.

A 19-page **"Independent Student Handbook"** is conveniently located in the back of the book and provides helpful self-study strategies for students to become better independent learners.

LESSON B | EXPLORING SPOKEN ENGLISH

Grammar

Comparisons with As ... As

We use as + adjective + as to talk about two things that are equal in some way.
*Ken is **as tall as** his brother.* (Ken and his brother are equally tall.)

We use not as + adjective + as to talk about two things that are not equal. When we compare unequal things, we say the smaller or lesser thing first.
*Ponies are **not as large as** horses.* (Ponies aren't equal to horses in size. Ponies are smaller.)

Note: Some common expressions formed with as ... as are:
as soon as possible   as much as possible   as many as possible

A | With a partner, make comparisons using as ... as and the words and phrases below. Give your own opinions and say complete sentences.

1. baby elephants/baby tigers/cute *I don't think baby elephants are as cute as baby tigers.*
2. oranges/chocolate/delicious
3. oranges/chocolate/nutritious
4. black bears/baboons/aggressive
5. camels/reindeer/large
6. lions/tigers/beautiful

B | Read the information about two kinds of penguins. With your partner, make as many comparisons as possible using as ... as, the adjectives below, and your own adjectives.

| colorful | heavy | long-lived | numerous | short | tall |

> Rockhopper penguins are not as heavy as Adélie penguins.

Penguin Fact File

Adélie Penguin		Rockhopper Penguin
20" (50 cm)	**Average Height**	20" (50 cm)
9 lbs.(kg)	**Average Weight**	7 lbs.(kg)
20 years	**Average Lifespan**	10 years
4.9 million	**Estimated Population**	3.3 million

178 | UNIT 9

UNIT 9

ENGAGE: Giving an Individual Presentation

You are going to choose a topic for a short presentation. Think about details to include, and then practice your presentation before you present to the whole class. Your teacher will tell you how long your presentation should be.

A | **Brainstorming.** Use the question below to brainstorm ideas for your presentation. Write a list of your ideas in your notebook. How is the natural world important to you?

B | **Using a Graphic Organizer.** Look at your list of ideas from exercise **A**. Choose the ideas that you want to use in your presentation. Then follow the steps below. *(See pages 214-215 of the Independent Student Handbook for more information on using Graphic Organizers.)*

- Choose a topic from your notes. Put a check (✔) next to it.
- Choose three or four main ideas to support your topic. Circle them.
- In your notebook, draw a "spider map" similar to the one below.
- Write your topic in the center of your spider map.
- Write three to four main ideas at the end of the lines, or "arms."
- Write a few details for each main idea.

Detail

Main Idea

Topic:
The natural world is important to me because it makes me feel healthy and happy.

Main Idea
Hiking is my favorite kind of exercise.

Detail
I go hiking every Saturday.

Presentation Skills: Ending a Presentation

At the end of a presentation, you need to give a strong conclusion. Your conclusion reminds your audience about the most important ideas from your presentation. It also tells your audience why they should care about the topic of your talk. For example, a presentation about a nearby lake might conclude in this way:

Lake Ripley is a home for wildlife as well as a popular place for people to have fun. As long as we take care of the lake, people will be able to enjoy it for a long, long time.

C | **Planning a Presentation.** Use your spider map from exercise **B** and follow these steps.

- Decide which of your ideas you will talk about first, second, and so on, and make notes for your talk. Think of a strong conclusion for your presentation.
- You may want to look back at page 60 in Unit 3 for information about speaking from notes.

D | **Practicing Your Presentation.** Work with a partner. Take turns practicing your presentations and making helpful suggestions for improvement. You may want to use a Presentation Checklist to help you. *(See page 218 of the Independent Student Handbook for information on Presentation Checklists.)*

E | **Presentation.** Give your presentation to the class.

180 | UNIT 9

BUILDING YOUR VOCABULARY

Independent Vocabulary Learning Tips

Keep a Vocabulary Journal

- If a new word is useful, write it in a special notebook. Also write a short definition (in English if possible) and the sentence or situation where you found the word (its context). Write a sentence that uses the word.
- Carry your vocabulary notebook with you at all times. Review the words whenever you have a free minute.
- Choose vocabulary words that will be useful to you. Some words are rarely used.

Experiment with New Vocabulary

- Think about new vocabulary in different ways. For example, look at all the words in your vocabulary journal, and make a list of only the verbs. Or list the words according to the number of syllables (one-syllable words, two-syllable words, and so on).
- Use new vocabulary to write a poem, a story, or an email message to a friend.
- Use an online dictionary to listen to the pronunciation of new words. If possible, make a list of words that rhyme. Brainstorm words that relate to a single topic that begin with the same sound (*student, study, school, skills, strategies, studious*).

Use New Words As Often As Possible

- You will not know a new vocabulary word after hearing or reading it once. You need to remember the word several times before it enters your long-term memory.
- The way you use an English word—in which situations and with what other words—might be different from a similar word in your first language. If you use your new vocabulary often, you're more likely to discover the correct way to use it.

Use Vocabulary Organizers

- Label pictures.

A Volcanic Eruption

- Make word maps.

Dairy: yogurt cheese milk

Proteins: meat fish poultry → **Food groups** ← **Fruits:** bananas apples kiwi

Vegetables: broccoli spinach carrots

- Make personal flashcards. Write the words you want to learn on one side. Write the definition and/or an example sentence on the other.

208   INDEPENDENT STUDENT HANDBOOK

For the Teacher:

Perfect for integrating language practice with exciting visuals, **video clips from National Geographic** bring the sights and sounds of our world into the classroom.

The Assessment CD-ROM with Exam*View*® is a test-generating software program with a data bank of ready-made questions designed to allow teachers to assess students quickly and effectively.

Bringing a new dimension to the language learning classroom, the **Classroom Presentation Tool CD-ROM** makes instruction clearer and learning easier through interactive activities, audio and video clips, and Presentation Worksheets.

A **Teacher's Guide** is available in an easy-to-use format and includes teacher's notes, expansion activities, and answer keys for activities in the student book.

For the Student:

The **Student Book** helps students achieve academic success in and outside of the classroom.

Audio CDs contain the audio recordings for the exercises in the student books.

ELT. Powered by MyELT, the **Online Workbook** has both teacher-led and self-study options. It contains 10 National Geographic video clips, supported by interactive, automatically graded activities that practice the skills learned in the student books.

Visit elt.heinle.com/pathways for additional teacher and student resources.

CREDITS

LISTENING AND TEXT

17 Adapted from "Interview With Sylvia Earle (oceanographer)," http://kids.nationalgeographic.com/kids/stories/peopleplaces/sylvia-earle/: National Geographic Kids, 24 Adapted from "Funny Business," by David George Gordon: National Geographic World, April 1999, 35 Adapted from "City Parks: Space for the Soul," by Jennifer Ackerman: National Geographic Magazine, October 2006, 44 Adapted from "Searching for Cleopatra," by Marylou Tousignant: National Geographic Extreme Explorer, February 2011, 47 Adapted from "The Presence of the Past," by Allison Lassieur: National Geographic World, May 1998, 54 Adapted from "Tang Shipwreck," by Simon Worrall: National Geographic Magazine, June 2009, 55 Adapted from "Shipwreck in the Forbidden Zone," by Roff Smith: National Geographic Magazine, October 2009, 75-77 Adapted from "Viking Weather," by Tim Folger: National Geographic Magazine, June 2010, 79 Adapted from "Changing Rains," by Elizabeth Kolbert: National Geographic Magazine, April 2009, 84-87 Adapted from "Far-Out Foods," by Diane

Wedner: National Geographic Explorer, November-December 2010, 90 Adapted from "Bugs as Food: Humans Bite" by Maryann Mott, National Geographic News, April 16, 2004, 94 Adapted from "Into the Heart of Dim Sum," by Jodi Helmer: National Geographic Traveler, March 2011, 94 Adapted from "Sweet Homecoming," by Jodi Helmer: National Geographic Traveler, March 2011, 117 Adapted from "Egypt "Greens" Deserts to Stem Housing, Food Shortages," by Steven Stanek: National Geographic News (online) http://news.nationalgeographic.com/news/2008/01/080108-egypt-greening.html, January 2008, 118 Adapted from "Straw Houses: No Need to Fear the Big, Bad Wolf," by Catherine Clarke Fox: National Geographic Kids, 124 Adapted from "Space Quest," by Don Thomas: National Geographic Explorer, January-February 2011, 129 Adapted from "Life on Mars?," by Jennifer Eigenbrode: National Geographic Extreme Explorer, September 2010, 134 Adapted from "Cosmic Vision," by Timothy Ferris: National Geographic Magazine, July 2009, 145 Adapted from "Pictures: "Bodies" Fill Underwater Sculpture Park," with reporting by Fritz Faerber: National Geographic News http://news.nationalgeographic.com/news/2011/01/pictures/110105-

underwater-sculpture-park-garden-cancun-mexico-caribbean-pictures-photos-science/, January 5, 2011, 147 photo gallery w/notes about Jim Denevan, http://channel.nationalgeographic.com/episode/cobra-town-amazing-mummies-and-hogzilla-4756/Photos/8305#tab-Photos/0, 149 Adapted from "Painting Elephants Get Online Gallery," by Hillary Mayell: National Geographic News http://news.nationalgeographic.com/news/2002/06/0626_020626_elephant.html, June 26, 2002, 164-165 Adapted from "Amazing World Cultures and the Animals in Their Lives," by Sean McCollum: National Geographic Kids, September 2004, 179 Adapted from "Incredible Animal Friends: Caracal Guides Blind Bobcat," by Amanda Sandlin: National Geographic Kids, April 2011 194 Adapted from "Big Idea: Clearing Space," by Michael D. Lemonick: National Geographic Magazine, July 2010

LISTENING AND TEXT SOURCES

145 "Artist Profile: Jason De Caires Taylor," Sources: http://www.underwatersculpture.com/, http://news.nationalgeographic.com/news/2011/01/pictures/110105-underwater-sculpture-park-garden-cancun-mexico-caribbean-pictures-photos-science/ 146 Listening: A PowerPoint Lecture, Sources: http://channel.nationalgeographic.com/episode/cobra-town-amazing-mummies-and hogzilla-4756/Photos/8305#tab-Photos/1; http://www.cbsnews.com/stories/2008/03/02/sunday/main3897559.shtml; http://www.snowfes.com/english/index.html; http://www.greendiary.com/entry/jim-denevans-sand-art-is-strictly-for-arts-sake/ 149 "Are These Elephants Really Artists?," Sources: http://www.thailandelephant.org/en/ and http://news.

nationalgeographic.com/news/2002/06/0626_020626_elephant_2.html; http://www.baliadventuretours.com/profile_ramona.html 169 "Black Bear Research: Two Places and Two Methods," Sources: http://www.bear.org/website/introduction-from-dr-lynn-rogers.html and http://www.state.nj.us/dep/fgw/bearfacts_resandmgt.html 175 "Mountain Gorilla Facts," Source: African Wildlife Foundation: http://www.awf.org/ 176 Listening: A Conversation, Source: Journal of Sustainable Development in Africa (Volume 9, No.2, 2007) ISSN: 1520-5509 Svotwa, E., J. Ngwenya O. T. Manyanhaire and J Jiyane, Fayetteville State University, Fayetteville, North Carolina http://www.jsd-africa.com/Jsda/V9N2-Summer2007/ARC_ResidentsPerception.pdf 178 "Penguin Fact File," Source: Data from: New England Aquarium www.neaq.org 185 "National Geographic Emerging Explorer Ken Banks," Sources: http://ap.ohchr.

org/documents/dpage_e.aspx?si=A/HRC/17/27; http://travel.nationalgeographic.com/travel/traveler-magazine/one-on-one/ken-banks/; http://www.openplanetideas.com/our_blog/national-geographic-news/solving-eco-challenges-with-grassroots-messaging/ 187 Listening: A News Report, Sources: http://ap.ohchr.org/documents/dpage_e.aspx?si=A/HRC/17/27; http://travel.nationalgeographic.com/travel/traveler-magazine/one-on-one/ken-banks/; http://www.openplanetideas.com/our_blog/national-geographic-news/solving-eco-challenges-with-grassroots-messaging/ 197 "Low-Tech Recycling of Electronics," "High-Tech Recycling of Electronics," Sources: http://news.cnet.com/8301-11128_3-20031323-54.html; *High-Tech Trash*; By Chris Carroll National Geographic Staff http://ngm.nationalgeographic.com/2008/01/high-tech-trash/carroll-text

PHOTOS

1: Lynn Johnson/National Geographic Image Collection, 2: Paul Chesley/National Geographic Image Collection, 2: Ira Block /National Geographic Image Collection, 2: Peter Stanley/National Geographic Image Collection, 3: Alex Treadway/National Geographic Image Collection, 3: Justin Guariglia/National Geographic, 3: Frontpage/Shutterstock.com, 4: Beverly Joubert/National Geographic Image Collection, 5: William Allen/National Geographic Image Collection, 6: Annie Griffiths/National Geographic Image Collection, 7: Annie Griffiths/National Geographic Image Collection, 7: Annie Griffiths/National Geographic Image Collection, 7: Annie Griffiths/National Geographic Image Collection, 8: Yuri Arcurs/Shutterstock.com, 8: Catherine Yeulet/istockphoto.com, 10: Rob Marmion/Shutterstock.com, 10: Fritz Hoffman/National Geographic Image Collection, 10: Mike Theiss/National Geographic Image Collection, 10: Carsten Peter/Speleoresearch & Films/National Geographic Image Collection, 10: Mike Theiss/National Geographic Image Collection, 11: Moshimochi/Shutterstock.com, 11: Andrey Novikov/Shutterstock.com, 11: Gualtiero boffi/Shutterstock.com, 12: Simon Marcus/Corbis Super RF/Alamy, 13: Fancy/Veer/Corbis/Jupiter Images, 14: Artistic Endeavor/Shutterstock.com, 14: Michaeljung/Shutterstock.com, 14: Rgerhardt/Shutterstock.com, 17: Tyrone Turner/National Geographic Image Collection, 18: Robert Adrian Hillman/Shutterstock.com, 19: Vicki Reid/iStockphoto.com, 20: Bob Daemmrich/Alamy, 21: Bill Hatcher/National Geographic Image Collection, 22-23: Ralph Lee Hopkins/National Geographic Image

Collection, 23: Lisa F. Young/Shutterstock.com, 23: Stephan Zabel/iStockphoto.com, 23: Joel Sartore/National Geographic Image Collection, 23: Max blain/Shutterstock.com, 24: Wesley Jenkins/iStockphoto.com, 25: Joel Sartore/National Geographic Image Collection, 26: StockLite/Shutterstock.com, 26: Kristian sekulic/iStockphoto.com, 27: James L. Stanfield/National Geographic Image Collection, 27: Yagi Studio/Jupiter Images, 28: National Geographic Image Collection, 29: Julia Pivovarova/Shutterstock.com, 31: Steve Raymer/National Geographic Image Collection, 31: Joel Sartore/National Geographic Image Collection, 32: Reuters/Thomas Mukoya /Landov, 32: Hemis/Alamy, 32: Georg Gerster/National Geographic Image Collection, 33: Reuters/Thomas Mukoya /Landov, 34: Huntstock/Photodisc /Jupiter Images, 34: Huchen Lu/iStockphoto.com, 34: Clerkenwell_Images/iStockphoto.com, 34: Flashon Studio/Shutterstock.com, 35: Amy Toensing/National Geographic Image Collection, 35: Catherine Karnow/National Geographic Image Collection, 36: Michael S. Yamashita/National Geographic Image Collection, 37: Diane Cook and Len Jenshel/National Geographic Image Collection, 38: Agnieszka Kirinicjanow/iStockphoto.com, 39: Gerd Ludwig/National Geographic Image Collection, 41: Bill Curtsinger/National Geographic Image Collection, 42-43: Tim Laman/National Geographic Image Collection, 43: Bates Littlehales/National Geographic Image Collection, 43: Don Kincaid/National Geographic Image Collection, 43: Jonathan Blair/National Geographic Image Collection, 44: Raj Singh/Alamy, 44: George Steinmetz/National Geographic Image

Collection, 45: Javarman/Shutterstock.com, 47: AP Photo/Ben Curtis, 49: Catherine Karnow/National Geographic Image Collection, 50: David Mclain/National Geographic Image Collection, 50: Interfoto/Alamy, 51: Emory Kristof/National Geographic Image Collection, 52: Ira Block/National Geographic Image Collection, 52: S Murphy-Larronde/Age fotostock/Photolibrary, 52: George Oze/Alamy, 53: Dominik Dabrowski/Istockphoto.com, 53: Arena Creative/Shutterstock.com, 53: K.L. Kohn/Shutterstock.com, 55: Tony Law/National Geographic Image Collection, 57: Tony Law/National Geographic Image Collection, 58: Harris & Ewing Collection/Library of Congress, 59: Branislav Senic/Shutterstock.com, 60: Bill Aron/PhotoEdit, 61: Mike Theiss/National Geographic Image Collection, 62: Paul Chesley/National Geographic Image Collection, 62: Jason Edwards/National Geographic Image Collection, 62: Jodi Cobb/National Geographic Image Collection, 62: Jim Lopes/Shutterstock.com, 62: Vlasov Pavel /Shutterstock.com, 62-63: Kevin Mcelheran/National Geographic Image Collection, 64: Petr Bukal/Shutterstock.com, 64: Galyna Andrushko/Shutterstock.com, 66: James P. Blair/National Geographic Image Collection, 66: Sergey_Ryzhenko/Shutterstock.com, 66: Ellen McKnight/Alamy, 67: Vlad Siaber/Shutterstock.com, 69: Grady Reese/iStockphoto.com, 70: Rich Reid/National Geographic Image Collection, 71: Tyler Olson/Shutterstock.com, 72: Mike Theiss/National Geographic Image Collection, 73: Carsten Peter/National Geographic Image Collection, 73: Robert Clark/National Geographic Image Collection, 73: MikeTheiss/National Geographic Image Collection,

continued on p.226

Living for Work

Think and Discuss

1. Look at the photo and read the caption. Would you like to do this job? Explain.
2. What do you think makes a good job?
3. Read the title of this unit. What do you think it means?

A construction worker climbs up a crane near tall buildings in Pittsburgh, Pennsylvania, USA.

1

Exploring the Theme: Living for Work

Look at the photos and read the captions. Match the photos with the places on the map. Then discuss the questions.

1. Which job looks the most interesting? Explain.
2. Which job do you think is the most difficult? Explain.
3. Which jobs would you like to do? Explain.

Firefighters put out fires and help people. Their work is very dangerous, so they need to learn special skills. This firefighter works in New York City, **USA**.

Policemen and **policewomen** help people in many different ways. Some police officers ride horses when they work. This **policewoman** is from **Canada**.

Farmers usually work outdoors. They need to know how to plant and grow food. These farmers in **Ethiopia** are harvesting wheat.

Teachers help their students learn important information and skills. This teacher in **India** teaches young children.

Waiters and **waitresses** work in cafés and restaurants. Their work can be difficult because they need to bring people food and drinks quickly. This waiter works in Perugia, **Italy**.

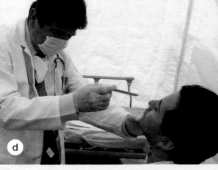

Doctors help their patients get well and tell them how to stay healthy. This doctor is helping a patient in Mexico City, **Mexico**.

A | **Using a Dictionary.** Read and listen to the words. Then match each word with its definition. These are words you will hear and use in Lesson A.

track 1-2

1. __c__ travel   a. (n.) a chance to do something
2. ____ opportunity   b. (adj.) likely to hurt or harm you
3. ____ experiences   c. (v.) to go from one place to another
4. ____ skills   d. (n.) things you do or that happen to you
5. ____ dangerous   e. (n.) things you are able to do well

B | **Meaning from Context.** Read and listen to the article. Notice the words in blue. These are words you will hear and use in Lesson A.

track 1-3

Dereck and Beverly Joubert filming and photographing a meerkat in Africa.

Beverly and Dereck Joubert

Beverly Joubert and her husband Dereck are creative people. Together, they write and make interesting films about animals in Africa. They love to explore different parts of Africa, and the result is 22 films, 10 books, and many articles!

In order to work together, the Jouberts need to communicate well and understand one another. Their films win many awards[1], but for the Jouberts, making films is an adventure. It is also a way to do something good for endangered[2] animals. They started the Big Cats Initiative fund[3]. With this money, the Jouberts can help the lions and other animals they love. Says Dereck, "If there was ever a time to take action, it is now."

[1]An **award** is a prize for doing something well.
[2]Something that is **endangered** might soon disappear or become extinct.
[3]A **fund** is money to be used for a certain purpose.

C | Write each word in blue from exercise **B** next to its definition.

1. ___creative___ (adj.) having imagination and artistic ability
2. _____ (v.) to go different places and learn about things
3. _____ (n.) an exciting time or event
4. _____ (v.) to share information with others
5. _____ (v.) to do something good for someone or something

D | **Using a Dictionary.** Work with a partner. Complete the chart with other forms of the words from exercises **A** and **B**. Use your dictionary to help you. (*See page 209 of the Independent Student Handbook for more information on using a dictionary.*)

Noun	Verb	Adjective
exploration	explore	exploratory
	communicate	
	help	
		creative

A | Work with a partner. Read the conversation and fill in each blank with a word from the box. Then practice the conversation.

| communicate | creative | explore | help | opportunity |

A: Guess what! I have a new job (1) _____.

B: That's great! What's the job?

A: I get to go to Kenya and take photos for a book. It's pretty (2) _____ work, and I can (3) _____ Kenya while I'm there.

B: Good for you! Can you (4) _____ by email or telephone from there?

A: Oh, sure. I can send you an email message every day.

B: Good. Then I won't worry about you.

A: By the way, can you (5) _____ me with something now?

B: No problem. What do you need?

A: I need you to pick up my camera from the camera shop.

B | Read the article. Then fill in each blank with a word from the box. Use each word only once. Then listen and check your answers.

track 1-4

| adventure | dangerous | experiences | skills | travel |

Photographer Annie Griffiths

Photographer Annie Griffiths on location in Petra, Jordan

Annie Griffiths is famous for her beautiful photographs. The photos come from countries all over the world, so it's just a normal part of life for Griffiths to (1) _____.

Living in other countries is not for everyone, but for Griffiths and her children, it's an (2) _____. Her children especially love the Middle East, and their (3) _____ in that part of the world helped them to learn about other cultures.

Griffiths' work can also be (4) _____. Traveling is not always safe. In the Galápagos Islands, Griffiths found herself in the water with sharks one day!

Besides writing and taking pictures, Griffiths teaches photography (5) _____ to people who want to become photographers. They know they are learning from one of the best photographers in the world.

Before Listening

Predicting Content. You are going to listen to an interview with Annie Griffiths. Look at the photo and information. What do you think Griffiths will talk about? Discuss your ideas with a partner.

About My Photo

Where: Victoria Falls, Zambia

When: around sunset, in 2006

What: a swimmer

Why: beautiful light, amazing place

Listening: An Interview

Critical Thinking Focus: Identifying Main Ideas

The main idea or ideas of a talk are the speaker's most important ideas. The details of a talk give more information about the main ideas.

A | Listening for Main Ideas. Listen to an interview with Annie Griffiths. Check (✔) the main idea of the interview.

❏ Annie Griffiths' work is dangerous sometimes.
❏ Annie Griffiths' job as a photographer is very interesting.
❏ Annie Griffiths knows how to communicate with the people she meets.

B | Listening for Details. Read the statements and answer choices. Then listen to the interview again and choose the correct word or phrase.

1. Annie Griffiths' favorite place is _____.
   a. New Zealand
   b. The Middle East
   c. Southern Africa

2. Annie Griffiths loves taking pictures of wildlife and _____.
   a. landscapes
   b. beaches
   c. cities

3. Annie Griffiths took her children with her because her assignments were _____.
   a. two or three months long
   b. three or four months long
   c. four or five months long

4. When Annie Griffiths doesn't know the local language, she gestures and _____.
   a. writes
   b. smiles
   c. translates

5. Annie Griffiths describes the day she took the photo at Victoria Falls as _____.
   a. hot and humid
   b. unforgettable
   c. adventurous

Annie Griffiths' children in Petra, Jordan, wearing Bedouin clothing and pretending to drink tea.

After Listening

A | **Making Inferences.** Read the statements and circle **T** for *true* or **F** for *false*. The answers are not in the speakers' exact words. You need to think about what you heard.

1.	Annie Griffiths likes her life of adventure.	**T**	**F**
2.	Griffiths knows how to make friends with strangers.	**T**	**F**
3.	Griffiths does not go to places that are dangerous.	**T**	**F**
4.	Griffiths' children do not like to travel.	**T**	**F**

B | **Self-Reflection.** Discuss the questions with a partner.

1. Griffiths takes her children to work. Is it a good idea to take your family to work? Explain.
2. What places do you like to travel to? What do you think is fun and interesting about traveling?

Ancient acacia trees grow near the huge red sand dunes of the Namib Desert. Photo by Annie Griffiths

Galápagos sea lions resting on a white beach. Photo by Annie Griffiths

Language Function

Communicating that You Don't Understand

We use these expressions and others to communicate that we don't understand what someone says. *(See pages 210-211 of the Independent Student Handbook for more information on useful phrases and expressions.)*

I don't understand.   *I'm sorry?*   *I'm not sure what you mean.*
Do you mean . . .?   *I'm sorry, I missed that.*

🎧 track 1-6 **A** | Read and listen to the conversation. Then <u>underline</u> the expressions that show when the speakers don't understand.

A: I took a job aptitude test today.

B: A job aptitude test? What's that?

A: Well, it's a test of your skills and interests.

B: I see. And did you get the job?

A: I'm not sure what you mean.

B: I mean—you took a job test, right? Did you do well on the test and get the job?

A: Oh, no. The test only shows which job might be good for you.

B: Ah, I see. It helps you to choose the right job.

A: Exactly!

👥 **B** | Practice the conversation from exercise **A** with a partner. Then switch roles and practice it again.

👥 **C** | Practice the conversations below with your partner. Student B uses one of the expressions from the box. Then switch roles and practice the conversations again using different expressions.

1. **A:** You need a lot of special skills to be a builder.
   B: ...
   A: Well, to build houses, you need to know how to do many things.

2. **A:** Being a teacher is an adventure.
   B: ...
   A: Every day in the classroom is different. You never know what will happen.

Grammar

The Simple Present vs. The Present Continuous

We use the *simple present* for:
1. Repeated actions or habits: *He **goes** to work at eight o'clock every day.*
2. Things that are always true: *Fish **swim** in the ocean.*

Note: We use an *-s* ending with third person singular verbs in the simple present.

   *It/She/He always **arrives** late.*

We use the *present continuous* for:
1. Things that are happening now: *She is **taking** a photo.*
2. Things that are happening around this time: *I **am traveling** a lot these days.*

A | Read the conversations below. Fill in each blank with the simple present or the present continuous form of a verb from the box. You will need to use one verb twice.

cook	help	sell	show	teach	text	~~work~~	write

Peter: What do you do, Jorge?

Jorge: I (1) ___work___ in a restaurant.

Peter: What are you doing right now?

Jorge: I (2) _____ a new meal for tonight.

Peter: Smells delicious.

Brenda: Hi, Steve. What are you working on?

Steve: I (3) _____ a new computer program.

Brenda: Sounds fun.

Cho: You're a real estate agent, right Raquel?

Raquel: Yes, that's right. I (4) _____ and (5) _____ homes.
I (6) _____ a house to a buyer at the moment.

Lana: What are you doing on your smartphone?

Dennis: I (7) _____ Bill.

Lana: Bill?

Dennis: You know, Professor Bill Franks. He (8) _____ right now.
Hopefully he can meet us after his lecture.

Eduardo: What do you do for your job?

Frank: I'm a police officer. I (9) _____ people who are in trouble.

B | Work with a partner. Look at the photo. Then read the story and fill in each blank with the verb in parentheses. Use the simple present or present continuous.

This is Cynthia Lauber and her son Mark. Cynthia (1) _____works_____ (work) in a clothing store in Lincoln, Nebraska, in the United States. She (2) _____ (help) people find the right clothes. Unfortunately, Cynthia (3) _____ (not make) much money at the store. She (4) _____ (look) for a different job. At the moment, Mark (5) _____ (help) her search for jobs online. They (6) _____ (make) a list of possibilities, but Cynthia (7) _____ (not have) the skills for every job.

C | With your partner, look at the photos. Then answer the questions and discuss the different jobs.

In which job   . . . do you explore different places?

. . . do you need good communication skills?

. . . do you travel a lot?

. . . do you help people?

. . . do you need special skills?

Chef

Fisherman

Reporter

Construction Worker

D | **Discussion.** Work with your partner. Follow the instructions below.

1. Look around the room. Talk about three things that are happening in the room right now.
2. Think of someone you know well. Tell your partner three things that person is probably doing right now.
3. Think of a job you both know about. Make a list of three things a person with that job does every day.

Doing an Interview

A | **Note-Taking.** Work with a partner. Take turns asking and answering the questions from the Career Aptitude Test. Take short notes on your partner's answers.

Career Aptitude Test	
A career aptitude test can help you decide which job or career is right for you.	
Interview Questions	**My Partner's Answers**
1. Are you a creative person?	
2. Do you like to travel and explore new places?	
3. Are you afraid of dangerous situations? For example, working with animals or with electricity?	
4. Do you have good communication skills?	
5. Do you like to spend time with other people, or do you prefer to spend time alone?	
6. Do you like to keep fit?	
7. Are you a good problem-solver?	
8. Do you like to help people?	

News reporters have good communication skills.

Computer programmers are good problem-solvers.

Teachers like to help people.

B | Look back at your notes from exercise **A**. Then tell your partner which jobs in the box below might be good for him or her. Explain your reasons.

business executive	doctor/nurse	firefighter	photographer	salesperson
computer programmer	farmer	news reporter	restaurant worker	teacher

C | Form a group with another pair of students and follow the steps below.

1. Tell the group which job might be best for your partner. Explain your reasons.
2. Tell the group your opinion of your partner's choice of job for you. Is it really a good job for you? Why, or why not?

BUTLER SCHOOL

Before Viewing

A | Prior Knowledge. Look at the photo of a butler. Then read each sentence and circle **T** for *true* or **F** for *false*.

1. Butlers usually work in England.   **T**   **F**
2. Butlers work for rich people in large houses.   **T**   **F**
3. Butlers wear informal clothes.   **T**   **F**
4. Butlers speak in a formal way.   **T**   **F**

B | Using a Dictionary. Match each word from the video to its definition. Use your dictionary to help you.

1. refreshments (n.) ____
2. fetch (v.) ____
3. practice (v.) ____
4. tradition (n.) ____

a. to go and get something
b. to do something again and again in order to improve
c. a custom or belief that has existed for a long time
d. things to drink or eat

While Viewing

A | Watch the video. Circle the correct word or phrase for each sentence.

1. In the past, there were (many/few) butlers.
2. Nowadays, there are (many/few) butlers.
3. The students at the school come from (one country/many countries).
4. Butler school is (easy/difficult) for the students.

B | Using the Simple Present. Watch the video again. Check (✔) the things students do at the butler school.

❑ graduate from the school   ❑ learn to walk correctly
❑ iron newspapers   ❑ practice saying things
❑ learn from books   ❑ wash clothes

After Viewing

A | Discussion. With a partner, read the list of careers and the words and phrases in the box below. Then discuss each career using some of the words and phrases from the box and your own ideas.

I think doctors work very long hours.

That's true, but they make a high salary.

Careers:

butler	news reporter
businessperson	scientist
doctor	waiter/waitress

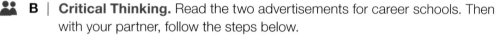

dangerous	high salary	low pay
difficult job	interesting work	opportunities to learn new things
easy work	long hours	travel opportunities

B | Critical Thinking. Read the two advertisements for career schools. Then with your partner, follow the steps below.

Learn to be a Medical Assistant!

Doctors and nurses are not the only people in a hospital. Medical assistants work in:

- Medical offices
- Medical laboratories

At Liverton Technical College, students receive six weeks of interesting classes and three weeks of training at a hospital.

To learn more about this exciting career, call or email now: (963) 555-4362; info@LT.com

---

APT School for the Culinary Arts since 1952

At APT, food and restaurants are everything. Choose from the following 16-week courses:

- *Head Chef*
- *Dessert Chef*
- *Food Server*
- *Dining Room Manager*

You could soon have a career as a restaurant worker! Call or email today. (217) 555-7090; chef@apt.com

---

1. Use some of the words and phrases from exercise **A** to describe the careers in the advertisements: medical assistant and restaurant worker.
2. Tell your partner which career might be better for you. Explain your reasons.
3. Tell your partner which career-school advertisement you think is better and why.

🎧 track 1-7 **A** | **Meaning from Context.** Read and listen to three interviews. Notice the words in blue. These are words you will hear and use in Lesson B.

Q: What kind of people make good nurses?

A: Well, you have to be **organized**. For example, I'm **in charge of** my patients' medicine. I have to give them the correct medicine, so I write everything down in a chart. I get the medicine. Then, I check on my chart that it's the correct one. Nobody gets the wrong medicine that way.

Q: You *are* well organized!

A: Thanks. It has a big **effect** on my patients' health, so it's important to me. Nurses also have to be fit because the work is very **physical**.

Q: What kind of physical work do you do?

A: I stand or walk all the time, and sometimes I have to lift patients up from their beds.

Q: Is teaching a difficult job?

A: Sometimes it is. **Although** the students are wonderful, the school has a rule I don't like.

Q: What kind of rule?

A: Well, I teach math and science, and I think they're very important subjects. But students here don't have to take both subjects. They can take one or the other and still **graduate**.

Q: Do you mean they can finish school and never take math, for example?

A: Yes, they can. It's not a good idea, in my opinion.

Q: What does an engineer do every day?

A: Well, there are many kinds of engineers. I'm an industrial engineer. I look at our processes here at the factory, and I **search** for any problems.

Q: What do you do if you find a problem?

A: I give a **presentation** to my **managers**. We have a meeting, and I explain the problem to them. We try to find ways to solve it.

Q: What happens next?

A: They usually follow my suggestions.

Q: So the managers here have a lot of respect for you.

A: Yes, I **believe** they do respect me. It's one of the reasons I like my job.

B | **Using a Dictionary.** Check (✔) the words you already know or understand from the context in exercise **A**. Use a dictionary to help you with any words you are unsure of.

❏ although (conj.)   ❏ in charge of (phrase)   ❏ graduate (v.)   ❏ organized (adj.)   ❏ presentation (n.)
❏ believe (v.)   ❏ effect (n.)   ❏ managers (n.)   ❏ physical (adj.)   ❏ search (v.)

A | Complete each sentence with a word from the box.

although	effect	graduate	physical	presentations	search

1. It's a good job, _____ the salary is not very high.
2. Roland needs to _____ for a new job.
3. He speaks well and gives good business _____.
4. Each year more than 4000 students _____ from the school.
5. They exercise and they're very fit, so they can do very _____ work.
6. A good manager can have a positive _____ on the employees' work.

B | Read the conversation. Then fill in each blank with a word or phrase from the box.

although	believe	graduated	in charge of	organized

Interviewer:	So, you (1) _____ a creative job is the best thing for you?
Jenny:	Yes, I do. I (2) _____ from college with a degree in photography.
Interviewer:	What other job skills do you have?
Jenny:	Well, I'm very (3) _____. At my last job we moved offices. I managed the move. I had to make sure everything arrived in the new office.
Interviewer:	Can you manage other employees?
Jenny:	Yes. In my last job I was (4) _____ five other employees. (5) _____ it was hard work, I enjoyed it a lot.

C | **Role-Playing.** Work with a partner. Role-play the situation below. Then switch roles.

Student A: You are the manager at a workplace. Ask your partner the job interview questions from the conversation in exercise **B**.

Student B: You are at a job interview. You really want the job. Answer the interview questions with your own ideas.

D | **Critical Thinking.** Discuss the questions with your partner.

1. What **effect** does each worker in exercise **A** on page 14 have on the world? For example, what **effect** does the nurse have on her patients' health?
2. What does the engineer **believe** about his **managers**? Do you think he is right? Explain.
3. Besides nursing, what other jobs are very **physical**? Are they good jobs in your opinion?
4. In what ways are you an **organized** student? How could you be more **organized**?

Pronunciation

Syllable Stress

We can divide words in English into one or more syllables. For example, *doctor* has two syllables (doc-tor). In words with more than one syllable, one syllable usually receives the main stress. For example, in the word doctor, *doc* is stressed. The syllable with the main stress is louder and longer than the other syllables.

Examples:

track 1-8

One syllable:	Two syllables:	Three syllables:
book	**doc**-tor	**com**-pan-y

track 1-9 **A** | Listen and <u>underline</u> the main stress in each word.

1. nurse
2. study
3. travel
4. remember
5. reporter
6. creative
7. receive
8. skills

track 1-10 **B** | Write each word from the box in the correct column of the chart below. Then listen and check your answers.

adventure	cook	know	officer	travel
amazing	fly	money	teacher	yesterday

One-syllable Words	Two-syllable Words	Three-syllable Words
cook	*money*	*adventure*

Before Listening

track 1-11 Here are some words you will hear in the Listening section. Listen and repeat the words. Then answer the questions below.

billion	marine biologist	ocean	pollution	tuna

1. How many syllables are in each word? Write the number of syllables next to each word.
2. Which syllable in each word receives the most stress? <u>Underline</u> the syllables with the most stress.

Listening: An Informal Conversation

A | You are going to listen to a conversation between two students. Listen to the first part of the conversation. What are the students talking about? Check (✔) the correct answer.

- ❏ a presentation that Becca missed
- ❏ a presentation that Franco missed
- ❏ a presentation that was not very good

B | **Listening for Main Ideas.** Listen to the entire conversation. Check (✔) the main idea of the conversation.

- ❏ Becca was not in class on Thursday because she was sick.
- ❏ The presentation was very good.
- ❏ Dr. Earle says the world's people are having a bad effect on the oceans.

C | **Listening for Details.** Listen again. Check (✔) any ideas that are NOT part of the conversation.

- ❏ Becca feels better today.
- ❏ Dr. Earle gave a presentation to the class on Thursday.
- ❏ Dr. Earle earns a high salary.
- ❏ There are almost seven billion people on earth now.
- ❏ It's fine to eat tuna and other large ocean fish.

Dr. Sylvia Earle

After Listening

A | **Self-Reflection.** Read each statement below and circle *Agree* or *Disagree*.

1. Dr. Earle's career might be a good career for me.   **Agree**   **Disagree**
2. When you're sick, it's better not to go to class.   **Agree**   **Disagree**
3. The large number of people in the world is a problem.   **Agree**   **Disagree**
4. What people eat has a big effect on the oceans.   **Agree**   **Disagree**

Student to Student: Giving Feedback while Listening

Use these expressions to show someone that you're listening and interested in the conversation.

Really? I see.   *Interesting!*   *I see what you mean.*   *Wow!*

B | **Discussion.** Form a group with two or three other students. Discuss the statements in exercise **A**. Give reasons why you agree or disagree with each statement. Use the expressions from the box to show interest in your classmates' ideas.

Grammar

👥 **A** | Work with a partner. Practice the conversation. Then switch roles and practice it again.

Terry:	What are you doing, Chris?
Chris:	I'm writing in my journal.
Terry:	Interesting! How often do you do that?
Chris:	Well, I always write something before I go to bed.
Terry:	And you sometimes write during the day, too—like you're doing now.
Chris:	That's right. Are you surprised?
Terry:	A little bit. People are usually on their smartphones and laptops nowadays. I seldom see anyone writing in a journal.
Chris:	I guess I'm strange, but you probably knew that already.
Terry:	Very funny. You might be a little strange, but in a *good* way.
Chris:	Thanks, Terry.

👥 **B** | **Discussion.** With your partner, discuss the questions about the conversation from exercise **A**.

1. Does Chris write in his journal every night? How do you know?
2. Does Chris write in his journal every day? How do you know?
3. Does Terry see people writing in a journal very often? How do you know?

Adverbs of Frequency

We use adverbs of frequency to talk about how often we do things. These adverbs go before most verbs, but after the verb *be*.

> I **always** <u>brush</u> my teeth in the morning.
> This bus <u>is</u> **usually** on time.

100%	**always**	*My children **always** do their homework.*
	usually	*That photographer **usually** takes good pictures.*
	often	*Archaeologists are **often** outdoors.*
	sometimes	*My uncle **sometimes** gives me money.*
	occasionally	*The weather here is **occasionally** very hot.*
	rarely/seldom	*Lorna is **rarely** in the library. She **seldom** works there.*
0%	**never**	*I am **never** late for class.*

C | Complete each sentence with an appropriate adverb of frequency. There may be more than one correct answer.

1. Butlers _____ wear formal clothes at work.
2. Annie Griffiths _____ takes beautiful photos.
3. Good students _____ forget to do their homework.
4. Doctors _____ work at more than one hospital.
5. Marine biologists _____ swim in the ocean.
6. Archaeologists _____ work indoors.

D | Compare your answers from exercise **C** with a partner's. When you have different answers, compare the meanings of the adverbs of frequency.

Language Function: Using Adverbs of Frequency

A | Work with a partner. Read the work schedule of a hotel housekeeper named Erica. Then answer the questions below.

1. Which days does Erica work at the hotel? Which days does she not work?
2. Which day is Erica's longest workday? Which is the shortest?
3. What does Erica have to do for her job?

B | With your partner, discuss Erica's weekly schedule using adverbs of frequency. Use the language from exercise **A** and your own ideas.

Hotel Avalon

Weekly work schedule: Erica S.

Tuesday	Wednesday	Thursday	Friday	Saturday
start: 7:00 a.m.	start: 7:00 a.m.	start: 7:00 a.m.	start: 7:00 a.m.	start: 7:00 a.m.
				end: 12:00 p.m.
end: 3:30 p.m.	end: 3:30 p.m.		end: 3:30 p.m.	
		end: 5:30 p.m.		

Job Duties:
Every day: *clean the guest bathrooms; make beds; remove trash*
Tuesday through Friday: *get clean sheets and towels from the hotel laundry room*
Wednesday and Friday: *clean the restaurant dining room after breakfast*
Saturday: *put new menus and information cards in the guest rooms*

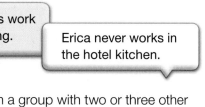

Erica always starts work early in the morning.

Erica never works in the hotel kitchen.

C | **Discussion.** Form a group with two or three other students. Discuss which words you might use to describe Erica's job. Then think of two more words that describe her job.

dangerous	difficult	easy
high-paying	interesting	physical

ENGAGE: Giving a Short Presentation about Yourself

You are going to introduce yourself and give a short presentation about yourself.

A | Planning a Presentation. Write your answers to the questions in the chart below or in your notebook. Then share your answers with a partner.

Questions	Answers
1. What's your name *(the name you want to be called in this class)*?	
2. Where are you from?	
3. What subjects are you studying?	
4. What do you like to do in your free time?	
5. What is one interesting fact about you?	

Presentation Skills: Introducing Yourself

When you give a presentation, you can use these expressions to introduce yourself.

Hi, I'm (your name).   *Hello, my name is (your name).*
I'm from (your city, country, university, etc.)

B | Planning a Presentation Read and listen to one student's presentation. Then follow the steps below.

track 1-14

Hi, everyone. My name is Alejandro, but please call me Alex. I'm from Bogotá. As you know, that's the capital city of Colombia. I'm studying English now, and I'm also studying international relations. In my free time, I like to play tennis or send text messages to my friends. One interesting fact about me is that I have a pretty large family. I live with my parents, two sisters and one brother, and two grandparents as well.

1. Underline the expressions Alex uses to introduce himself.
2. Circle the information Alex gives about the place he's from.
3. Decide which expressions you will use to introduce yourself.

C | Presentation. Introduce yourself to the class or to a small group. Then tell them about yourself using the information from exercise **A**. You can use the student's presentation from exercise **B** to help you.

Good Times, Good Feelings

Think and Discuss

1. Look at the photo. What is this man doing? Why?

2. How do you think the man in the photo feels?

A man greets the sun after several days of rain
at Mavora Lakes, South Island, New Zealand.

21

Exploring the Theme:
Good Times, Good Feelings

A | Look at the photos and read the captions. Then discuss the questions.

1. What activities make people feel good?
2. Do you do any of these activities? Do they make you feel good? Why, or why not?
3. What other activities make you feel good? Why?

Hot air balloons float above a crowd at a Balloon Fiesta, Albuquerque, New Mexico, USA.

Activities That Make Us Feel Good

Research says that when we **help other people**, we feel good.

We feel good when we do **physical exercise**.

Having **close friendships and family connections** makes us feel good.

Having regular **vacations** and **time away from work** helps us feel good.

track 1-15 A | Listen and check (✔) the words you already know. These are words you will hear and use in Lesson A.

❑ funny (adj.)	❑ joy (n.)	❑ led (v.)	❑ recorded (v.)	❑ situations (n.)
❑ joke (n.)	❑ laughter (n.)	❑ noise (n.)	❑ researchers (n.)	❑ unique (adj.)

track 1-16 B | Meaning from Context. Read and listen to the article and notice the words in blue.

a chimpanzee

From Pant-Pant to Ha-Ha

Look at the photo. Does this look like laughter? New research says that apes laugh when they are tickled[1]. **Researchers** at the University of Portsmouth **led** a 'tickle team.' The group of researchers tickled the necks, feet, hands, and armpits of young apes. The team **recorded** more than 800 of the resulting laughs on tape. The research suggests that the apes' panting[2] **noise** is the sound of **laughter**. They think that this panting is the basis[3] for human expressions of joy— the 'ha-ha' sound we make when we laugh. When we find something **funny**, such as a joke, we laugh. When apes find something funny, such as a tickle, they laugh. Humans find many **situations** funny—such as jokes, tickles, TV comedy shows—but we are not **unique** because animals laugh, too.

[1]When you **tickle** someone, you touch them lightly with your fingers to make them laugh.
[2]When people or animals **pant**, they breathe very hard.
[3]The **basis** for something is the starting point from which it develops.

C | Write each word in blue from exercise **B** next to its definition below.

1. ___funny___ (adj.) able to make one smile or laugh
2. _____ (adj.) the only one, one of a kind
3. _____ (n.) a sound (often unpleasant)
4. _____ (n.) people who study or investigate something scientifically
5. _____ (n.) great happiness
6. _____ (v.) directed, showed the way
7. _____ (n.) a story that makes people laugh
8. _____ (v.) made an audio or written copy of something
9. _____ (n.) sounds of happiness or amusement
10. _____ (n.) the way things are at a certain time and place

A | Fill in each blank with a word in **blue** from exercise **A** on page 24. Use each word only once.

1. **A:** Social ___situations___ such as parties sometimes make me nervous.

   B: Me too.

2. **A:** They felt great _____ when they held their first grandchild.

   B: I'm sure they were really happy.

3. **A:** So, who _____ the group discussion yesterday?

   B: Adriana did. She asked some really good questions about the topic.

4. **A:** There are several new _____ on Professor Watson's team.

   B: Interesting. What are they studying?

5. **A:** I like your new CD. The singer is very unusual.

   B: Yes, she has a _____ style.

6. **A:** Larry told a _____, but it wasn't _____. Nobody even smiled.

   B: Poor Larry!

7. **A:** I can hear _____ coming from next door.

   B: Yeah, they're watching their favorite TV sitcom[1].

8. **A:** I missed the lecture.

   B: Don't worry. I _____ the lecture on my computer. We can listen to it again later.

9. **A:** Your car is making a really odd _____.

   B: Really? Perhaps I should take it to a mechanic.

B | **Self-Reflection.** Form a group with two or three other students. Discuss the questions.

1. When was the last time you **laughed** a lot? What was **funny**?
2. What **situations** do you find **funny**? What makes you **laugh**?

> My children tell jokes. The jokes are so bad I laugh.

[1]**Sitcom** is short for situation comedy. A **sitcom** is a funny TV series.

Before Listening

A | **Discussion.** Look at the photos. Then discuss the questions with a partner.

1. Both of these activities can be enjoyable. How are the people in the photos enjoying themselves?
2. Who in the photos is likely to laugh? Explain.

B | **Predicting Content.** You are going to hear a lecture about laughter. With your partner, check (✔) the topics you think you will hear about.

❏ reasons people laugh   ❏ animal laughter

❏ examples of jokes   ❏ things that people are afraid of

Listening: A Lecture

Critical Thinking Focus: Understanding the Speaker's Purpose

When we listen to a lecture or a conversation, we need to know *why* the speaker is giving the talk, lecture, etc. This is the speaker's purpose. Sometimes speakers directly state their purpose, but often they do not. Listening to what speakers say and how they say it will help you understand their purpose.

Here are some examples.
The purpose of a political speech is often <u>to persuade or convince the audience to vote.</u>
The purpose of a TV sitcom is <u>to entertain the audience.</u>
The purpose of a college lecture is <u>to inform the audience.</u>

🎧 track 1-17
A | **Understanding the Speaker's Purpose.** Read the questions and answers. Then listen to the first part of the lecture and choose the correct answers.

1. What is the speaker's main purpose?

   a. to make us laugh   b. to give us information

2. Does the speaker directly state his purpose?

   a. yes   b. no

B | Checking Predictions. Look back at the predictions you made in exercise **B** on page 26. Then listen to the entire lecture. Which of your predictions were correct?

track 1-18

C | Listening for Main Ideas. Read the statements and answer choices below. Then listen again and choose the best word or phrase to complete each statement.

track 1-18

1. People usually laugh _____.
   a. at good jokes
   b. after they learn to talk
   c. when other people laugh

2. For rats, laughter is a form of _____.
   a. communication
   b. play
   c. research

3. People will probably *not* laugh _____.
   a. in a social situation
   b. when they're with friends
   c. when they're alone

D | Listening for Details. Read the statements. Then listen again and complete each statement with information from the lecture.

track 1-18

1. Professor Panksepp, the rat researcher, works at _____ State University.

2. The rats' laughter is at a very _____ frequency, so people can't hear it.

3. More than _____ percent of laughter is *not* because of jokes.

4. TV comedy shows often use a _____ track to make the audience laugh.

After Listening

Critical Thinking. Discuss the questions with a partner.

1. Do you think some people laugh more than others? If so, what do you think the reason is for this?

2. Is it always a good thing to laugh? Or, are there times when it is not good to laugh? Explain.

Language Function

Asking Questions to Show Interest

When we have a conversation, it is polite to show interest in what the other person is saying. Sometimes, we use an expression of interest followed by a question to find out more information.

A: *I don't like my new job.*
B: **Oh,** *why not?*

A: *The movie was just awful!*
B: **Oh, that's too bad.** *What didn't you like about it?*

A: *My vacation was fabulous. I'm so relaxed now.*
B: **Good for you.** *Do you have any photos?*

A: *It was a fascinating lecture.*
B: **Really?** *Why?*

A | Complete each conversation below with an appropriate expression from the box.

Good for you!	Really?	How funny!	Oh, that's too bad.	Oh, why?

1. **A:** I hate that new TV sitcom.
   B: _____
   A: It wasn't funny!

2. **A:** Oh, I love this weather. It makes me happy.
   B: _____ Most people don't like rain and cold.

3. **A:** I'm going shopping. I just got my paycheck.
   B: _____ Don't spend it all at once!

4. **A:** I'm studying to be a chef.
   B: _____ That's exactly what I want to do.

5. **A:** I didn't pass the test.
   B: _____ Better luck next time.

B | Practice the conversations with a partner. Then switch roles and practice them again.

C | Work with your partner and have a conversation. Student A: Ask Student B about what makes him or her laugh. Student B: Use the expressions of interest from exercise **A**. Then switch roles.

Grammar

The Simple Present Tense: *Yes/No* Questions

Yes/No questions are questions that we can answer with the words *yes* or *no*.

For *yes/no* questions with the verb *be*, we put *am, is,* or *are* before the subject.

Questions	**Answers**
Is the movie funny?	Yes, it is. OR No, it isn't.
Are researchers interesting people?	Yes, they are. OR No, they're not.

For *yes/no* questions with other verbs, we put *do* or *does* before the subject, and use the base form of the verb.

Questions	**Answers**
Do you **laugh** a lot?	Yes, I do. OR No, I don't.
Does he **tell** jokes all the time?	Yes, he does. OR No, he doesn't.
Do we **laugh** in lectures?	Yes, we do. OR No, we don't.

A | Complete the questions in the survey below. Use *do/does* or *are* and the verbs from the box.

have	do	like	have	keep

Survey: How Happy Are You?

1. ____Are____ you a social person?   **Yes   No**
2. _____ you _____ activities with other people?   **Yes   No**
3. _____ you _____ fun with people?   **Yes   No**
4. _____ you _____ a vacation every year?   **Yes   No**
5. _____ you middle-aged?   **Yes   No**
6. _____ you married?   **Yes   No**
7. _____ you _____ fit?   **Yes   No**
8. _____ you _____ being outside?   **Yes   No**

B | Answer the questions in the survey. Circle *Yes* or *No*.

C | **Discussion.** Compare your answers from exercise **B** with a partner's.

Answer: *If you answered Yes to all the questions, you are likely to be a very happy person!*

Pronunciation

track 1-19 **The Intonation of *Yes/No* Questions**

Intonation is the rise and fall of your voice. When you ask a *yes/no* question, your voice rises or goes up on the last content word. Content words are *nouns, verbs, adjectives,* and *adverbs.*

Examples:

*Do you think it is **funny***?   *Is she really **laughing**?*

track 1-20 **A** | Listen to and read these *yes/no* questions and answers. Underline the words where the voice rises.

1. **A:** Do you laugh a lot?
   B: Yes, I do.

2. **A:** Do you like weddings?
   B: I love weddings!

3. **A:** Do you like sitcoms?
   B: Some of them are OK.

4. **A:** Do you go to many parties?
   B: No, not really.

B | With a partner, practice the conversations from exercise **A**.

C | Take turns asking your partner *yes/no* questions about what he or she does to have fun.

| dance | go to parties | watch sitcoms | socialize with friends | play games |

Do you like to dance?

No, I don't. Do you?

Yes, I do!

D | Form a group with two or three other students. One member of the group thinks of a well-known sitcom or movie. Other members of the group ask *yes/no* questions to find out what the name of the show or movie is.

Student A:	Is it a movie?
Student B:	No, it's a sitcom.
Student A:	Does this show come on at the same time every week?
Student B:	Yes, it does.
Student C:	Do older people like to watch this show?
Student B:	No, they don't.

Discussing Celebrations and Holidays

A | **Self-Reflection.** Think of a fun celebration or holiday. Read the questions. Then complete the chart with your answers.

	My Answers	My Partner's Answers
1. What's the name of the celebration or holiday?		
2. Do you celebrate it every year?		
3. Is this celebration in your home?		
4. Does your family get together?		
5. Do you eat a big meal together?		
6. Do you sing or dance?		
7. Do you give gifts?		
8. Is this a fun time for you? Explain.		

B | With a partner, ask and answer the questions from exercise **A**. Complete the chart with your partner's answers. Show interest and ask follow-up questions.

Yes, we sing.

Really? What songs do you sing?

C | Form a group with another pair of students. Report what you learned about your partner in exercise **B**.

A dragon float in a Chinese lunar new year procession, Singapore Island, Singapore

A family celebrating Thanksgiving together in Lincoln, Nebraska, USA

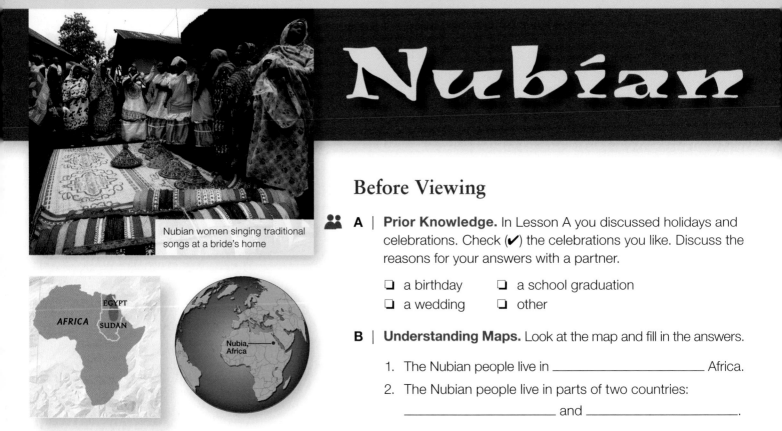

Nubian

Nubian women singing traditional songs at a bride's home

Before Viewing

A | **Prior Knowledge.** In Lesson A you discussed holidays and celebrations. Check (✔) the celebrations you like. Discuss the reasons for your answers with a partner.

- ❏ a birthday
- ❏ a school graduation
- ❏ a wedding
- ❏ other

B | **Understanding Maps.** Look at the map and fill in the answers.

1. The Nubian people live in _____ Africa.

2. The Nubian people live in parts of two countries: _____ and _____.

C | **Using a Dictionary.** Read about the Nubian wedding celebration you are going to see in the video. The celebration includes both Nubian and Muslim traditions. Use a dictionary to help you with the underlined words.

A Nubian Wedding

The music: At the beginning of the video, we see people from a <u>village</u> in Egypt. They are playing <u>drums</u>, singing <u>songs</u>, and dancing. It's all part of a wedding celebration.

The couple: The <u>groom</u>'s name is Sherrif. He met the <u>bride</u>, Abeer, two years before the wedding.

The food: In many cultures, a <u>feast</u> is part of a wedding celebration. In the video, the whole village eats a meal of rice and meat.

A man playing a drum

Women baking flat bread for a large wedding

Wedding

D | With a partner, take turns asking and answering the questions about the Nubian wedding. Use the information from exercise **C** to answer the questions.

1. Where is the wedding?
2. Who is getting married?
3. How do the people at the wedding celebrate?
4. What do the people eat at the wedding feast?

While Viewing

A | Read the questions. Then write the answers while you watch the video.

1. How many days and nights is the wedding celebration?

   _____

2. Who comes to the wedding celebration? _____
3. Where do the people eat the feast? _____
4. When do the bride and groom arrive at the party? _____
5. What does the bride wear to the party? _____

Nubian women carrying wedding gifts for a bride and groom

B | Read the statements. Then watch the video again and circle **T** for *true* or **F** for *false*.

1. Life changed for the Nubian people in the 1950s.	**T**	**F**
2. The Nubians had to move because of the Aswan dam.	**T**	**F**
3. Mohammed Nour came here when he was 12 years old.	**T**	**F**
4. Nour thinks life is better now, in the new village.	**T**	**F**
5. Nour talks about the Nubian language.	**T**	**F**

After Viewing

Critical Thinking. Form a group with two or three other students and discuss the questions.

1. What surprised you about the video? Explain.
2. How is the Nubian wedding in the video similar to weddings in your country? How is it different?
3. What was the main purpose of the video?
   a. to tell us about life in a Nubian village
   b. to tell us about a Nubian wedding
   c. to tell us about Nubian history
4. In Lesson B, you will learn about how people use their free time to be happy. What do you do in your free time that makes you happy?

track 1-21 **A** | **Meaning from Context.** Read and listen to what four people say about their free time. Notice the words in blue. These are words you will hear and use in Lesson B.

I don't have much free time because I have a full-time job. I also have children, so I like to spend time with them. Sometimes we go to the beach, and sometimes we go to the park. For me, playing with my children has some important benefits: It makes me feel young and gives me great joy.

I enjoy taking walks in the park. I love being outdoors—seeing the trees and feeling the sun on my face. Basically, I'm always moving. Walking is good exercise. All that exercise keeps me healthy.

What do I do in my free time? Well, my hobby is cooking. It's a pretty common hobby, so I know a lot of other people who like to cook. Sometimes, my friends come over and we cook together. We laugh and tell stories.

When I want to relax, I listen to music at home. My favorite music is classical, especially Mozart. There's only one drawback to spending my free time at home: I almost never spend time outside.

B | Match each word in blue from exercise **A** with its definition.

1. free time (n.) _____
2. benefits (n.) _____
3. enjoy (v.) _____
4. outdoors (adv.) _____
5. healthy (adj.) _____
6. common (adj.) _____
7. together (adv.) _____
8. exercise (n.) _____
9. relax (v.) _____
10. drawback (n.) _____

a. physical activity that keeps you fit
b. in the open air, outside a building
c. strong and well, not sick
d. a period when you are not working
e. to get pleasure or satisfaction from something
f. to spend time doing something calm and peaceful
g. advantages, good results of doing something
h. a disadvantage, something that can create a problem
i. with another person or people
j. usual, happening often

A | Read the article. Fill in each blank with a word in blue from exercise **A** on page 34.

An Urban Escape

In a big city such as Paris, people need places to live, shop, and work. Empty space can be hard to find. But the city government finds and keeps these empty spaces. People need places to spend their (1) _____, and parks are places that most people (2) _____.

The city of Paris spends a lot of money to create more parks and gardens. Some people think that the cost is a big (3) _____. So, why does the city do this? What are some of the (4) _____ of parks and other green spaces?

- **Better Health.** Having places to (5) _____ after work helps people feel good. Parks allow people to get (6) _____ such as walking and jogging. Being (7) _____ in the sunlight is good for people.

- **Better Environment.** Trees help to clean the air and make cities cooler. Clean air helps people stay (8) _____.

- **Less Crime.** Crime, such as robbery and murder, is (9) _____ in big cities. Research says that there is less crime in places with green areas around them.

- **Improved Education.** Parks are also a place for children to learn and play (10) _____. According to one study, children learn better after they play in a park.

A woman and her granddaughter spinning in the Jardin de Reuilly, Paris.

A woman reading on a bench in the Jardin du Luxembourg, Paris, France.

B | **Critical Thinking.** Discuss the questions with a partner.

1. Why do people **enjoy** parks?
2. What are some **drawbacks** of spending money on parks?

Before Listening

Predicting Content. You are going to listen to a guest speaker talk about city parks. Look at the photo and discuss the question with a partner. What do you think the speaker will say about the relationship between parks, or green spaces, and crime?

Central Park, Manhattan, New York City, USA

Listening: A Talk with Questions and Answers

A | **Listening for Main Ideas.** Read the statements. Then listen and complete each statement with the information you hear. _track 1-22_

1. The speaker is there to talk about some of the _____ of public parks.
2. The speaker says that parks provide _____ benefits and social benefits.
3. The speaker says that _____ is lower in places with a lot of trees and green spaces.
4. The speaker says that healthy, happy people have fewer _____.

B | **Listening for Details.** Read the statements and answer choices. Then listen again and choose the correct answer. _track 1-22_

1. The first question the speaker answers is about _____.
   a. the things families do together at parks
   b. the types of exercise people get at parks
   c. the number of people who go to parks

2. The second question the speaker answers is about _____.
   a. the health benefits of parks
   b. the education benefits of parks
   c. the environmental benefits of parks

3. The third question the speaker answers is about _____.
   a. the types of city parks
   b. the drawbacks of city parks
   c. the importance of city parks

After Listening

A | Ranking Information. In the Listening section you learned that city parks have several benefits. Rank the benefits of city parks 1 through 5 in order of importance (1 = most important; 5 = least important).

_____ People have a place to exercise.   _____ Cities are cleaner and cooler.

_____ Cities have less crime.   _____ People have a place to relax.

_____ Children learn better.

B | Giving Opinions. Work with a partner. Compare your answers from exercise **A**. Discuss the reasons for your decisions.

> I think the most important benefit is that cities have less crime.

> Really? I disagree. I think the most important benefit is that parks give children a place to play.

Pronunciation

The Intonation of *Wh-* Questions

In *wh-* questions, the speaker's voice rises on the last content word and falls at the end of the question.

track 1-23

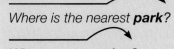

*Where is the nearest **park**?*

*When are you **going**?*

The High Line is an elevated park on an old railway in New York City.

track 1-24 **A |** Read the two conversations. Mark the intonation you think you will hear in the *wh*-questions. Then listen and check your answers.

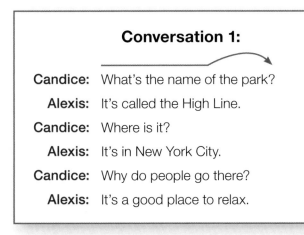

Conversation 1:
Candice: What's the name of the park?
Alexis: It's called the High Line.
Candice: Where is it?
Alexis: It's in New York City.
Candice: Why do people go there?
Alexis: It's a good place to relax.

Conversation 2:
Sam: What do you do in your free time?
Devon: I like to jog in the park.
Sam: Why do you do that?
Devon: It's good exercise, and I enjoy being outdoors.
Sam: When are you going next?
Devon: Tomorrow morning. Do you want to come?

B | With a partner, practice the conversations in exercise **A**. Then switch roles and practice them again.

Language Function

Making Small Talk

When people do not know each other well, they can be friendly by making small talk. One way to make small talk is to ask and answer questions about the weather and other topics.

Examples: *So, who goes to River Park?*
What's the temperature today?

🎧 track 1-25 **A** | Read and listen to the conversation. <u>Underline</u> examples of small talk.

Shelli:	There are a lot of people here today.
Omar:	I'm sorry?
Shelli:	I said there are a lot of people at the park today.
Omar:	There sure are. It's a beautiful day to be outdoors.
Shelli:	It really is. What's the temperature today?
Omar:	I don't know, but it feels perfect. I'm here with my son.
Shelli:	Oh, which one is your son?
Omar:	That's him over there.
Shelli:	Really? He's playing with my son!
Omar:	That's your son? What's his name?
Shelli:	Robert, and my name is Shelli.
Omar:	Nice to meet you, Shelli. I'm Omar, and my son is Andy.
Shelli:	It's great that the kids can play here.
Omar:	It really is.

👥 **B** | Compare your answers from exercise **A** with a partner's. Then practice the conversation. Switch roles and practice it again.

Grammar

The Simple Present Tense: *Wh-* Questions

We use *wh-* words (*What, Where, When, How, Why, Who(m), and Which*) to ask for information.

> For *wh-* questions with the verb *be,* we put the *wh-* word before *am, is,* or *are.*
> **What is** the name of your favorite park?
> **Where are** your parents?

> For *wh-* questions with other verbs, we put the *wh-* word before *do* or *does.*
> **When does** the next train **arrive**?
> **Who do** they usually **stay** with in Portugal?

A | Complete the questions using the simple present tense.

1. When / you / get up ___*When do you get up*___ in the morning?
2. What / be _____ your favorite food?
3. Who / you / send _____ a lot of text messages or emails to?
4. How / you / relax _____ on the weekends?
5. Where / be _____ the closest park in this city?
6. Why / be _____ trees good for the environment?

B | With a partner, take turns asking and answering the questions from exercise **A**.

C | **Discussion.** Talk to your partner about one of the topics below. Your partner will listen and ask you questions. Then switch roles and discuss a new topic.

| a hobby | a favorite book or movie | a beautiful place | a family member |

> I want to tell you about my older brother.

> What's your brother's name?

Student to Student:
Asking for Repetition

Sometimes we don't hear part of a conversation. Here are some expressions you can use to let people know you didn't understand them.

Could you say that again?
What's that?
What did you say?
Could you repeat that, please?

D | Listen to the conversation. Then practice it with your partner.

track 1-26

A: Everyone's having a good time!

B: What did you say?

A: I said everyone's having a good time.

B: They sure are—it's a fun party!

E | Work with your partner and follow the instructions below.

Student A: Say the sentences below to your partner. When you see //////////, don't speak clearly.

Student B: Ask your partner for repetition when you don't understand something. Your partner will repeat the information using his or her own ideas.

Example: **A:** I heard that ////////// are on the exam.
B: Could you say that again? What are on the exam?
A: Verb tenses.
B: Oh, OK. Thanks.

A crowd at a foam party at a water park in Sudak, Russia

1. There's a free concert in the park on //////////.
2. The weather is beautiful today! It's //////////.
3. I like this class because //////////.
4. That's my friend over there. Her name is //////////.
5. The park is easy to find. It's next to the //////////.
6. My favorite way to enjoy nature is //////////.

You are going to give a short presentation about something that makes you feel good, such as a celebration, a holiday, or an activity you like to do in your free time.

A | Brainstorming. Write down some ideas for your presentation topic in your notebook.

B | Planning a Presentation. Choose one of your ideas from exercise **A**. In your notebook, write short notes to help you plan your presentation. Include ideas for your Introduction, Details, and your Conclusion. Use the example below to help you.

Topic: Chuseok in Korea

Introduction: Chuseok in Korea

                —important holiday; families get together; in autumn

                —eat special foods

Details: Food

                —feast for the whole family

                —always make songpyeon (rice cakes)

        Activities

                —some families go to cemetery to remember ancestors

                —my family remembers ancestors while we eat Chuseok foods

Conclusion: Chuseok celebrates family (living and dead)

        I love being with my family for Chuseok.

Presentation Skills: Speaking to a Group

When you are speaking to a group, you need to speak loudly enough for everyone to hear you. Try to speak clearly with good pronunciation. This will help your audience understand what you are saying.

C | Presentation. Form a group with two or three other students. Follow the steps below.

1. Decide who will present first, second, and so on.
2. While one person presents, the audience listens carefully.
3. After the presenter finishes, each person in the audience must ask one question—either a *yes/no* question or a *wh-* question.
4. The presenter answers each question.
5. Repeat steps 1 to 4 for each member of the group.

Treasures from the Past

Think and Discuss

1. What man-made objects do we find at the bottom of the ocean?

2. What can we learn about the past from these objects?

These coins and jewelry are from the Whydah Galley shipwreck.
The ship sank in 1717 near the coast of Massachusetts, USA.

Look at the photos and read the captions. Then discuss the questions.

1. What kinds of man-made objects do you see on these pages? Where did people find them?
2. How do you think people used these objects in the past?
3. Why do people want to find these objects now?
4. Do you think it is important to try to find objects like these? Explain.

A diver explores the wreck of the ship *Liberty*, sunk by the Japanese in 1942, Bali, Indonesia.

Gold beads, chains, and coins found in a Spanish Armada shipwreck, Ireland

A diver discovered this **gold plate** by accident off the Florida Keys, Florida, USA.

A scuba diver examines a **bottle** found in the Aegean Sea off Serce Limani, Turkey.

A | **Using a Dictionary.** Listen and check (✔) the words you already know. Use a dictionary to help you with any new words. These are words you will hear and use in Lesson A.

track 1-27

❑ dishes (n.)   ❑ find (v.)   ❑ looked like (v.)   ❑ objects (n.)   ❑ ruled (v.)

❑ exhibit (n.)   ❑ image (n.)   ❑ nearby (adj.)   ❑ recently (adv.)   ❑ tools (n.)

B | Match each word with its definition.

1. tools _____
2. nearby _____
3. recently _____
4. dishes _____
5. find _____

a. a short distance away, not far away
b. things used to make or repair things
c. plates or bowls used to serve food
d. to locate, or to discover
e. not very long ago

C | **Meaning from Context.** Read and listen to the information. Notice the words in blue. Then write each word or phrase in blue next to its definition below.

track 1-28

New Exhibit Opens Today

Queen Cleopatra VII ruled Egypt for fewer than 20 years. People are still very interested in her more than 2000 years later. But until recently, no one knew much about Cleopatra at all. We didn't even know what she looked like because there were no pictures of her.

Now, a new exhibit tells us more about Cleopatra's life. The exhibit has hundreds of objects such as jewelry, tools, and dishes. For the first time we can see Cleopatra's face! There are coins with Cleopatra's image on them.

An image of Cleopatra on an Egyptian coin

1. _____ (n.) things you can see or touch
2. _____ (n.) a picture of someone or something
3. _____ (n.) a thing or group of things you can see in a museum
4. _____ (v.) governed or led a country
5. _____ (v.) had a similar appearance to another person or thing

Bas relief of Cleopatra with her son by Julius Caesar, Dendera, Egypt

A | Read the conversations. Fill in each blank with the correct form of a word from exercise **A** on page 44.

Devon: Where did Cleopatra VII live?

Brenda: She grew up in Alexandria and two
(1) _____ cities.

Devon: So, when did she become queen?

Brenda: She became queen in her teens, I think. Then, she
(2) _____ for nearly 20 years.

Marc: What happened to Cleopatra?

Hitomi: Well, the Romans became the rulers of Egypt, and Cleopatra killed herself.

Marc: Wow, I didn't know that.

Hitomi: Then, after Cleopatra's death, the Romans destroyed anything with her (3) _____ on it— statues, pictures, coins, and so on. They didn't want the Egyptians to remember her. So, for a long time we didn't know what she (4) _____.

Kim: What happened to Alexandria?

Larry: Earthquakes[1] destroyed it. But (5) _____, archaeologists discovered parts of the city under the ocean.

Kim: Really? What did they (6) _____?

Larry: They discovered over 20,000 (7) _____, including beautiful (8) _____ for serving food and useful (9) _____ to help people do all kinds of jobs.

Alexandria, Egypt

Boats above Cleopatra's lost city, Alexandria, Egypt

B | Work with a partner. Compare your answers from exercise **A**. Then practice the conversations.

C | **Discussion.** With your partner, discuss the questions below.

1. Talk about a person who **ruled** a country you know about. Where was the person from? What did he or she **look like**?
2. Think of an **object** that is very important to you. What is it? Why is it important?
3. What kinds of museum **exhibits** do you enjoy? Explain.
4. Do you like to visit historic places? Why, or why not?

[1]An **earthquake** is a sudden, violent movement of the earth's surface.

Pronunciation

> ### The Simple Past Tense -ed Word Endings
>
> For regular verbs in the simple past tense, add -ed to the base form of the verb (-d to verbs that already end in -e). Usually the -ed ending adds the sound /t/ or /d/ to the verb.
>
> **Examples:**
>
> track 1-29
>
> look → look**ed**   live → live**d**   play → play**ed**
> My grandfather **looked** like his father.
>
> If a verb ends in a /t/ or /d/ sound, the -ed ending adds a syllable. We pronounce this syllable /əd/.
>
> **Examples:**
>
> want → want**ed**   need → need**ed**   start → start**ed**
> They **decided** to make a map.

track 1-30 Listen and check (✔) the sound you hear for each word.

	/t/ or /d/	/əd/			/t/ or /d/	/əd/
1. painted	❑	❑	5. closed	❑	❑
2. explored	❑	❑	6. rested	❑	❑
3. talked	❑	❑	7. shouted	❑	❑
4. divided	❑	❑	8. watched	❑	❑

Before Listening

Understanding Visuals. You are going to listen to a talk about the lost city of Alexandria. Look at the map and read the statements below. Circle **T** for *true* or **F** for *false*.

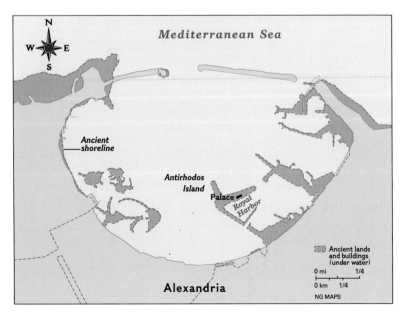

1. Ancient Alexandria is on land. **T** **F**
2. Cleopatra's palace was on an island. **T** **F**
3. Cleopatra's Royal Harbor[1] was to the north of Antirhodos Island. **T** **F**

[1]A **harbor** is a place on the coast that protects ships from the ocean.

Listening: A Talk about an Ancient City

🎧 track 1-31 **A | Listening for Main Ideas.** Listen to part of the talk. Choose the best phrase to complete each sentence.

1. The ancient city of Alexandria _____.
   a. is only a legend
   b. was very rich and important
   c. disappeared 1000 years ago

2. Goddio's discoveries _____.
   a. give us new information about Cleopatra's world
   b. do not answer our most important questions about Cleopatra
   c. came too late to help historians today

3. Goddio knew that the underwater ruins[1] were _____.
   a. parts of the ship he was looking for
   b. ancient lost cities
   c. small enough to explore alone

Franck Goddio shows a bronze statue that was in the Temple of Isis.

🎧 track 1-32 **B | Note-Taking.** Listen to the entire talk. Complete the notes about Goddio.

Archaeologist Franck Goddio	Goddio's Team
• found cities that disappeared almost (1) _____ ago	• uncovered statues, (5) _____, musical instruments, (6) _____, and many other objects
• went to Egypt in (2) _____ to look for a sunken[2] ship	• made maps of (7) _____ Alexandria and two other cities
• found the (3) _____ of whole cities in the sand deep underwater	• explored Cleopatra's (8) _____
• started The European Institute of (4) _____ Archaeology	• found statues of (9) _____ and (10) _____ that were once in temples

🎧 track 1-32 **C | Making Inferences.** Listen again. Read the statements below and circle **T** for *true* or **F** for *false*. The answers are not in the speaker's exact words. You need to think about what you hear.

1. At first, Goddio did not know the importance of his discovery.   **T**   **F**
2. We still don't know what Cleopatra looked like.   **T**   **F**
3. It is taking a lot of time to study the ruins of the cities.   **T**   **F**

After Listening

👥 **Critical Thinking.** Discuss the questions with a partner.

1. Do you think museums are important? Explain.
2. What can we learn by studying the past? Do you think it is useful or not? Explain.

[1]**Ruins** are the remaining parts of a destroyed building, town, etc.
[2]If something is **sunken**, it is under the ocean.

Grammar

The Simple Past Tense

We use the simple past tense to talk about completed actions in the past.
> It **rained** for three hours yesterday.   They **watched** a movie last night.

We add -*ed* to the base form of a regular verb to form the simple past tense.
We add -*d* if the verb already ends in -*e*.
> talk - talk**ed**   learn - learn**ed**   close - close**d**   like - like**d**

We need to make spelling changes when we add -*ed* or -*d* to some regular verbs.
> tr**y** - tr**ied**   carr**y** - carr**ied**   ro**b** - ro**bb**ed   sto**p** - sto**pp**ed

Many verbs are irregular in the simple past tense.
> leave - left   eat - ate   go - went   read - read
> find - found   give - gave   know - knew   quit - quit
> fight - fought   come - came   take - took   meet - met

A | Fill in each blank with the simple past tense of the verb in parentheses.

1. The show _____*started*_____ (start) at 8:00 p.m.

2. My family _____ (live) in Taipei until 1998.

3. Linda _____ (move) to Buenos Aires when she (leave)
   _____ home.

4. Teodoro _____ (try) to call his parents last night.

5. That's a great book! I _____ (read) it in 2009.

6. Max and Ramona _____ (meet) in 1996.

B | With a partner, read the conversation and <u>underline</u> each verb in the simple past tense. Then decide how many syllables are in each verb. Look back at page 46 if you need help.

Sam:	Wow! I <u>learned</u> a lot from that class.
Coty:	Me too. I took a lot of notes.
Sam:	I heard a lot of noise from the hallway, though.
Coty:	I think the professor wanted to close the door, but it was too hot in the room.
Sam:	Yes. Oh, by the way, I finished my archaeology assignment.
Coty:	That's great! Were you at the library last night?
Sam:	No, I stopped going there to work. I don't like the library.
Coty:	Me neither. I studied in my room last night.

C | Practice the conversation in exercise **B** with your partner. Then switch roles and practice it again.

Language Function

An informal way to agree with a speaker's affirmative statement is by using *Me too*.

A: *I traveled to Alexandria.*
B: ***Me too!*** *I went there in 2007.*

An informal way to agree with a speaker's negative statement is by using *Me neither*.

A: *I didn't like that museum.*
B: ***Me neither.*** *It was very small.*

A | Complete the conversations with *too* or *neither*.

Josie:	You know, I really liked the exhibit.
Frank:	Me (1) _____. Cleopatra was a very interesting person.
Josie:	She really was. I didn't know she killed herself.
Frank:	Me (2) _____.

Cho:	Did you see the movie *Cleopatra* in Price Hall last night?
Jacqui:	Um, no, I didn't.
Cho:	Me (3) _____.

Lupe:	I want to learn more about the *Titanic*.
Bruce:	Me (4) _____!

B | Work with a partner. Follow the instructions.

1. Choose one person to be Student A and one to be Student B.
2. Read your statements below and circle the word or phrase in **bold** that is correct for you.
3. Take turns saying your sentences to your partner. Your partner agrees with you by using *Me too* or *Me neither*.

Student A

1. I **like/dislike** historical museums.
2. I **got/didn't get** a lot of sleep last night.
3. I **like/don't like** the weather today.
4. I **studied/didn't study** a lot last night.

Student B

1. I **took/didn't take** the bus today.
2. I **like/dislike** chocolate ice cream.
3. I **got/didn't get** a lot of exercise last week.
4. I **like/don't like** learning about history.

Grammar

Yes/No Questions in the Simple Past Tense

We form *yes/no* questions with *be* by changing the order of the subject and verb.

Statements: *The* Titanic **was** *a big ship.*
A lot of people **were** *on the* Titanic.

Questions: **Was** *the* Titanic *a small ship?*　　　*No, it* **wasn't**.
Were *a lot of people on the* Titanic?　　　*Yes, there* **were**.

We use the auxiliary *did* to form *yes/no* questions with other verbs.

Statements: *Bob Ballard found the* Titanic *in 1985.*　　*He* **used** *robots with cameras.*
Questions: **Did** *Bob Ballard* **find** *the* Titanic *in 1980?*　*No, he* **didn't**.
Did *he* **use** *robots with cameras?*　　　*Yes, he* **did**.

Read the fact file below about the *Titanic*. With a partner, take turns asking and answering *yes/no* questions about the information. Use the words and phrases below.

1. the *Titanic* / leave Liverpool / April
2. the *Titanic* / arrive / New York / May
3. all the passengers / get into / lifeboats
4. the *Titanic* / sink / at night
5. Ballard / find / the *Titanic* / the Atlantic Ocean
6. Ballard / return / 1996

> Did the *Titanic* leave Liverpool in April?

> No, it didn't. It left Southampton.

The *Titanic*—Fact File

- April 10, 1912: The *Titanic* left Southampton, England. It never arrived in New York.

- April 14, 1912: The *Titanic* hit an iceberg[1] just before midnight.

- April 15, 1912: Some passengers got into small lifeboats, but there wasn't enough room for most of them.

- April 15, 1912: When the *Titanic* sank at 2:00 a.m., 1500 people were still on the ship.

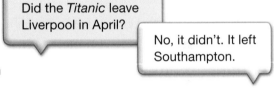

In 1912, on its first trip across the Atlantic, the *Titanic* hit an iceberg and sank.

- August 31, 1985: Ocean explorer Bob Ballard found the *Titanic* on the bottom of the Atlantic Ocean. He used cameras and an underwater robot to see the ship.

- 1986: Ballard returned to the *Titanic*. He used a new robot to explore inside the ship.

Bob Ballard found the *Titanic* in 1985.

[1]An **iceberg** is a huge piece of ice floating in the ocean.

Talking about the Past

Understanding Visuals. Read the timeline about Bob Ballard.

The wreck of the *Titanic*

Childhood: Bob Ballard read books about shipwrecks[1] and dreamed of finding the *Titanic*.

July 1, 1985: Ballard and a team of scientists went to the area where the *Titanic* sank. They searched the area for several weeks.

August 31, 1985: Ballard's team found the *Titanic* in very deep water. They also saw many objects such as shoes and suitcases that once belonged to the passengers.

1986: Ballard returned to the *Titanic*. He sent a robot camera inside, and the team saw the grand staircase, the gym, and even the captain's bathtub.

2009: Two new research boats went into the water. Ballard designed them with the latest electronic equipment. Within hours, the boats started finding shipwrecks all over the world.

[1]A **shipwreck** is a ship that has been destroyed or damaged by an accident or storm.

Grammar

Wh- Questions in the Simple Past Tense

We form most *Wh-* questions in the simple past tense in the same way as *yes/no* questions, except we add a *Wh-* word, such as *why, where, when,* or *how* to the beginning of the question.

Was the Titanic *hard to find?*	***Why** was the* Titanic *hard to find?*
Did the ship hit an iceberg?	***When** did the ship hit an iceberg?*

Do not use *did* with *who, what,* and *which* when they talk about the subject.

✓ *Who discovered the* Titanic?   X *Who did discover the* Titanic?

Discussion. With a partner, discuss Bob Ballard's life. Use the time line and your own ideas to ask and answer *Wh-* questions. Use *where, when, why,* or *how.*

> Why did Ballard look for the *Titanic*?

> As a child, he dreamed of finding it.

Treasures in Old San Juan

Fort San Felipe del Morro, Old San Juan, Puerto Rico

Puerto Rico, U.S.

The Capitol building, Old San Juan, Puerto Rico

Before Viewing

> The hospital is in a very old building.

> There are ancient coins at the museum.

A | Work with a partner. In Lesson A, you learned about some historical places and things. Make a list of three old or historical places or things in your city or town. Take turns talking about the historical places and things on your lists.

B | **Identifying the Simple Past Tense.** Read the information about Old San Juan, Puerto Rico, and underline the words in the simple past tense.

The Government Mansion, *La Fortaleza*

Old San Juan Quick Facts

- The Spanish explorer Ponce de Leon came to the island that is now Puerto Rico in 1508.

- San Juan became a city in 1521.

- There were huge stone walls around the city in the 16th century. A fortress[1] called *La Fortaleza* protected the city.

- Today, the governor of Puerto Rico lives in *La Fortaleza*.

[1]A **fortress** is a castle or other strong building that protects an area.

C | **Predicting Content.** Check (✔) the things you think you will see in the video.

❏ an airport	❏ new shopping centers	❏ a statue of Ponce de Leon	❏ tourists
❏ *La Fortaleza*	❏ old houses	❏ the ocean	❏ residents[2] of Old San Juan

[2]A **resident** is a person who lives in a place.

While Viewing

A | Checking Predictions. Watch the video. Check your predictions from exercise **C** in the Before Viewing section.

B | Note-Taking. Watch the video again. Write down three other things that interest you in the video.

1. _____ 2. _____ 3. _____

C | Watch the video again. Match each person in the video with the topic he talks about.

Person	Topic
1. Ricardo Rivera _____	a. the nice weather in Puerto Rico
2. Ricardo Alegría _____	b. the culture of Old San Juan: the music, artists, writers, and so on
3. Domingo Deleon _____	c. the way Old San Juan used to be in the 1950s

A street in Old San Juan

After Viewing

A | Discussion. With a partner, discuss the questions below.

1. Why is the historical part of San Juan a good place to live?
2. Why is the historical part of San Juan a good place for tourists?
3. Which do you prefer for a vacation—historical cities or modern cities? Explain.

B | Using the Simple Past Tense. Read the information about Juan Ponce de Leon. Complete each sentence with the simple past tense of a verb from the box. Use each verb only once.

go	give	fight	become	die

Colorful buildings in Old San Juan

Juan Ponce de Leon

At the end of the 15ᵗʰ century, explorers from Spain and Portugal began arriving in the Americas. One of the explorers from Spain was Juan Ponce de Leon.

- He (1) _____ in the Spanish army before he came to the Americas.

- He (2) _____ the first governor of Puerto Rico.

- He (3) _____ the state of Florida its name. Florida is now part of the United States.

- Some people say he (4) _____ to Florida to look for the Fountain of Youth—a place with water that keeps people young forever. (The fountain has never been found.)

- He (5) _____ in 1521 after the Calusa Indians attacked him and his men in Florida.

A statue of Juan Ponce de Leon

A | **Using a Dictionary.** Listen and check (✔) the words you already know. Use a dictionary to help you with any new words. These are words you will hear and use in Lesson B.

track 1-33

- ❏ were made of (v.)
- ❏ carry (v.)
- ❏ everyday (adj.)
- ❏ goods (n.)
- ❏ route (n.)
- ❏ sailed (v.)
- ❏ ship (n.)
- ❏ silk (n.)
- ❏ traded (v.)
- ❏ valuable (adj.)

B | **Understanding Maps.** Look at the map and read the statements below. Circle **T** for *true* or **F** for *false*.

1.	The ship sailed to China.	**T**	**F**
2.	It took a route past Indonesia.	**T**	**F**
3.	The ship went to the Middle East.	**T**	**F**

C | **Meaning from Context.** Read the article. Circle the correct word in blue. Then listen and check your answers.

track 1-34

The Shipwreck of an Arab *Dhow*

This is the story of an Arab (1) (ship/sail) called a *dhow*. The *dhow* left the Middle East, and it (2) (traded/sailed) east to China. There, the sailors bought (3) (everyday/valuable) objects such as simple dishes, but also (4) (valuable/everyday) goods such as gold and (5) (ship/silk). Sadly, the ship sank near Belitung Island in Indonesia, and the sailors never returned home.

Travel was difficult in the ninth century, but not impossible. By land, there was the Silk Road. It was a way for people in one part of the world to (6) (trade/carry) with people in other parts of the world. By sea, there was the Maritime Silk (7) (Route/goods).

MARITIME SILK ROUTE
DURING THE NINTH CENTURY A.D.
—— Main route
--- Probable route of the Belitung dhow

SHIPWRECK SITE
circa A.D. 826

SCALE VARIES IN THIS PERSPECTIVE.
PRESENT-DAY PLACE-NAMES AND BOUNDARIES SHOWN.
FERNANDO G. BAPTISTA, NG STAFF. MAP BY VIRGINIA W. MASON
AND LISA R. RITTER, NG STAFF

A | Read the rest of the article. Fill in each blank with a word or phrase from exercise **A** on page 54. Then listen and check your answers.

track 1-35

More about the Belitung *Dhow*

A *dhow* was a type of ship that was common in the Indian Ocean and the Arabian Sea. *Dhows* were not very large, but they could (1) _____ a lot. Around the year 826, one *dhow* (2) _____ from the city of Al Basrah (now Basra, Iraq) to Guangzhou, China. There, the sailors (3) _____ with the local people, and they loaded the ship with the new (4) _____ they bought.

When the ship left China, it carried thousands of simple dishes and other (5) _____ objects. It also carried (6) _____ for making fine clothes, and a few very beautiful and (7) _____ objects. Some of these objects (8) _____ gold. (Recently, archaeologists studied the objects, and they think the gold objects were probably gifts for a royal wedding.)

The *dhow* chose an unusual (9) _____ home. Nobody is sure why the sailors took their (10) _____ so far south. Because of a storm, or perhaps an accident, the *dhow* sank between two Indonesian islands. Centuries later, in 1999, divers[1] found the dishes and other objects, as well as small pieces of the *dhow* itself.

The *dhow* carried 55,000 dishes that were made in China.

[1]A **diver** is a person who goes underwater, usually with special equipment.

B | **Discussion.** With a partner, discuss the questions below.

1. Which is more **valuable**, gold or silver? Explain.
2. In the ninth century, how long do you think it took to **sail** from the Middle East to China?
3. When did people find the Arab *dhow* shipwreck? How many years was it lost?
4. How do countries **trade** with each other today?
5. What **goods** does your country buy from other countries? What **goods** does your country sell to other countries?

Before Listening

Prior Knowledge. Discuss the questions with a partner. Look back at pages 54 and 55 if you need help.

1. Where did the *dhow* come from?
2. What did the *dhow* carry away from China?
3. What happened after the *dhow* left China?
4. Who found the *dhow* many years later?

Listening: A Conversation

A | Listening for Main Ideas. Listen to the conversation. Choose the correct answer for each question.

track 1-36

1. What kind of homework assignment do the speakers need to do?
   a. write a paper
   b. give a presentation
   c. write a paragraph

2. What does the woman think about the homework assignment?
   a. It will take a long time.
   b. It's not an interesting topic.
   c. It's very easy.

3. What does the man suggest?
   a. asking some questions
   b. getting help from the teacher
   c. borrowing a book

B | Listening for Details. Listen again. Choose the correct word to complete each sentence.

track 1-36

1. The homework assignment is due on _____.
   a. Monday
   b. Tuesday
   c. Wednesday

2. The man says he doesn't know anything about the goods from _____.
   a. The Middle East
   b. China
   c. Indonesia

3. The woman wants to know where the _____ came from.
   a. divers
   b. sailors
   c. archaeologists

4. The woman also wants to know _____ people made the beautiful dishes.
   a. when
   b. how
   c. why

After Listening

A | Making Inferences. Read the statements below. Circle **T** for *true* or **F** for *false*. Then discuss the reasons for your choices with a partner.

1. The speakers are classmates.   **T**   **F**
2. They are discussing the man's problem.   **T**   **F**
3. They don't solve the problem.   **T**   **F**

B | Role-Playing. Form a group with two or three other students. Imagine that you are going to do the assignment you heard about on page 56. Decide which information each person in your group needs to find. Practice making informal suggestions to each other.

> Why don't you find out about the divers? How did they find the shipwreck?

> OK, and maybe you could write about the reasons for the shipwreck.

C | Discussion. With your group, discuss the questions below.

1. Why do you think the woman wasn't interested in the shipwreck?
2. Why do you think some people aren't interested in history?
3. Finding and exploring shipwrecks is expensive. Is it a good way to spend money? Explain.

Student to Student: Making Informal Suggestions

When you are working with a partner or in a group, you will sometimes want to make informal suggestions. Here are some expressions you can use to make informal suggestions.

Maybe you could find some information about Indonesia.
Why don't you ask the teacher for help?

A bracelet and cup made of gold were some of the objects on the Belitung *dhow*.

Grammar

Recognizing Past Tense Signal Words

Some words and phrases tell us that we need to use the past tense. These are called signal words.

ago	*yesterday*	*last night/week/month/year*
in (a past year)	*on (a past date)*	

*Archaeologists **discovered** an important shipwreck **last year**.*
*William **finished** the chemistry assignment two weeks **ago**.*
*The president **made** an important announcement **yesterday**.*
***In 2002**, over a million tourists **visited** the city.*
*Celine **celebrated** her birthday **on September 22**.*

Past tense signal words or phrases usually come at the beginning or at the end of a sentence. They may be followed by a comma at the beginning of a sentence.

A | Fill in each blank with a word or phrase from the box. Then underline the words in the simple past tense.

1. The library closed an hour _____ *ago* _____, so we can't go there now.
2. I took both children to see the doctor _____ July 18.
3. _____ week, we had meetings every afternoon.
4. _____ 1841, a musician named Adolphe Sax invented the saxophone.
5. _____ year, I went on vacation in April.

A street scene of Washington, D.C., USA around 1913-1918

B | Take turns asking and answering the questions with a partner. Use your own information in your answers.

1. What did you do yesterday morning?
2. What did you do last night?
3. On what date did this English course begin?
4. When were you born?
5. What important events happened last year?
6. What important events happened more than 10 years ago?

A | **Critical Thinking.** Follow the steps below to practice recalling facts.

1. Fill in each blank with information about your past. You can use real information or invent information if you prefer. Use the correct verb tense.

- Yesterday I _____.
- I _____ last month.
- In 2008, I _____.
- I learned how to _____ about _____ (years/months/weeks) ago.

2. Take turns saying your sentences from Step 1 to a partner.
3. Work with a new partner. Take turns talking about the information you learned in Step 2.
4. Discuss the questions below with your original partner.
   - Which information did you remember correctly?
   - What helped you to remember that information?
   - Which information did you forget?

> Yesterday Kim bought a birthday card for his sister.

track 1-37 **B** | Read and listen to the magazine article. Rank the four steps in *Improve Your Memory* from 1 (most helpful) to 4 (least helpful).

Critical Thinking Focus: Recalling Facts

Recalling information is an important skill. Deciding that you want to remember information is an important first step. Looking at your notes before class can help you recall important information that you might need for an exam or a class discussion.

Improve Your Memory: Four Easy Steps

Do you remember names, phone numbers, and other information easily? If not, here are some things you can do to improve your memory.

- **Get a good night's sleep.** Getting eight or more hours of sleep can improve your memory and your ability to learn new information by as much as 30 percent.

- **Eat a healthy diet.** Good foods such as fish, olive oil, fruits, and vegetables help your brain stay healthy. A healthy brain means a better memory.

- **Exercise your body.** Any kind of exercise—walking, swimming, playing sports—keeps the blood moving around your body and helps your brain work better.

- **Exercise your mind.** Exercising your brain is helpful. One of the best exercises for your brain is learning a new language.

C | **Collaboration.**

1. Form a group with two or three other students. Make a list of other things you do that help you remember information (e.g., making notes, repeating information after you hear it).
2. Which ideas on your group's list work best for you when you are studying English? Take turns telling your group.

A | Planning a Presentation. You are going to tell your classmates about your past. Check (✔) the ideas that are true for you. Write two more ideas about your past.

❑ I lived with my family.
❑ I learned to do something interesting (e.g., to play a musical instrument).
❑ I moved from one place to live in another place.
❑ I graduated from school.
❑ I got a job.
❑ I decided to do something important (e.g., to leave home).

Your idea: _____

Your idea: _____

Presentation Skills: Speaking from Notes

We often use notes when presenting to help us remember important points. It's important to make helpful notes and use them correctly. Here is some advice for making helpful presentation notes.

- Write your topics in the same order you plan to talk about them.
- Make simple notes that are large enough to read.
- Hold your notes down and keep them away from your face.
- Look down at your notes only when you really need to. Then look up and speak to your audience.

B | Organizing Ideas. Look at the student's notes below. Then make notes for your own presentation in your notebook. Use your ideas from exercise **A** and add interesting details about your past.

- My family lived in Pusan—12 years
- We moved to Seoul
- I learned to drive a car—18 years old—(funny story)
- I graduated last year
- I got my first job six months ago–in a bank

C | Presentation. Stand up and give your presentation for a small group.

D | Self-Reflection. Discuss the questions with a partner.

1. How well did you follow the advice about making and using your notes?
2. How helpful were your notes during the presentation?
3. How did you feel during your presentation?

Weather and Climate

Think and Discuss

1. Look at the photo and read the caption. When do you
   usually see this kind of weather?
2. Are you afraid of thunderstorms and lightning? Explain.

A bolt of lightning strikes the ground during a
thunderstorm in Kansas City, Missouri, USA.

Exploring the Theme:
Weather and Climate

A | Look at the photos and read the captions. Then discuss the questions.

   1. What kinds of weather do you see on these pages?
   2. What is your favorite kind of weather? Explain.

B | Look at the information in the Extreme Weather chart. Then discuss the questions.

   1. Which place has the highest temperature? The lowest temperature?
   2. Which place usually has the most rain in one year? The least rain in one year?

Different Kinds of Weather

People shoveling snow after a snowstorm, **Colorado**, **USA**

Small, colorful boats tied up on a **sunny** day on Nusa Lembongan Island, **Bali**, **Indonesia**

People walking in Piazzo San Marco on a **rainy** day, **Venice**, **Italy**.

Palm trees on a **windy** day in **Florida**, **USA**

Extreme Weather

		Location	Date
Highest Temperature:	136°F (58°C)	El Azizia, Libya	September 13, 1922
Lowest Temperature:	−129°F (-89°C)	Vostok, Antarctica	July 21, 1983
Highest Annual Rainfall:	524 inches (1331 cm)	Lloro, Colombia	average over 29 years
Lowest Annual Rainfall:	0.03 inches (0.1 cm)	Arica, Chile	average over 59 years

Lightning and storm clouds over yellow canola fields, Calgary, Alberta, Canada

A | **Using a Dictionary.** Listen and check (✔) the words you already know. Use a dictionary to help you with any new words. These are words you will hear and use in Lesson A.

track 1-38

❏ amount (n.)	❏ drought (n.)	❏ forecast (n.)	❏ predict (v.)	❏ storm (n.)
❏ destroy (v.)	❏ flooding (n.)	❏ measure (v.)	❏ rainfall (n.)	❏ temperature (n.)

B | **Meaning from Context.** Read the magazine article. Circle the correct word in blue.

Water from the Sky: Too Much or Not Enough?

"How much rain did we get?" It's a question we often hear, and it's important because all life on Earth depends on (1) (storms/rainfall). As long as our part of the world gets the usual (2) (forecast/amount) of rain, we're happy.

The problem comes when we get too much rainfall or not enough. In Queensland, Australia, for example, March of 2011 was a month of (3) (storms/destroy) that brought far too much rain. The rain caused (4) (drought/flooding) in much of the state. Roads were closed, and thousands of people didn't have electricity.

That same spring, very little rain fell in eastern Africa. That caused (5) (drought/flooding) in Somalia, Kenya, and Ethiopia. The terrible conditions

Flooding in Detmarovice, Czech Republic

(6) (destroyed/measured) food crops, which couldn't grow without water. There was little grass for animals as well.

The problems are different when the (7) (temperature/predict) is cold. Then, it's the amount of *snowfall* that matters. In February of 2011, a huge snowstorm hit the eastern coast of South Korea. It was the biggest snowfall in South Korea since they began to keep records in 1911!

Because rainfall is so important to us, scientists called meteorologists try to (8) (destroy/predict) the amount of rainfall different parts of the world will receive. To do this, they (9) (measure/flooding) air and ocean temperatures. They also watch weather conditions around the world to see how the air is moving.

Meteorologists then make weather (10) (storms/forecasts) to let us know how much rain to expect. They're not always exactly right, but they do know when we'll probably have large amounts of rain or not enough.

A dry valley in Namibia

C | Listen and check your answers from exercise **B**.

track 1-39

A | Fill in each blank with a word in **blue** from exercise **A** on page 64. Use each word only once.

1. I remember the _____ of 1987. There was no rain from May through September.

2. Storms with very strong winds can _____ houses. They can be very dangerous.

3. I listened to the weather _____ this morning. The meteorologist said it's going to snow this afternoon!

4. There was a very small _____ of rain yesterday. It wasn't enough to ruin our day at the beach.

5. During the _____, Mike stayed inside the house because he is afraid of lightning.

6. There was a lot of _____ that year—up to 90 inches (229 centimeters) in some parts of the country. It caused a lot of _____, and hundreds of homes and businesses were under water.

7. The _____ on Friday was 98 degrees Fahrenheit (37 degrees Celsius). It was too hot for me!

8. Meteorologists use special instruments to _____ changes in the weather.

9. It's difficult to _____ the weather, so meteorologists are not always correct.

B | **Self-Reflection.** Take turns asking and answering the questions with a partner.

1. Did you hear or see a weather **forecast** this morning? If so, what did the **forecast predict**?

2. Do you usually watch or listen to weather **forecasts**? Explain.

3. As a child, what kind of weather or **storms** were you afraid of?

4. In your opinion, what **temperature** is too hot? Too cold?

5. What do you remember about the worst **storm** you've ever experienced?

6. In your opinion, what is "perfect weather"?

C | Match each word with a statement about the weather.

1. flooding _____
2. forecast _____
3. storm _____
4. drought _____
5. temperature _____

a. It will be sunny on Wednesday.
b. It rained for five days. There was water everywhere!
c. It's cold today—only 45 degrees Fahrenheit (7.2 degrees Celsius).
d. I'm not going outside! There's too much wind and lightning.
e. After three years of little rain, it's too dry here for plants or animals.

Before Listening

A | **Prior Knowledge.** With a partner, discuss each photo. Why are weather forecasts important to these people?

B | **Discussion.** Form a group with another pair of students. Share your ideas from exercise **A**. Then discuss the question below.

Which people in the photos probably pay the most attention to weather forecasts? Explain.

Listening: A Radio Show

track 1-40 **A** | **Listening for Main Ideas.** Read the questions. Then listen and choose the correct answers.

1. The title of Brad Jameson's book is *Weather in Your Backyard: The Limits of* _____.
   a. *Measuring*
   b. *Predicting*
   c. *Forecasting*

2. Jameson's book talks about weather _____.
   a. all over the world
   b. in one country
   c. in small areas

3. Jameson says that meteorologists _____.
   a. can make forecasts about the big picture
   b. are almost never correct
   c. cannot help farmers

🎧 **B** | **Listening for Details.** Listen again. Choose the correct word or phrase
track 1-40   to complete each sentence.

1. The meteorologist says that today's forecast was _____.
   a. correct   b. incorrect

2. According to the meteorologist, forecasts are correct _____ these days.
   a. more often   b. less often

3. The meteorologist's first example happened at a _____ party.
   a. birthday   b. wedding

4. The meteorologist's second example was about _____.
   a. rain   b. snow

5. The meteorologist says that weather forecasts are very important to _____.
   a. farmers   b. gardeners

After Listening

👥 **Critical Thinking.** Form a group with two or three other students. Discuss the question below.

The meteorologist says, " . . . we're getting it right more often these days." Why do you think
weather forecasts are correct more often now than in the past?

Pronunciation

Reduced *of*
When people speak English quickly, they don't always pronounce every word fully. In fast speech, the word *of* is often reduced to just a vowel sound, schwa: /ə/. Listen to the phrases and pay attention to reduced *of*.

🎧 track 1-41

Careful Speech		Fast Speech
a lot of snow	→ (sounds like)	*a lot- ə snow*
most of my friends	→	*most- ə my friends*
a glass of water	→	*a glass- ə water*
the rest of the lecture	→	*the rest- ə the lecture*

👥 With a partner, practice saying the sentences below. Use reduced *of*.

1. I have a couple of questions for you.
2. A lot of people want to know.
3. The information comes from many parts of the world.
4. Suddenly, a strong gust of wind hit them—wham!
5. Most of the storms were still far away.
6. We could get a lot of rain.

Language Function

Expressing Likes and Dislikes

In a conversation, we may say that we like or dislike something. There are many different ways to express likes and dislikes. *(See pages 210–211 of the Independent Student Handbook for more information on useful phrases.)*

A | Read and listen to an interview between a student and a meteorologist.

track 1-42

Student:	Do you like being a meteorologist?
Meteorologist:	Oh, yes. I really like it.
Student:	Do people get angry with you when your forecast is wrong?
Meteorologist:	Yes, sometimes they do, but that's understandable. Even I hate it when I want to do something outdoors and it rains!
Student:	Did you ever work in a weather station?
Meteorologist:	Yes. I worked at a station in Antarctica. I loved it!
Student:	So you like cold weather then.
Meteorologist:	Oh, no. I can't stand it! But Antarctica is very interesting.
Student:	I'm actually studying to be a meteorologist.
Meteorologist:	Really? That's great!

B | Practice the interview from exercise **A** with a partner. Then underline the four expressions that tell you what the speakers like and dislike.

C | Take turns telling your partner about weather you like and dislike. Use the ideas and expressions from the box below. Do you have the same likes and dislikes?

I like . . .	rainy days
I enjoy . . .	cloudy days
I love . . .	electrical storms
I dislike . . .	hot weather
I can't stand . . .	sunny weather
I hate . . .	strong wind
	cold weather
	snowstorms

I enjoy sunny weather.

I hate snowstorms.

D | Discussion. Form a group with two or three other students. Talk about some of your likes and dislikes. Use expressions from exercise **C** on page 68 and the topics below. Add at least two new topics.

How do you feel about classical music?

I love classical music!

chocolate	sports	cold weather
science classes	classical music	_____

Grammar

Count and Noncount Nouns

In English, nouns are either count or noncount.

Count nouns can be singular or plural.
> **Singular Count Nouns:** *a **tree**, an **egg**, a beautiful **day**, an awful **storm***
> **Plural Count Nouns:** *three **trees**, two **eggs**, several **days**, bad **storms***

Noncount nouns are always singular.
> **Noncount Nouns:** *the **weather**, a lot of **rain**, some **ice**, bright **sunshine***

Some nouns can have both count and noncount meanings.
> *The world's **climate** is changing.* (noncount)
> *People in different **climates** grow different kinds of food.* (count)

A | Using a Dictionary. Work with a partner. One of you will be Student A and the other will be Student B. Each of you has a list of words below. Look for information about your list of words in your dictionary. Discuss your words. Then work together to complete the chart that follows.

Student A		Student B	
water	snow	wind	drought
street	flooding	lightning	person
cloud	thunder	sand	food

Count	Noncount	Both Count and Noncount
cloud	sand	

B | Talk about the photo with your partner. Use count and noncount nouns.

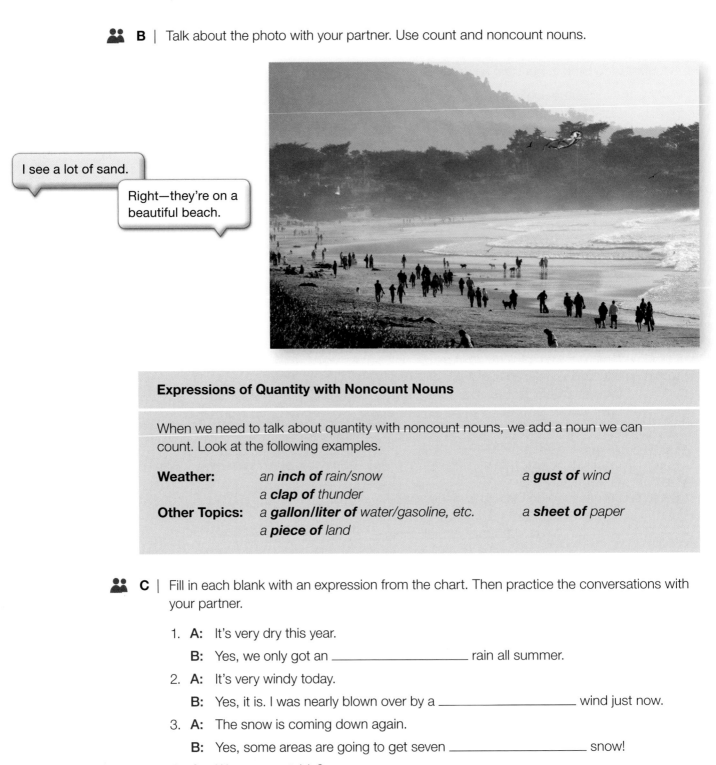

I see a lot of sand.

Right—they're on a beautiful beach.

Expressions of Quantity with Noncount Nouns

When we need to talk about quantity with noncount nouns, we add a noun we can count. Look at the following examples.

Weather: an *inch of* rain/snow   a *gust of* wind
                 a *clap of* thunder
Other Topics: a *gallon/liter of* water/gasoline, etc.   a *sheet of* paper
                 a *piece of* land

C | Fill in each blank with an expression from the chart. Then practice the conversations with your partner.

1. **A:** It's very dry this year.

   B: Yes, we only got an _____ rain all summer.

2. **A:** It's very windy today.

   B: Yes, it is. I was nearly blown over by a _____ wind just now.

3. **A:** The snow is coming down again.

   B: Yes, some areas are going to get seven _____ snow!

4. **A:** Were you outside?

   B: Yes, but I heard a _____ thunder, so I came in.

5. **A:** I forgot my notebook. Could you give me a few _____ paper?

   B: No problem. Here you go.

6. **A:** You found a very nice _____ land to build your new house on.

   B: Thanks. We love the view of the lake.

Planning an Itinerary

Form a group with two or three other students. Follow the steps below.

1. Imagine that you are going to take a three-day vacation together. Read the list of possible vacation activities. Ask yourselves, *What else do I like to do on a vacation?* Then add three or more new ideas to the list.

- *go hiking at a mountain park*
- *have a picnic at the beach*
- *go shopping*
- _____

- *visit museums*
- *go on a boat tour of the harbor*
- _____
- _____

Critical Thinking Focus: Making a List

In many situations, it's helpful to make a list. A simple shopping list, for example, helps you at the store. In an academic paper, a formal list of sources or references at the end helps people locate specific information about your topic. Making a list also helps you explore or think about a topic or idea. It makes you ask yourself, *What else?* or, *Is this everything?* as you complete the list.

2. Read the three-day weather forecast.

Friday	Saturday	Sunday
A lot of sunshine today; expect cooler temperatures in the morning; hot by early afternoon 	Morning rain showers; thunderstorms possible in the afternoon; clear and cool at night 	Partly cloudy and warmer; windy in the afternoon, with gusts up to 30 mph (48 kph) 

3. Look back at your ideas from Step 1. In your group, decide on two activities for each day of your vacation. Then write one morning (a.m.) and one afternoon (p.m.) activity for each day in the itinerary below.

What do you want to do on Saturday?

It's going to rain. Let's do something indoors.

Friday	Saturday	Sunday
a.m. p.m.	a.m. p.m.	a.m. p.m.

Tornado Chase

A tornado, Campo, Colorado, USA

Before Viewing

A | **Critical Thinking.** Discuss the questions with a partner.

1. How can the weather be dangerous? Make a list; for example, *Very high temperatures can make people sick.*
2. What is the most dangerous kind of weather in your country?

B | **Using a Dictionary.** Read the information below and use your dictionary to help you with the underlined words.

Tornado Quick Facts

- Tornadoes form during thunderstorms. Their wind speeds can be over 200 mph (320 kph), and they can destroy almost everything in their <u>path</u>.

- Although most of the world's tornadoes happen in North America and northern Europe, tornadoes happen on every continent except Antarctica.

- Meteorologists can't forecast tornadoes accurately. They can only tell people when conditions are right for tornadoes.

- In areas where tornadoes happen, people should have some kind of tornado <u>shelter</u>—a safe place to go during a tornado.

- In order to study tornadoes, some scientists actually <u>chase</u> them! They get as close as possible, and then try to deploy[1] special probes[2] to measure wind speed and other conditions inside the tornado.

---

[1]To **deploy** means to put something or someone in position.
[2]A **probe** is a scientific instrument used for collecting information.

C | Discuss the questions with a partner.

1. What new information did you learn in exercise **B**?
2. What surprises you about the information in exercise **B**?
3. How do you think people feel when they are close to a tornado?

A storm chaser deploys a probe in the path of a tornado in South Dakota, USA.

While Viewing

A | Watch the video. Check (✔) the things the tornado chasers do.

- ❑ find a road that takes them close to the tornado
- ❑ go to a store to buy a map
- ❑ deploy all of Tim Samaras' probes
- ❑ go inside a tornado shelter
- ❑ escape from a tornado

B | Watch the video again. Choose the correct answer to complete each sentence.

Tim Samaras holds a probe that calculates tornado wind speeds.

1. In the video, another word for *tornado* is _____.
   a. cyclone
   b. twister
   c. thunder cloud

2. When a tornado begins to form, the team is _____ miles away.
   a. five
   b. six
   c. seven

3. The team finds a road that goes _____, directly toward the tornado's path.
   a. east
   b. north
   c. west

4. Tim Samaras has _____ probes to deploy.
   a. five
   b. six
   c. seven

After Viewing

Critical Thinking. Form a group with two or three other students. Discuss the questions.

1. Why do you think tornado chasers do such dangerous work?
2. Do you think this might be a good career for you? Why, or why not?
3. What do you think is the most dangerous kind of storm in the world? Explain.

A van thrown into a hotel by a tornado in Kansas, USA

A | **Meaning from Context.** Read and listen to the information below. Notice the words in blue. These are words you will hear and use in Lesson B.

track 1-43

Climate Change

While the *weather* changes from day to day, the word *climate* refers to common weather patterns over a long time. Let's look at how the earth's climate is changing.

Higher Average Temperatures

Although some days are warm and some are cool, the earth's average temperature is higher now than in the past. With more heat, some plants can now grow in places that used to be too cold.

Stronger Storms

The world's oceans are also somewhat warmer than in the past. This means that the right conditions exist for stronger storms, especially hurricanes and typhoons.

Melting Ice

Much of the world's water is in the form of ice—polar ice at the north and south poles and glaciers in high mountain areas. With higher average temperatures, much of that ice is melting. We now see bare ground high in the mountains instead of glaciers.

Rising Sea Levels

When polar ice and glaciers melt, more water enters the world's oceans and sea levels rise. This means that islands and areas of low land along a country's coast may soon be under water.

B | Write each word in blue from exercise **A** next to its definition.

1. _____ (n.) land near the ocean
2. _____ (v.) changing from ice to water
3. _____ (adj.) mathematically normal
4. _____ (adv.) a little
5. _____ (v.) to go up
6. _____ (n.) repeated ways in which something happens
7. _____ (n.) a high temperature
8. _____ (v.) to live and develop, become larger
9. _____ (prep.) in place of
10. _____ (v.) to be present

A | With a partner, complete each sentence. Use your own ideas.

1. The **average** high temperature here on a summer day is about
   _____ degrees.

2. Nowadays, I use my bicycle **instead of** _____. It's better for the
   environment.

3. Two kinds of plants that **grow** here are _____
   and _____.

4. Living on a **coast** is nice because you can _____.

5. One thing that frightens me **somewhat** is _____.

6. My great-grandparents never used a _____. That kind of
   technology didn't **exist** then.

B | Fill in each blank with a word or phrase from the box. There is one word or phrase you will
not use.

coast	heat	instead of	melting	pattern	rising

The whole world is getting warmer, but temperatures in some places are (1) _____ faster than in other places. Greenland is one example. In the past, the weather (2) _____ there was always about the same—cool in the summer and very cold in the winter.

Now, however, the summers are a little longer and a little warmer. People in Greenland are growing more food (3) _____ buying all their food from other countries. Although ice still covers most of Greenland, some of the ice is (4) _____. That means there is now a little more land, and the land holds the (5) _____ from the sun, so even more ice is disappearing. Greenland's ice won't go away completely anytime soon, but life is changing quickly for Greenland's people.

GREENLAND
(KALAALLIT NUNAAT)
(Denmark)

Qeqertarsuaq
(Disko Island)

Ilulissat
Sermeq Kujalleq
(Jakobshavn Isbræ)

60°W

20°

70°N

ARCTIC CIRCLE

30°W

Denmark Strait

WESTERN
SETTLEMENT
Nuuk
(Godthåb)

Norse settlement
(circa 985-1450)

0 mi   100
0 km   100
NGM MAPS

40°

Narsaq
50°
Qassiarsuk
Ipiutaq
Qaqortoq

Tasermiut
fjord   EASTERN
SETTLEMENT

ATLANTIC OCEAN

North
Pole
Greenland
North   --DENMARK
America
ICELAND

C | **Critical Thinking.** Form a group with two or three other
students. Discuss the questions.

1. What information in exercise **B** is new to you?
2. Look at the map. Where do most people in Greenland
   live? Why do you think they live there?
3. Greenland's ice will probably continue to melt. What effects
   will this have on Greenland? On the rest of the world?

Before Listening

A man harvesting potatoes in Greenland

Activating Prior Knowledge

Prior knowledge means all the things you already know. Using your prior knowledge can help you understand what you hear. Here are some examples.

Topic: A TV show about dangerous weather
Ask yourself: What do I know about this topic? (*Some storms are dangerous. Perhaps they will talk about tornadoes or lightning or typhoons. They might give some advice about staying safe.*)

Topic: Friends talking about going to see a movie
Ask yourself: What do I know about this situation? (*They need to choose a movie and a time. Then, they probably need to decide where to meet before the movie. Perhaps they will ask me if I want to go.*)

When you think about the topic or situation first, you can often predict the things you will hear.

A | **Critical Thinking.** In this section, you will listen to a conversation about the effects of climate change on Greenland. Make a list of things you already know about this topic in your notebook. Use the information on page 75 and your own ideas.

B | Compare your list from exercise **A** with a partner's. Which topics do you think the speakers will probably talk about?

Listening: A Conversation among Friends

track 1-44 **A** | **Listening for Main Ideas.** Listen to the conversation. Then answer the questions.

1. Who are Douglas, Eric, and Lenora? _____

2. Where does Eric live?_____

3. Where do Douglas and Lenora live? _____

4. What are Doug, Eric, and Lenora doing? _____

🎧 track 1-44 **B | Note-Taking.** Listen again and complete the T-chart. (*See page 214 of the Independent Student Handbook for more information about using T-charts.*)

Climate Change in Greenland

Benefits (good things)	Drawbacks (bad things)
1. _____	1. *Possible for oil to get into ocean water*
2. _____	2. _____

🎧 track 1-44 **C | Listening for Details.** Listen again. Choose the correct answer to complete each sentence.

1. Average temperatures in Greenland are rising _____ as fast as in other places.

   a. two times   b. three times   c. four times

2. If all of Greenland's ice melts, sea levels will rise _____ feet.

   a. 24   b. 34   c. 44

3. Greenland's oil is under _____.

   a. land   b. cities   c. ice

After Listening

A | Self-Reflection. Discuss the questions with a partner.

1. Is the climate in your country changing? If so, in what ways?
2. Are you worried about climate change? Explain.
3. What can people do about climate change?

B | Role-Playing. Form a group with two other students. Role-play the rest of the dinner conversation. Start with the conversation below. Then continue with your own ideas.

Douglas:	Here it is—my delicious chicken with rice!
Eric:	That looks really good!
Lenora:	It's one of my favorite dishes.

A family grows grass to feed their 700 sheep, Tasiusaq, Greenland.

Student to Student: Showing Thanks and Appreciation

There are many situations when you want to thank a classmate, a friend, a coworker, etc. Here are some expressions you can use to thank someone.

Thank you.   *Thanks.*   *I appreciate it.*   *Thank you for (doing something).*

Grammar

A, An, Any, and Some

We can use *a, an, any,* and *some* to talk about count and noncount nouns.

	Singular Count	Plural Count	Noncount
Affirmative	It's **an** instrument.	There are **some** clouds.	We saw **some** lightning.
Negative	It's not **a** strong storm.	There aren't **any** hurricanes in my country.	We never get **any** snow.
Question	Do you want **an** apple?	Did you read **any** articles yesterday?	Is there **any** thunder?

A | Fill in each blank with *a, an, any,* or *some.*

Jake: Hello?

Trina: Hi, Jake. Listen to this: "Climate change is affecting the world's rainfall."

Jake: Really? Where did you read that?

Trina: It's in (1) _____ magazine article.

Jake: I thought there weren't (2) _____ effects on rainfall—only on temperatures.

Trina: The article lists a lot of effects. (3) _____ of them will happen here.

Jake: Which ones?

Trina: The article says we will probably get (4) _____ very strong storms.

Jake: Well, we did have (5) _____ huge hurricane last year.

A dry lake in Istanbul, Turkey

A flooded street in Oklahoma, USA

B | Compare your answers from exercise **A** with a partner's. Then practice the conversation. Switch roles and practice it again.

C | **Using a, an, any, and some.** Underline *a, an, any,* and *some* in the questions below. Then look at the photos and practice asking and answering the questions with your partner.

1. Which picture shows a drought? A flood?
2. Are any places in the world having a drought or a flood right now? If so, where?
3. In which picture do they need some rain? Some warm weather and sunshine?

Language Function

Comparing Quantities or Amounts

When we want to compare how much of something we have, we can use *more* or *fewer/less*.

> **Count:** *There are **more** clouds today than yesterday, and **fewer** people in the park.*
> **Noncount:** *These days we get **more** rain in the winter and **less** rain in the summer.*

We can also be more specific when we compare quantities or amounts. These expressions show a large difference.

> **Count:** *There are **a lot/many more** clouds today, and **a lot/many fewer** people.*
> **Noncount:** *These days we get **a lot/much more** rain in the winter, and **a lot/much less** rain in the summer.*

A | Understanding Visuals. Form a group with two or three other students. Look at the map below and discuss the questions.

1. In the future, which parts of the world will probably get a lot more rain? A lot less rain?
2. Which parts of the world will probably get a little more rain? A little less rain?

B | Collaboration. With a partner, make a list of the countries or parts of the world that will get more rain in the future. Then make another list of the countries that will get less rain in the future.

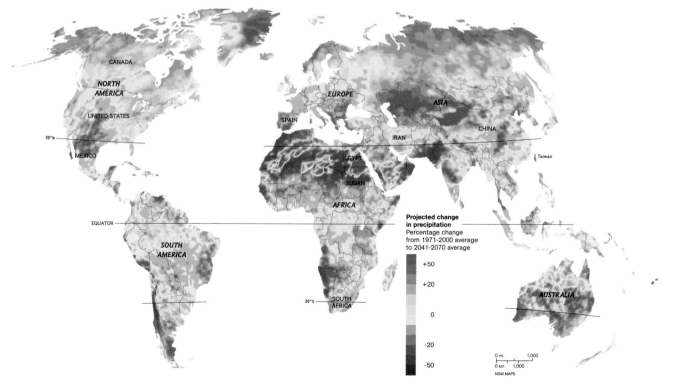

Projected change
in precipitation
Percentage change
from 1971-2000 average
to 2041-2070 average

+50
+20
0
-20
-50

0 mi   1,000
0 km   1,000
NGM MAPS

ENGAGE: Discussing Ways to Reduce Greenhouse Gases

🎧 **A** | **Note-Taking.** Listen to a short conversation about global warming. Take notes about the effects of greenhouse gases.
track 1-45

👥 **B** | **Understanding Visuals.** Look at the diagram below. Use the words in the diagram, your notes from exercise **A**, and your own ideas to explain the process of global warming to a partner. Then switch roles.

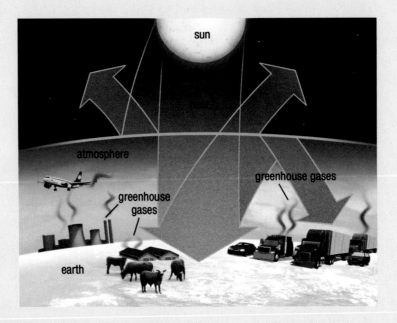

When we burn gasoline, oil, coal, and other fuels, greenhouse gases are the result.

👥 **C** | **Collaboration.** With your partner, rank the ways people can reduce greenhouse gases in the air from 1 (most helpful) to 5 (least helpful).

_____ ride a bicycle or take the bus most places

_____ use less electricity at home

_____ plant more trees in cities

_____ buy local food instead of food from other countries

_____ recycle old bottles and cans

Presentation Skills: Making Eye Contact

Whether you are making a formal presentation or just speaking to the class, it is important to make eye contact. Eye contact lets your audience know you are talking to them, and it makes your audience *want* to listen to you.

If you are using notes, look up often and make eye contact. Each time you look up, look into the eyes of a different audience member.

👥👥 **D** | Form a group with another pair of students. Tell them how you ranked the items in exercise **C**. Explain your reasons. Practice making eye contact while you speak.

Focus on Food

ACADEMIC PATHWAYS

Lesson A: Listening to a Talk by an Anthropology Professor
Conducting a Survey
Lesson B: Listening to a Conversation between Students
Creating a Description with Interesting Details

Think and Discuss

1. What do you see in the photo?
2. What are some foods you eat almost every day?
3. What foods do you eat on holidays or on special occasions?

Farmers spread out apricots to dry in Anatolia, Turkey.

Exploring the Theme:
Focus on Food

Look at the photos and read the captions. Then discuss the questions.

1. What foods do you see in the photos?
2. Which of these foods do you like? Dislike? Explain.
3. Where are papayas from?
4. What are some foods that people typically eat every day in your country?

Foods from around the World

Cheese and other **dairy products** are popular in **Europe**.

African yams are a starchy vegetable.

Rice is part of many meals in **Asia**.

Many animals are raised for **meat** in **North America**. For example, cattle are raised for **beef**.

Papayas are a kind of fruit. They grow in **Central and South America**.

Australia and New Zealand are surrounded by water, so many people in these countries eat **seafood** such as **prawns**.

Bananas grow in the floodplains of the Nyabarongo River, Kigali, Rwanda.

A | **Meaning from Context.** Look at the photos and read the captions. Then read and listen to the sentences below. Notice the words in **blue**. These are words you will hear and use in Lesson A.

track 2-2

The puffer fish can be dangerous to eat.

In some countries, people eat insects.

The durian has sharp spines on the outside and soft fruit on the inside.

1. The puffer fish is a poisonous fish, but the Japanese government will **allow** certain chefs to prepare it. They know how to make the fish safe to eat.
2. India is not the **only** country where people like hot foods. There are many other countries, too.
3. Insects are small but very **nutritious**. They are full of things that your body needs.
4. Many people can't **imagine** eating insects for dinner. It is a strange thing to think about.
5. I visited a rainforest in Colombia where the **local** people eat insects called termites.
6. Some people eat only **raw** foods. They think cooking food makes it less nutritious.
7. Many people eat honey. They like the sweet **taste** in their mouths.
8. Lingonberries are an **unusual** fruit. You find them in Sweden and just a few other places.
9. You can hurt yourself if you **touch** a durian fruit. You need to wear gloves to open it.
10. People in some parts of Asia think large water insects are **delicious**, so they eat a lot of them.

B | Write each word in **blue** from exercise **A** next to its definition.

1. _____ (v.) to let someone do something
2. _____ (adj.) uncooked
3. _____ (v.) to feel with your fingers
4. _____ (adj.) not found very often, or interesting because it is different
5. _____ (adj.) shows that no others exist or no others are present
6. _____ (adj.) tasting very good
7. _____ (adj.) belonging to the area where you live, or to the place you are talking about
8. _____ (v.) to see something in your mind, not with your eyes
9. _____ (adj.) describes food that is good for your health
10. _____ (n.) the flavor of something, e.g., sweet or salty

A | Read the article. Fill in each blank with a word in **blue** from exercise **A** on page 84. Use each word only once.

Sharing Food and Making Friends

Dr. Wade Davis is an anthropologist. Anthropologists study people and cultures around the world. In each place he travels to, Dr. Davis likes to share meals with the (1) _____ people. One food that made a big impression on him is the durian fruit. You might not have durian where you live. Southeast Asia is the (2) _____ part of the world where it grows.

Sometimes it's hard to (3) _____ why people eat the things they do. But everybody likes different things. In Malaysia, the durian is the "king of the fruits." Malaysians love it! They think it's (4) _____. Some people say durian has a (5) _____ that's like vanilla ice cream with a little bit of onion.

The durian is a huge fruit—as big as a man's head. It's also heavy. You can only eat this fruit after it falls from the tree. But you can't just run up and (6) _____ it with your hands. A durian has sharp spines growing on it, and they can hurt you. Inside, though, the durian is soft. Some people like to cook it. Others prefer to eat it (7) _____. There's something else that's (8) _____ about the durian. It has a very strong smell. Some people say it smells like dirty feet! Some people won't (9) _____ a durian inside their house.

People know that the durian is a healthy, (10) _____ food for the body. So people who don't really like the fruit hold their noses and eat it. For Dr. Davis, eating durian and other unusual foods shows respect for people and their customs. He also says that durian is good in pies!

B | **Self-Reflection.** Complete each sentence with your own ideas. Then share your ideas with a partner.

1. I think _____ is **delicious**.
2. Sometimes I like the **taste** of _____, and sometimes I don't.
3. I can't **imagine** how people eat _____.
4. I love to eat **raw** _____.
5. I think that _____ is/are **nutritious**.

Before Listening

Prior Knowledge. You are going to listen to a professor talk about the importance of food in her work. The professor is also going to answer questions from students in the class. Discuss the following questions with a partner.

1. Do you feel comfortable asking questions in a small class? In a large class?
2. Do you think teachers want you to ask questions in class? Explain.
3. What do you think is the best way to ask a question in class? Circle your answer.

   ❏ Raise your hand and say nothing.
   ❏ Raise your hand and say the professor's name.
   ❏ Use a phrase such as *Could I ask a question*? or *I have a question.*
   ❏ Just ask your question when there is a quiet moment.

Listening: A Talk by an Anthropology Professor

track 2-3 **A** | **Listening for Main Ideas.** Read the statements and answer choices. Then listen to the talk and choose the correct answer.

1. The professor is _____.
   a. a biologist
   b. a psychologist
   c. an anthropologist

2. The professor showed the students _____.
   a. travel photos
   b. family photos
   c. interesting Web sites

3. The professor eats _____.
   a. anything except insects
   b. only foods from her home country
   c. everything the local people eat

track 2-3 **B** | Look back at the list in the Before Listening section. Then listen again. Check (✔) the ways you hear students ask questions.

Nopal cactus fields near Tlayacapan, Mexico

Prickly pear cactus leaves, *nopalitos,* ready for the grill in Yucatan, Mexico

Cassava

🎧 **C | Listening for Details.** Listen again. Fill in each blank with the word or words that you hear.
track 2-3

1. For the professor, it's very important to become a part of the _____.
2. The professor eats unusual foods such as _____ ants.
3. *Cassava* is a kind of _____.
4. If it is raw, *cassava* can make people _____.
5. The professor never gets sick when she _____.
6. The professor likes to eat cactus with _____.

After Listening

👥 **A | Self-Reflection.** Form a group with two or three other students. Discuss the questions.

1. Do you like to try new foods? Why, or why not?
2. What non-nutritious foods do you like to eat? Explain.

👥 **B | Critical Thinking.** Discuss the questions with your group.

1. What foods from your culture might seem strange to other people? Explain.
2. What can we learn about people from the kind of foods they eat?

Pronunciation

Can and *Can't*

In a sentence, the word *can* is usually unstressed. That means the vowel is reduced to schwa /ə/. The word *can't* is usually stressed and has a full vowel sound.

🎧 *I **can** eat it, too.*
track 2-4 *You **can** use it to make bread.*

*I **can't** eat any kind of cheese.*
*You **can't** eat it raw.*

There are two ways to hear the difference between *can* and *can't* in a sentence:

1. Listen for the final /t/ sound in *can't*.
2. Listen for the reduced vowel schwa /ə/ in *can*, and the full vowel /æ/ in *can't*.

In fast speech, we often don't hear the final /t/ sound, but the vowel sound can help you understand *can* and *can't* correctly.

👥 With a partner, practice saying each pair of sentences. Use a reduced vowel for *can* and a full vowel (as in *cat* or *math*) for *can't*.

1. You can eat raw apples.
2. You can eat cactus raw or cooked.
3. I can help you tomorrow.
4. We can work on our homework together.

You can't eat raw *cassava*.
You can't eat cactus with the spines.
I can't help you on Sunday.
We can't work on the test together.

Language Function

Expressing Opinions

In a conversation, we often use these expressions to show we are giving a personal opinion.

🎧 track 2-5

***In my opinion**, trying new foods is a lot of fun.*
***I think** the food in India is very good.*
***I don't think** durian fruit tastes very good.*
***For me,/To me**, this dish is too salty.*
***Personally**, I don't like the food at that restaurant.*

🎧 track 2-6 **A** | Listen to the conversations and <u>underline</u> the expressions for giving a personal opinion.

   1. **Lydia:** I think these fried potatoes are delicious.

      Henri: I don't think they're good for you, though.

      Lydia: You're probably right.

      Henri: Personally, I don't like to eat any fried foods.

   2. **Lee:** Do you like the chicken curry?[1]

      Zachary: In my opinion, it's a little too hot.

      Lee: Really? For me, it's perfect.

   3. **Natalia:** What are you cooking? It smells great!

      Jenny: It's *falafel*. It's a vegetarian[2] dish.

      Natalia: Are you making any meat dishes to go with it?

      Jenny: Not tonight. Personally, I think we eat too much meat.

B | Practice the conversations in exercise **A** with a partner. Then switch roles and practice them again.

C | Work with your partner. Fill in each blank with a word or phrase from the Expressing Opinions box. Then practice the conversations.

   1. **A:** _____ puffer fish is too dangerous for people to eat.
      B: _____ you're right.

   2. **A:** _____ eating insects is a terrible idea.
      B: _____ I would like to try them.

   3. **A:** _____ Frank is a very good chef.
      B: _____ he cooks eggs very well, however.

[1] **Curry** is a flavorful dish that is common in India and other parts of the world.
[2] A **vegetarian** dish has no meat in it.

Grammar

Can and Can't

We use *can* and *can't* to talk about <u>ability</u>.
> I **can** ride a bicycle, but I **can't** drive a motorcycle. I don't know how.

We use *can* and *can't* to talk about <u>possibility</u>.
> You **can** write your paper about nutrition or about strange foods. You **can't** write it on any other topic.

We use *can* and *can't* to ask for or give <u>permission</u>.
> **Can** I come in? Yes, but you **can't** stay very long. I have to leave soon.

The negative form of *can* is *cannot*. *Can't* is a contraction. It is usually used in spoken English.
> Instructors **cannot** enter the building before 7:00 a.m.
> Could you speak up? I **can't** hear you very well.

Note: In short answers with *can*, we use the full vowel sound.
> Can you hear me?   Yes, I **can**. (/æ/)

A | Fill in each blank with *can* or *can't*.

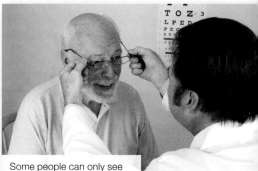

Some people can only see well when they wear glasses.

1. Lyle _____ pick you up at the airport. He'll be at work at that time.

2. You _____ use *cassava* like you use potatoes. It's delicious!

3. I'm sorry, you _____ go in there. They're having a meeting.

4. Students _____ meet with professors during their office hours.

5. Paula got new glasses, so she _____ see much better now.

6. I _____ eat this food. It's too hot for me.

B | Work with a partner. Take turns asking questions and giving short answers about the abilities below.

Can you speak more than two languages?

No, I can't.

speak more than two languages	play tennis well
cook Italian food	take beautiful photos
run very fast	eat very hot foods
play a musical instrument	name all seven continents

track 2-7 **C** | Read and listen to the article. Underline *can* and *can't*.

Eating Insects: More Common Than You Might Think

Do you like to eat bugs? Some people do, and some people don't. But here's the surprise—even if you don't like eating insects, you are probably eating them anyway.

"It's estimated that the average human eats one pound (around half a kilogram) of insects each year unintentionally,"[1] says Lisa Monachelli, director of youth and family programs at New Canaan Nature Center in Connecticut. In the United States, the U.S. Food and Drug Administration (FDA) allows some insects and insect parts in food, as long as they don't make people sick.

The food in your refrigerator can contain some surprises.

For example, for every 3.5 ounces (100 grams), chocolate can have up to 60 insect parts and peanut butter can have 30 insect fragments,[2] according to the FDA. Tomato sauce can't contain more than 30 fly eggs per 3.5 ounces (100 grams).

And food is not the only place you can find insects and insect parts. Cochineal insects give a red or pink coloring to foods, lipsticks, and beverages. The small bugs are listed as "cochineal extract" on the ingredient[3] list. The fact is—you can't always avoid eating insects.

[1] **Unintentionally** means by accident.
[2] A **fragment** is a small piece or part of something.
[3] An **ingredient** is an item you need to make a meal or food product.

D | Ask a partner questions 1-3. Your partner will give short answers using the information in the article. Then switch roles for questions 4-6.

1. Can 3.5 ounces (100 grams) of chocolate have more than 60 insect parts in it?
2. Can you avoid eating insects?
3. Can insects be used in some drinks?
4. Can 3.5 ounces (100 grams) of tomato sauce have 35 fly eggs in it?
5. Can 3.5 ounces (100 grams) of peanut butter have 25 insect parts in it?
6. Can the insect parts in peanut butter make you sick?

E | **Critical Thinking.** Form a group with two or three other students. Discuss the questions. Use some of the expressions for giving opinions on page 88.

1. Besides the foods in the article, do you think other foods can contain insects? Explain.
2. Do you think a vegetarian can eat these foods? Why, or why not?
3. Do you think it is safe to eat foods with insects or insect parts? Explain.
4. In general, who should make sure our food is safe (e.g., farmers and other food producers; government agencies such as the FDA; customers who buy food; grocery stores that sell food)?

Conducting a Survey

Staple Foods

Staple foods are foods that make up a large part of the diet. People eat them every day, or almost every day. You are going to conduct a survey of your classmates' eating habits. You are going to talk to three of your classmates. Then you are going to share the information from your survey with a small group.

Some of the World's Staple Foods

Beans · Rice · Potatoes · Wheat · Corn

A | Note-Taking. Follow these steps. Take notes in the chart below or in your notebook.

1. Ask a classmate questions about his or her eating habits.
2. Take notes on your classmates' answers.
3. Then switch roles and answer the questions.
4. When you are finished, repeat the steps with two more classmates.

Survey Questions	Student 1	Student 2	Student 3
1. Where did you grow up?			
2. What staple food do you eat most often?			
3. How do you eat that food (e.g., made into bread, with a sauce, as a side dish, etc.)?			
4. Do you think this staple food is an important part of your culture? Explain.			
5. Are any of the foods in the photos new to you? Do you want to try them?			

B | Critical Thinking. Read your notes from exercise **A**. Think about the information you have. Decide which information might be interesting to talk about.

C | Presentation. Form a group with two or three other students. Share the interesting information you learned from your survey.

> The students in my survey come from cultures with different staple foods: corn, rice, and wheat. But they all said . . .

FORBIDDEN FRUIT

Durian fruit, Johore, Malaysia

Before Viewing

A | **Critical Thinking.** Discuss the questions with a partner.

1. What do you remember about durian fruit from Lesson A of this unit?
2. In Lesson A, you learned that only some people like to eat foods such as insects, cactus, and durian fruit. Why do you think other people dislike these foods?

B | **Using a Dictionary.** Use your dictionary to find out whether each word in the box has a positive (good) or negative (bad) meaning. Write each word in the correct side of the T-chart below.

awful	disgusting	fragrant	precious	smelly	smuggle

Positive Meaning	Negative Meaning

While Viewing

A | Watch the video. Choose the correct answer to complete each sentence.

1. Hotels don't want durian fruit in the rooms because it _____ bad.
   a. looks   b. tastes   c. smells
2. According to the video, durian fruit in Southeast Asia is as precious as _____.
   a. gold in India   b. cheese in France   c. gasoline in Bolivia
3. Hotel workers can use _____ to clean the air in hotel rooms.
   a. soap and water   b. a machine   c. flowers
4. Hotels want guests to eat their durian fruit _____.
   a. indoors   b. at home   c. outdoors

B | Watch the video again. <u>Underline</u> each word from exercise **B** in the Before Viewing section when you hear it.

After Viewing

A | **Meaning from Context.** Read and listen to the information about the video. Notice the <u>underlined</u> words.

track 2-8

Forbidden Fruit

In this video, hotels in Malaysian Borneo have a problem: Guests like to bring smelly durian fruit into their rooms. Then the hotel staff has to work hard to get rid of the smell. The video uses interesting words to talk about the problem. For example, it says that, "Hotels are on the <u>front lines</u> of the durian <u>war</u>." Of course, it's not really a war, but there are two sides: the hotels and the guests who bring durian fruit into the rooms. The video also says, "Hotel managers maintain a constant <u>vigil</u> to keep it out." But the managers can't see everything, so when a guest does bring in a durian fruit, there is "a durian <u>alert</u>," and the hotel staff must work quickly to make the room smell good again.

During durian season, hotels in Malaysian Borneo don't allow the fruit inside.

B | With a partner, write each <u>underlined</u> word or phrase next to its definition below.

1. _____ (n.) a time of watching and waiting
2. _____ (n.) fighting; usually between two or more countries
3. _____ (n.) places where most of the fighting happens
4. _____ (n.) emergency situation

C | **Expressing Opinions.** Form a group with another pair of students. Discuss the questions.

1. Is it a big problem for you if a hotel room has a bad smell? Explain.
2. What's one food that is disgusting to you? Why do you dislike it?
3. What's one food that almost everyone in your culture likes? Why do they like it?
4. Is the situation with hotels and durian fruit in Malaysian Borneo really like a war? How is it similar or different?

Meaning from Context. Read and listen to the information about three kinds of restaurants. *track 2-9* Notice the words in blue. These are words you will hear and use in Lesson B.

Three Kinds of Restaurants

Sugar Shacks

You can find *sugar shacks* in the Canadian province of Quebec. They're family restaurants, and you can go there in the early spring for good food and maple syrup—a sweet liquid from maple trees. After you finish your pancakes and hot coffee, order some maple taffy— a kind of candy. To make the taffy, a restaurant worker pours warm maple syrup onto cold snow. Then the worker quickly turns the maple syrup with a wooden stick, and the maple taffy is ready to eat!

Fresh maple taffy on a bed of snow

Chinese *dim sum*

Dim Sum Restaurants

In English, *dim sum* means, "a little bit of heart." In the United States, San Francisco is a great place to enjoy these small plates of delicious treats—all made with love. Why San Francisco? In the 1800s, many Chinese people moved to California to work. Their neighborhood in San Francisco was the first Chinatown in the United States. Today, there are numerous *dim sum* restaurants in San Francisco. They all serve this traditional Chinese food with a traditional Chinese beverage—hot tea.

Chocolaterías

Which European country makes the best chocolate? People disagree on that, but we do know that Spain was the first European country to buy cacao beans for making chocolate. Cacao arrived in Seville in 1585! Soon after that, Spanish people fell in love with a drink called hot chocolate. Today, you can find cafés called *chocolaterías* all over Spain. They're popular places for friends and families to meet, and some of them are open all night.

Hot chocolate is a favorite beverage in many parts of the world.

A | Fill in each blank with a word in **blue** from page 94. Use each word only once.

1. Welcome to Mom's Sugar Shack. Are you ready to _____?

2. On the cold snow, maple syrup changes from a _____ to a solid.

3. I don't want to drive very far. Are there any good restaurants in this _____?

4. This café is very _____. There are always a lot of people here.

5. Does that restaurant _____ seafood? I'd like to have some fish for dinner.

6. The class starts in 10 minutes. Let's walk _____ so we get there on time.

7. We often _____ at the library, and we all study together there.

8. My favorite _____ is water, but I also like tea.

9. There are _____ reasons to eat at home. For example, it's less expensive than eating at restaurants, and homemade food is more nutritious.

10. That restaurant has a lot of delicious _____ on its dessert menu such as chocolate cake, apple pie, and several kinds of ice cream.

B | **Collaboration.** Notice how the vocabulary words are used in exercise **A**. With a partner, write each word in the correct column of the chart below.

Noun	Verb	Adjective	Adverb

C | Take turns asking and answering the questions with your partner.

1. What's the name of a **popular** restaurant or café you know about? What do they **serve** there?

2. What's your favorite hot **beverage**? Your favorite cold **beverage**?

3. At a restaurant, what do you like to **order** for breakfast?

4. Do you usually eat **quickly** or slowly? Explain.

5. What are your two favorite sweet **treats**? Why do you like them?

A family enjoys *dim sum* at the May Flower restaurant in San Francisco.

Bread baked in a wood-fired oven, Paris, France

Before Listening

Listening for Specific Information

Listening for main ideas is almost always necessary. Listening for specific information, or smaller details, can also be very important. Here is an example.

This listener wants to know two things: Where is the restaurant? Is it expensive? Notice the specific information that the listener needs to hear.

🎧 track 2-10

Lucky Noodle is a new restaurant on the north side of the city. It's located at 314 Webster Street near the university campus. Students and other busy people will love the quick service at *Lucky Noodle,* and everyone will love the food. The prices are not bad either. A large bowl of noodle soup is $6.95, and the pan-fried noodles with chicken costs $8.95.

🎧 track 2-11 **Note-Taking.** Read the questions. Then listen to information about a school cafeteria[1] and write the answers.

1. Where is the cafeteria? _____

2. Who can eat there? _____

3. When is it open? _____

4. How much does the food cost? _____

Listening: A Conversation between Students

🎧 track 2-12 **A | Listening for Main Ideas.** Read the questions and answer choices. Then listen to a conversation between two university students and choose the correct answer.

1. What does Roger think about the cafeteria food?
   a. It's very bad.
   b. It's not very popular.
   c. It's too expensive.

2. What does Roger think about the cafeteria hours?
   a. The cafeteria opens too early.
   b. The cafeteria closes too early.
   c. The cafeteria hours are fine.

3. What does Aaron suggest?
   a. Roger should cook at home.
   b. Roger should meet him at the cafeteria.
   c. Roger should eat at the nearby restaurants.

Food sits uneaten on a school lunch tray.

[1] A **cafeteria** is a self-service restaurant, usually in a public building such as a school or hospital.

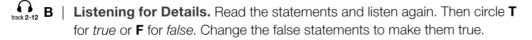

B | Listening for Details. Read the statements and listen again. Then circle **T** for *true* or **F** for *false*. Change the false statements to make them true.

track 2-12

1. Roger thinks the coffee in the cafeteria is good.   **T   F**
2. Roger usually eats dinner around 10:00 p.m.   **T   F**
3. Roger and Aaron both like the food at the Pink Rose Café.   **T   F**
4. Aaron says people can eat quickly at the cafeteria.   **T   F**
5. Roger and Aaron agree to meet at the cafeteria at 12:15 p.m.   **T   F**

After Listening

A | Self-Reflection. When you eat at a restaurant or cafeteria, what is important to you? Rank the following from 1 (most important) to 5 (least important).

_____ cost/price   _____ quality of food   _____ location

_____ service   _____ hours

B | Discussion. With a partner, compare and discuss your rankings in exercise **A**.

For me, the food is most important.

That's important to me, too, but the price is even more important.

Student to Student: Showing Agreement

In a conversation, you will often want or need to agree with someone. Here are some expressions you can use to show agreement.

Right!   *Exactly!*   *That's true.*   *I agree.*

C | Critical Thinking. Form a group with another pair of students. Think about the conversation between Roger and Aaron, and discuss the questions. Practice using expressions to show agreement.

1. What did you think about Roger? Were his reasons for not going to the cafeteria good reasons? Was his idea to eat at nearby restaurants a good idea? Explain.
2. What did you think about Aaron? Did he understand Roger's problem? Did he recommend a good solution? Explain.
3. Where do you usually eat? Do you eat at home, in restaurants, or in cafeterias? Explain.

🎧 track 2-13   **A** | Read and listen to the conversation. Notice the words the speakers use to describe food.

Mexican tacos

Korean *kim chee*

Mariana:	You should really try tacos. They're delicious!
Jen:	What are they like?
Mariana:	Well, they're made from fresh, warm tortillas—those are like little corn pancakes, but they're not sweet.
Jen:	OK. Fresh tortillas sound good.
Mariana:	They are! Then we put a little meat and raw onions and other vegetables on top.
Jen:	Well, I'll try tacos if you'll try *kim chee*.
Mariana:	Hmmm . . . What's *kim chee*?
Jen:	It's made from raw vegetables with salt, red chili, and fish sauce. Then, we wait several days before we eat it.
Mariana:	Really? It doesn't sound very good to me.
Jen:	Oh, it's great! You only eat a little, and you have it with other food such as rice or soup.
Mariana:	I could try it, I guess.
Jen:	Yes, try it! And I'll try tacos.

B | Practice the conversation with a partner. Then switch roles and practice it again.

Thai prawn curry soup

Grammar

Descriptive Adjectives

Adjectives give us more information about the nouns they describe. They usually come before nouns.

> I don't like **sweet** foods.   For some people, a **boiled** egg is a **good** snack.

Adjectives come after the verb *be* and some other verbs, for example: *taste/smell/look*.

> This soup is **salty.**   Potato chips are usually **crispy,** but these are **soft.**
>
> The fried rice smells **delicious!**   This curry is very **red.** It looks **spicy!**

Here are some adjectives to describe food:

salty	delicious	crunchy	raw
sweet	mild	soft	cooked
sour	spicy	crispy	fried/boiled

Chinese fried rice

A | Write sentences in your notebook using adjectives from the box and the words and phrases below. Then take turns saying your sentences to a partner.

| boiled | crunchy | delicious | fried | mild | raw | salty | spicy | sweet |

1. This chocolate cake/look *This chocolate cake looks delicious.*
2. The soup at the Blue Moon Café/be
3. I really/like/eggs
4. My favorite snack/be
5. This apple/taste
6. I/don't like/foods

B | **Describing a Favorite Food.** Follow the steps below.

1. Choose a food that you really like to eat.
2. Think about how people prepare the food and when and where you eat it.
3. Make a list of adjectives to describe the food. You can use your dictionary to help you.

C | With a partner, take turns describing the food you chose in exercise **B**. Use descriptive adjectives.

> I really like baked lasagna. It has a mild flavor, and it's hot and delicious. I make it on cold days when . . .

Critical Thinking Focus: Distinguishing between Main Ideas and Details

There are different kinds of information in every conversation, lecture, or reading passage. Some of the information gives you the main ideas—the most important things to know. Other ideas are details. These details give you more information about the main ideas. Knowing whether a piece of information is a main idea or a detail can help you to understand what you hear or read.

Critical Thinking. Read the two groups of statements below. Each group has one main idea and three details. With a partner, mark each statement with **M** for *main idea* or **D** for *detail*.

1. _____ We eat rice at almost every meal.	1. _____ The professor explains things well.
2. _____ Many dishes in my country, such as rice noodles, are made from rice.	2. _____ Algebra 362 is an excellent course.
3. _____ Many farmers in my country grow rice.	3. _____ We're using a very good textbook.
4. _____ Rice is very important in my country.	4. _____ The tests and quizzes are helpful.

Situation: You and your group are restaurant managers. You plan to add three new items to your restaurant's menu. Research shows that people order menu items with good descriptions. You will create the best description for each new menu item shown on this page.

Form a group with two other students. Then follow the steps below.

1. **Discussion.** Look at the photos below and discuss some of the details about each new menu item. For example, does it contain vegetables, nuts, or tomato sauce? Will you serve it hot or cold? Use your own ideas.
2. **Brainstorming.** For each new menu item, make a list of several descriptive adjectives in your notebook. Look back at the chart on page 98. Use your dictionary to help you with other adjectives.
3. **Planning a Presentation.** Assign one menu item to each person in your group. Write notes for a description of your menu item. The words you choose should make people want to order the food.
4. **Presentation.** Describe your menu item to your group. Remember to use descriptive adjectives. Ask your group members if your description makes them want to order the item. Can they think of ways to make the description even better?

Fried vegetable egg rolls

Pasta with chicken and tomato sauce

Brownie with vanilla ice cream and chocolate sauce

Presentation Skills: Giving Interesting Details

Giving details keeps your audience interested and makes your presentation more complete. You can use descriptive adjectives and other expressions to add interesting details. For example:

Without Details: *There were flowers in front of the building.*

With Details: *There were fragrant red roses in large wooden flower boxes in front of Murphy Hall.*

Housing

Think and Discuss

1. What do you see in the photo?
2. Would you like to live in a house like this? Explain.
3. What do you think you will learn about in this unit?

A wooden summer house, West Sussex, U.K.

101

Exploring the Theme:
Housing

Look at the photos and read the captions. Then discuss the questions.

1. Where was each photo taken?
2. Does the housing in the photos look similar to the housing in your country? Explain.
3. What are some of the advantages and disadvantages of each type of housing?

House

This house is in **Canada**. Houses like this usually hold one family, so they are often called "single-family homes."

Apartment Building

Tall apartment buildings are common in the world's large cities. These apartment buildings are in **Melbourne, Australia**. An "apartment complex" is several of these buildings together.

Row House

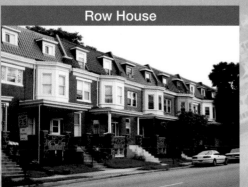

There is no space between one row house and the next. Instead, row houses such as these in the **United States** have shared walls.

Condominium

Like apartments, there can be many condominiums in one building. These vacation "condos" are on **Paradise Island** in the **Bahamas**.

The Palm Jumeirah is a man-made island with beach front homes in Dubai, United Arab Emirates.

A | **Using a Dictionary.** Listen and check (✔) the words you already know. Then use a dictionary to help you with any new words. These are words you will hear and use in Lesson A.

track 2-14

❏ apartments (n.) ❏ building (n.) ❏ residents (n.) ❏ spacious (adj.) ❏ style (n.)
❏ balcony (n.) ❏ comfortable (adj.) ❏ roof (n.) ❏ stairs (n.) ❏ walls (n.)

B | Complete each sentence with a word from exercise **A**.

1. My bedroom is small, but it's _____, so I like it.

2. The Willis Tower is a very tall _____ in Chicago.

3. I think there's a problem with the _____. Water gets into my bedroom every time it rains.

4. The _____ in this complex are all the same. They each have a living room, a dining room, and two bedrooms.

5. The elevator isn't working, so we'll need to take the _____ to the third floor.

6. We have a _____ living room, so we're buying a large sofa and chairs.

7. From my room on the fifth floor of the hotel, you can step outside onto the _____.

8. The _____ of this apartment building are friendly, and they're usually quiet.

9. All of the _____ in my new house are white, but I love color, so I'll probably paint them.

10. The _____ of this house is too modern for me. I prefer more traditional houses.

C | Read the information about the Spanish architect Antoni Gaudí. Fill in each blank with a word from exercise **A**. Then listen and check your answers.

track 2-15

Casa Milà

In Barcelona, Spain, both visitors and (1) _____ of the city know about the architect Antoni Gaudí. The Casa Milà is perhaps his best-known (2) _____. From the outside, the (3) _____ look like natural stone. On the (4) _____, several large, unusual works of art are actually chimneys—they carry away gases from cooking and heating from inside the (5) _____.

Casa Batlló

The Casa Batlló is another of Gaudí's apartment buildings. The outside of the building is very colorful, and it's easy to see that Gaudí was an artist as well as an architect. Not every apartment is (6) _____, but each apartment has a (7) _____ so residents can stand outside their bedrooms or living rooms and see the street below.

Park Güell

One of the most popular Gaudí sites isn't a building at all. The Park Güell is a large outdoor park, but Gaudí's architectural (8) _____ is everywhere—from the (9) _____ and stone columns to the beautiful artwork. There are (10) _____ places to sit, and the trees and gardens invite city residents to relax and enjoy nature.

A | **Discussion.** Look at the photos on this page and read the captions. Then discuss the questions with a partner.

1. What do you think about the **buildings** and park from exercise **C** on page 104?
2. Which of Gaudí's **apartment buildings** do you prefer? Would you like to live there? Explain.
3. What else do you know about Gaudí or about Barcelona, Spain?
4. What other famous architects do you know about?

Gaudí designed every part of the lobby of Casa Batlló, including the windows and the lighting.

A resident of Casa Batlló enjoys the evening air on one of the building's balconies.

B | Read the conversation. Choose the correct word in **blue**.

Katrina:	Do you like this (**apartment/resident**), Hector?
Hector:	I do like it. It's quite (**style/spacious**), so there's enough room for all our furniture.
Katrina:	I agree, and I like the (**comfortable/style**), too.
Hector:	What do you like about it?
Katrina:	It looks very modern.
Hector:	There is one problem, though. There's no (**balcony/building**).
Katrina:	True, but if we want to go outside, we can go up onto the (**roof/wall**).
Hector:	Really? We can go up there?
Katrina:	Sure. There's a seating area with tables and (**building/comfortable**) chairs.
Hector:	That sounds nice. Do we have to use the (**stairs/walls**)?
Katrina:	No, we can take the elevator.

C | Practice the conversation with a partner. Then switch roles and practice it again.

Before Listening

Using Context Clues

Clues are pieces of information that help us understand other ideas. When we listen to a talk, we often don't understand every word. Using context clues can help us understand the talk. Here are some common types of context clues.

- **Nearby words and phrases:** Listen for clues near the word you don't understand. *Jerry doesn't want to buy a house because he doesn't want the* commitment*. You have to **take care of a house**, and you have to **stay there a long time**. Jerry might want to move soon.*

- **Definitions:** Listen carefully after you hear a new word. Sometimes a speaker will explain the meaning of the word. *Paulina wants to rent an apartment, but she doesn't want to sign a* lease—*a legal agreement. She thinks it's enough just to pay her rent every month.* *(See page 204 of the Independent Student Handbook for more information on understanding meaning from context.)*

A | Read and listen to the conversation. Then work with a partner to find context clues that help you understand the underlined words.

track 2-16

Mrs. Ferrer:	I don't want to live in that neighborhood.
Mr. Ferrer:	Why not? It's close to your office.
Mrs. Ferrer:	Yes, but there's a lot of <u>congestion</u>. Everyone is looking for a place to park their cars, and it's hard just to cross the street sometimes.
Mr. Ferrer:	So where do you want to live?
Mrs. Ferrer:	I like the <u>demographics</u> in Riverdale. There are a lot of young families with good jobs there.
Mr. Ferrer:	OK, but we're getting older, and our children live on their own now.
Mrs. Ferrer:	True, but we're not <u>geriatric</u> yet. We're still young enough to enjoy a nice neighborhood.
Mr. Ferrer:	Then we'll ask the <u>real estate agent</u> to show us apartments in Riverdale.
Mrs. Ferrer:	Good. I think we'll like it there.

B | Practice the conversation with your partner. Then switch roles and practice it again.

Listening: A PowerPoint Presentation

A | **Listening for Main Ideas.** Listen and choose the main idea of the presentation.
(track 2-17)

    a. The La Costa apartment complex is in the Barceloneta neighborhood.

    b. There are nice apartments for sale in the new La Costa complex.

    c. Families will like the beach and the good schools.

B | **Listening for Details.** Listen again. Complete the statements with the numbers you hear.
(track 2-17)

    1. Each building has _____ floors.

    2. In all, there are _____ apartments!

    3. The next picture shows the lobby of building number _____.

    4. We have _____ elevators in each building for the residents to use.

    5. In addition, there is _____ large service elevator in each building.

C | **Using Context Clues.** Read the statements from the presentation. Listen again and write down some of the context clues that help you understand the underlined words.
(track 2-17)

    1. We have something for *all* of your <u>clients</u>. _____

    _____

    2. It's a colorful <u>mosaic</u>. _____

    _____

After Listening

Critical Thinking. Form a group with two or three other students. Follow the instructions.

1. What good things do you remember about the apartment complex?

2. What other questions might the real estate agents ask the developer?

3. Do you think the audience of real estate agents will bring their clients to see the apartments? Explain.

Grammar

Coordinating Conjunctions

We use coordinating conjunctions to join sentences and show a relationship between ideas.

The most common coordinating conjunctions are: *and, but, or,* and *so.*

> The kitchen is nice, **but** the living room is too small. (a contrast)
> We can live downtown, **or** we can live near the beach. (a choice)
> We want to buy a house, **so** we need to save our money. (a result)

Note: In writing, we use a comma before a coordinating conjunction.

> The condominium is clean. It's not expensive. (two sentences)
> The condominium is clean, **and** it's not expensive. (an addition; two good things)

A | Work with a partner. Circle the coordinating conjunction in each sentence. Then identify the relationship between the ideas.

1. We love nature, (so) we want to live near a park. ___*a result*___

2. It's a beautiful condo, but the rent is too high. _____

3. I can stay here, or I can move to a different apartment. _____

4. The living room is spacious, but the bedrooms are small. _____

5. We like the house, and the neighborhood is beautiful. _____

6. My real estate agent never answers his phone, so I'm looking for a new agent. _____

B | Complete each sentence with your own ideas.

1. Our apartment is large, so ___*we have a lot of parties there.*___

2. I like my neighborhood, but _____

3. The building has friendly residents, and _____

4. I can eat dinner at home, or _____

5. I love big cities, so _____

6. Apartments downtown are expensive, so _____

C | Say your sentences from exercise **B** to a partner. Decide whether each of you used conjunctions correctly.

Many people dream of owning a home, but taking care of a single-family house can be a lot of work.

Language Function

Agreeing and Disagreeing

When we agree with someone, we often use short expressions.
Here are some of the short expressions you can use to show that you agree with someone.

I agree.   *You're right.*   *Absolutely.*   *Definitely.*   *That's true.*

When we disagree with someone, it's more important to be polite, so expressions for disagreeing are often longer.

That's a good point, but I don't agree.
I see what you mean, but I think . . .
I'm afraid I disagree.

A | Work with a partner. One partner is Student A and the other is Student B. Take turns saying one of your statements below. Your partner will agree or disagree, using expressions from the box above.

Student A
- I like the houses in this neighborhood.
- Gaudí was very creative, so his buildings are beautiful.
- Our classroom is very spacious.
- White walls are light and bright, so they look the best.

Student B
- I don't like elevators. I prefer the stairs.
- An apartment building is a great place for a family.
- These chairs are old. We need new ones.
- The food at the cafeteria is delicious.

B | Read and listen to the conversation. Then <u>underline</u> the expressions for agreeing and disagreeing.

track 2-18

Sasha:	I'm so happy! I finally found a new place.
Janet:	That's great! Where are you living?
Sasha:	I'm living on the east side, and it's close to a bus line.
Janet:	Being close to the bus line is good, but the east side is dangerous.
Sasha:	That's a good point, but I think the neighborhood is improving.
Janet:	Really? What's happening there?
Sasha:	They're putting in better lighting, so the streets aren't so dark at night.
Janet:	That's good.
Sasha:	My new apartment is also in a safe building, and that's important.
Janet:	I agree.

C | Practice the conversation with a partner. Then switch roles and practice it again.

D | Collaboration. With your partner, look at the photos and read the information. Then list several good points about each place to live. Use the information and your own ideas.

Option 1

This clean, modern two-bedroom apartment is downtown and close to the university, so it's perfect for students. There is a resident manager who takes care of any problems.

close to the university

don't need a car

_____

_____

_____

Option 2

This beautiful traditional house is a comfortable place for a family. It's in a quiet area near schools and parks.

_____

_____

_____

_____

_____

Option 3

This spacious, elegant house has a swimming pool, five bedrooms, and six bathrooms. It's close to the beach and far from the noisy city.

_____

_____

_____

_____

_____

_____

Critical Thinking Focus: Evaluating Options

Every housing option on this page has good points, but not every good point has the same importance for everyone. When we choose a place to live, we must judge or evaluate the different options and decide which good points are more important to us, or a better match for the way we live.

E | Critical Thinking. Form a group with another pair of students. Compare your lists of good points from exercise **D**. Then discuss which option is the best for each person in the group.

> I have children, and Option 2 is close to schools. That's important to me.

> I don't have time to take care of a house, so Option 1 is the best for me.

Expressing Relationships between Ideas

A | Work with a partner. Look at the picture of Dylan and read the ideas about him in the chart below. Then take turns making statements about him using ideas from the chart. Decide if your partner's statements make sense or not. You may want to look back at the grammar chart on page 108.

Dylan loves music		he takes a train to work.
Dylan works downtown	and	he plays the guitar.
Dylan is an excellent cook	but	he travels to other countries a lot.
Dylan often calls me	or	he lives in the country.
Dylan has a car	so	he eats at restaurants a lot.
Dylan works for an international company		he sends me emails.

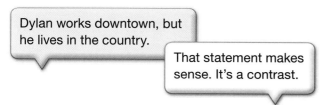

Dylan works downtown, but he lives in the country.

That statement makes sense. It's a contrast.

Dylan

B | Read the conversation and <u>underline</u> the expressions that show disagreement. Then practice the conversation with your partner.

Zach:	The climate here is too cold, so I want to move.
Hiroshi:	Where do you want to go?
Zach:	San Francisco, California.
Hiroshi:	Are you sure about that?
Zach:	I think so. California is really warm, right?
Hiroshi:	The southern part of California is warm, but the northern part is cooler.
Zach:	That's a good point. I'll move to Los Angeles, then.
Hiroshi:	Hmm, I don't know . . . That may not be the best place for you.
Zach:	Why not? You said it's warm in southern California.
Hiroshi:	It is warm, but you don't like big cities, and Los Angeles is very big.
Zach:	You're right. I probably need to think about this a little more.

Student to Student:
Expressing Disagreement to a Friend

When we're talking with our good friends, it's still important to be polite when we disagree. On the other hand, the expressions we use to disagree with our friends can be fairly informal. Here are some examples of informal expressions.

I don't know . . .

Hmm . . .

Maybe . . .

Are you sure about that?

Don't Believe Your Eyes!

Before Viewing

A | Self-Reflection. Discuss the questions with a partner.

1. In Lesson A of this unit, you saw several pictures of houses and buildings. Which house or building in Lesson A is the most beautiful to you? Explain.
2. For you, what usually makes a house or building beautiful? For example, is it the style, the color, the size, or something else?

track 2-19 **B | Using a Dictionary.** Read and listen to the information about the video. Use a dictionary to help you with the underlined words.

This video is about a kind of art called *trompe l'oeil*. It's a painting <u>technique</u> that is popular in an Italian village called Camogli. There, many people have *trompe l'oeil* paintings of windows, balconies, flowers, and even animals on the outside walls of their houses.

A *trompe l'oeil* painting

Houses in Camogli have always been colorful. In the past, <u>fishermen</u> wanted to see their houses from the sea, so they painted the houses in bright colors. Nowadays, people think the *trompe l'oeil* paintings make the houses look beautiful and <u>grand</u>.

These days, only a few artists know how to do *trompe l'oeil*, so some people worry about Camogli losing this <u>tradition</u>. Artists Raffaella Stracca and Carlo Pere are keeping the *trompe l'oeil* tradition alive, however. If you ever go to Camogli, take a careful look around. Things are not always what they <u>seem</u> to be.

C | Predicting Content. Check (✔) the things you think you will learn about in the video.

❑ how artists learn to make *trompe l'oeil* paintings
❑ the price of a house with *trompe l'oeil* paintings on it
❑ why some people don't like *trompe l'oeil* paintings
❑ the history of *trompe l'oeil* painting in Camogli, Italy

While Viewing

A | Checking Predictions. Watch the video. Check your predictions from exercise **C** in the Before Viewing section.

B | Read the statements. Then watch the video again. Choose the correct word or phrase to complete each statement.

1. Camogli is a fishing village near (Rome/Genoa).
2. People in Camogli started putting *trompe l'oeil* paintings on the houses in the (1600s/1700s).
3. Raffaella Stracca learned *trompe l'oeil* from her (grandmother/grandfather).
4. Some artists learn *trompe l'oeil* at an art school in (Florence/Venice).
5. Painters spend (a few years/a full year) at The Palazzo Spinelli Art School.
6. According to the video, Carlo Pere's style comes from (the art school/history).

After Viewing

A | Discussion. Form a group with two or three other students. Discuss the questions.

1. Did the *trompe l'oeil* paintings you saw in the video seem real to you? Why, or why not?
2. Why do you think people might want their houses to look grander or more expensive than they really are?
3. Why do you think there are fewer *trompe l'oeil* painters and teachers now than in the past?
4. Is *trompe l'oeil* something you might want on the inside or outside of your house? Explain.

B | Critical Thinking. In Lesson B of this unit, you will learn about new housing. Read the statement by Carlo Pere. Then discuss the question below with your group.

> "It's easy to see. If we lose the *trompe l'oeil* tradition, then very little of Camogli's culture will remain. We'll have museums, but that's not much. Culture should be seen."
>
> — **Carlo Pere, *trompe l'oeil* artist**

Do you think we can see culture in new houses, or only in old ones? Explain.

A | **Using a Dictionary.** Listen and check (✔) the words you already know. Use a dictionary to help you with any new words. These are words you will hear and use in Lesson B.

track 2-20

❑ belong (v.)	❑ damage (n.)	❑ especially (adv.)	❑ population (n.)	❑ rapid (adj.)
❑ build (v.)	❑ deserts (n.)	❑ locations (n.)	❑ property (n.)	❑ tourists (n.)

B | Write each word from exercise **A** next to its definition.

1. _____ to make or construct
2. _____ being more true for one thing than with other things
3. _____ people who visit a place on vacation
4. _____ places that get little rainfall, very dry areas of land
5. _____ a building and/or the land it is on
6. _____ places where things are or where things happen
7. _____ all the people who live in a country or area
8. _____ harm that happens to an object or place
9. _____ fast, happening very quickly
10. _____ to be owned by someone

C | **Discussion.** Work with a partner. Look at the photos at the bottom of this page and read the captions. Then imagine that you are going to take a vacation together. Discuss each vacation choice below.

On your vacation, would you rather . . .

visit a **location** in the **desert**, or near the ocean?
take a **rapid** kind of transportation such as an airplane, or a slower kind such as a car?
see a lot of other **tourists**, or a lot of local residents?
stay in a hotel, or in a house or other **property** that **belongs** to a friend?

Puerto Balandra, Baja California Sur, Mexico

A man rides a unicycle on a trail in the desert, Sedona, Arizona.

🎧 track 2-21 Fill in each blank with a word from exercise A on page 114. Use each word only once. Then listen and check your answers.

Vacation Homes: Owning a Piece of Paradise[1]

Q: What are vacation homes?

A: They're usually houses or condominiums. Families only use these homes during vacations, so they want them to be in beautiful (1) _____.

Q: Why is Baja California popular for vacations?

A: It has coasts on the Pacific Ocean and the Sea of Cortez, so (2) _____ can enjoy sea life such as dolphins, whales, and unusual fish. Its beautiful mountains and (3) _____ are also excellent for hiking and sightseeing.

New homes in Loreto, Baja California, Mexico

Q: Can anyone own a home in Baja California?

A: Yes. You don't have to be a Mexican citizen to own (4) _____ here. Many vacation homes (5) _____ to people from other countries, (6) _____ Canada and the United States.

Baja California, Mexico

Q: Are there a lot of new vacation homes for sale?

A: Yes. Most of Baja California's (7) _____ lives in the north, in cities such as Tijuana and Mexicali. Recently, though, there has been (8) _____ growth in the south, especially near Cabo San Lucas and La Paz. They want to (9) _____ a lot of new houses and hotels quickly in those places.

Q: Is everyone happy about the housing growth?

A: No. Some people worry about (10) _____ to the environment as more and more people move in. Baja California is also very dry, so having enough drinking water for everyone is another concern.

[1]**Paradise** is a perfect place.

🎧 track 2-22 ## Pronunciation

Contractions with *Be*

When we are speaking, we often form contractions with pronouns and *be*.

Each contraction below has one syllable. The contracted form of *be* does not add an extra syllable to the pronoun.

Examples:

I am → **I'm**	She is → **She's**	We are → **We're**
You are → **You're**	It is → **It's**	They are → **They're**
He is → **He's**	That is → **That's**	There is → **There's**

👥 Replace the words in parentheses with contractions. Then practice saying the sentences with a partner.

1. (We are) _____We're_____ going to Bali in April.
2. (That is) _____ a new apartment building.
3. (He is) _____ going to pay for the damage to your car.
4. (I am) _____ especially pleased to meet you.
5. (You are) _____ an excellent student.
6. (There is) _____ a huge desert a few miles from the town.

Before Listening

Prior Knowledge. You will hear a conversation about Egypt. Look at the photo and map on this page. Then read each statement and circle **T** for *true* or **F** for *false*. Check your answers at the bottom of page 117.

1. The Nile River is only in Egypt.		**T**	**F**
2. The population of Egypt is growing.		**T**	**F**
3. Most of Egypt's land is very dry.		**T**	**F**
4. Farmers can grow food in the desert.		**T**	**F**

Ramadan Affifi, 60, and his grandson Shady Mohammed Rafifi, 5, plant onions in Tahrir Province, Egypt.

Listening: A Conversation

A | **Listening for Main Ideas.** Read the statements and answer choices. Then listen and choose the best answer to complete each statement.

1. The speakers are talking about _____.
   a. a TV show
   b. an article
   c. a presentation
2. The government's plan is important because Egypt needs more _____.
   a. money for new buildings
   b. desert for tourists to visit
   c. places for people to live
3. The main reason some people disagree with the plan is _____.
   a. they're not sure who the Nile River water belongs to
   b. more tourists came to Egypt before the plan
   c. the plan damages the environment

B | **Listening for Details.** Read the sentences from the conversation. Then listen again and fill in each blank with a word or phrase that you hear.

1. It says the _____ of Egypt is growing.
2. _____ a pretty rapid increase—about 1.5 million people every year.
3. _____ where the water is, so it's the best location for houses and cities.
4. They're also selling _____ there at a low price.
5. The water _____ to Egypt, right?

After Listening

Critical Thinking. In your own words, explain the Egyptian government's plan to a partner. Then switch roles. Does the plan sound like a good idea to you? Explain.

The fertile Nile Delta is green from the river's water, Luxor, Egypt.

ANSWERS: 1. F (It's in several countries), 2. T, 3. T, 4. T (if they bring in water)

track **2-24** **A** | Read and listen to the information. Notice the underlined sections.

Straw Houses: Another Way to "Go Green"

What is your house made of? Building a house from concrete[1] or metal requires large amounts of energy and pollutes[2] the air. Building a house from wood means cutting down trees and damaging the environment.

Builder Michael Furbish has another idea: Use straw to make buildings. "Most other building materials require a lot of energy use in production and manufacturing at a factory," explains Furbish. Straw is a kind of grass, and it takes little energy to grow. It's not very nutritious for animals, however, so farmers normally dry it and use it for animals to sleep on.

After the straw is dry, farmers use a machine to make bales—large rectangular bricks of straw. Then, builders such as Furbish build walls with the bales. When they finish the walls, they cover them with plaster[3] inside and outside. That keeps out water as well as insects and small animals.

Furbish used about 900 straw bales for his family's two-story, three-bedroom house. His company used about 4000 bales to build an elementary school in Maryland, USA.

Do you think a straw-bale house is for you? You won't know until you try living in one, but for Furbish, it's a greener way to build.

1 Farmers grow straw in their fields.

3 People stack the bales to make walls.

2 A machine ties dried straw together into large bales.

4 People cover the walls with wire and a material such as plaster to keep out water.

[1]**Concrete** is a material used for building made from sand, water, and cement.
[2]To **pollute** means to make something dirty or dangerous to use.
[3]**Plaster** is a soft, wet, sticky mixture that becomes hard when it dries.

B | **Discussion.** Look at the photos and read the captions from exercise **A**. Then discuss the questions with a partner.

1. How do people make straw-bale houses? Explain the process.
2. Do you think straw-bale houses might be popular in your country? Why, or why not?
3. Do you try to "go green" in your own life? Explain.

Grammar

Time Relationships in the Simple Present Tense

In Lesson A, you learned about coordinating conjunctions. Another way to join sentences is with subordinating conjunctions. These subordinating conjunctions show time relationships: *when, after, before, until,* and *while.*

> **When** *you talk to a real estate agent, you usually ask a lot of questions.*
> *Residents can use the swimming pool* **after** *they pay a small deposit.*
> *Most people look at several properties* **before** *they buy one.*

Note: We only need to use a comma when the time clause comes first.

> **While** *you are here, you can get to know different neighborhoods in the city.*
> *Many people live with their parents* **until** *they get their first job.*

A | Look back at the photos on page 118. Then complete each sentence.

1. Before farmers make straw bales, _they dry the straw_____.
2. After the straw is tied together in bales, _____.
3. When people finish stacking the bales to make walls, _____.
4. After the plaster dries, _____.
5. People can live in the house when _____.

B | Say your sentences from exercise **A** to a partner. Then switch roles. Do both of you understand how to make a straw-bale house?

C | With your partner, complete each sentence. Use the simple present tense and your own ideas.

1. Many university students work part time while _they go to school_____.
2. It's important to ask questions about an apartment before _____.
3. When _____, I usually talk to my teacher.
4. Good students study for a test until _____.
5. After _____, many people buy new furniture.
6. I like to listen to music while _____.

D | Form a group with another pair of students. Share your sentences from exercise **C**.

Houses made of straw can be just as comfortable as other houses.

6

You and a partner are going to decide on the type of property you want to buy. Then you are going to hold a meeting with a team of real estate agents and tell them about your needs.

A | With your partner, decide what sort of property you are interested in. Choose one of the following:

- a vacation home
- a shared student apartment
- a family home

B | **Brainstorming.** In your notebook, make a list of everything you want in your property (e.g., three bedrooms, a nice yard, exercise room, fireplaces). Do not worry about money at this point.

C | **Critical Thinking.** Now it is time to be more realistic. Look at your list together. Decide which items are necessary, and which are less important or too expensive. Circle the items on your list that are the most important to you.

D | **Role-Playing.** Join another pair of students. You are going to role-play meetings between a team of real estate agents and a pair of clients.

- Take turns role-playing the agents and the clients.
- When you and your partner are the agents, ask questions to help your clients explain their needs. (Do they need a big yard? Do they expect to have a lot of visitors?)
- When you and your partner are the clients, use your list from exercise **C** to give plenty of details to help the agents find the right property for you.

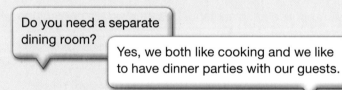

Do you need a separate dining room?

Yes, we both like cooking and we like to have dinner parties with our guests.

- At the end of each meeting, the team of real estate agents must describe a property for the clients to buy. The clients must decide whether or not it is a good property for them.

Presentation Skills: Role-Playing

Role-playing is a useful classroom tool. It lets you practice speaking and listening in a semi-realistic setting or situation. Role-playing can also be an excellent way to practice for a more formal presentation. A friend or family member can role-play an audience member and ask you questions about your presentation. To get the most from any kind of role-playing, it's important not to be embarrassed. Try to stay in character. You can learn a lot from role-playing.

Exploring Space

An astronaut moves himself through space with a guidance gun.

Think and Discuss

1. Look at the photo. What do you see?
2. Would you like to be an astronaut? Explain.
3. What do you think you will learn about in this unit?

Exploring the Theme:
Exploring Space

Look at the photos and read the captions. Then discuss the questions.

1. What kinds of space technology do the captions talk about?
2. What did the Soviet Union do first in space?
3. What did the United States do first in space?
4. What information on these pages do you find most interesting? Explain.

Satellites

The Soviet Union sent the first **satellite** (*Sputnik 1*) into space in 1957, the first man (Yuri Gagarin) in 1961, and the first woman (Valentina Tereshkova) in 1963.

The Moon Landing

Neil Armstrong stepping onto the moon during the Apollo 11 **moon landing** in 1969. The United States was the first country to put a man on the moon.

Space Agencies

Space agencies from around the world, including Japan, Russia, the United States, Europe, and Canada, work together on the International Space Station (ISS).

View of a distant galaxy from the Hubble Space Telescope. In the future, new telescopes will provide even better pictures of space.

track 2-25
A | **Using a Dictionary.** Listen and check (✔) the words you already know. Then use a dictionary to help you with any new words. These are words you will hear and use in Lesson A.

❑ ago (adv.)	❑ appears (v.)	❑ become (v.)	❑ gas (n.)	❑ in contrast (phrase)
❑ amazing (adj.)	❑ atmosphere (n.)	❑ even (adv.)	❑ gravity (n.)	❑ lasted (v.)

track 2-26
B | **Meaning from Context.** Read and listen to the article about stars. Notice the words in blue.

A Look at the Stars

Here on Earth, we like to look up at the stars in the night sky. In space, the stars look even more amazing!

Astronaut Don Thomas flew into space on the space shuttle *Columbia*. He said later, "I could see many more stars. I also could see stars of different colors. Some are white. Others are blue, red, or yellow like our sun."

For most of us, stars in the night sky appear to twinkle.[1] That's because light from the stars travels through the Earth's atmosphere before we see it. Gases in the atmosphere are always moving, and that makes the light from the stars look unsteady. In contrast, "They don't twinkle in space," says Thomas. "They look like steady points of light."

Our own sun is a yellow, average-sized star. It formed around 4.6 billion years ago—probably in a very large cloud of gas and dust[2] called a nebula. Bits of gas and dust came together, and then gravity began to pull the gas and dust into a ball. As the ball grew larger, its gravity grew stronger. Over time, the gravity became so strong that the ball collapsed[3] and the gas heated up. A star was born!

Stars last a very long time—for millions or even billions of years. Our sun will get cooler and die someday, but it won't happen any time soon.

An astronaut at work on the space shuttle *Columbia*

You can tell a star's temperature by its color. Blue means hot. Red stars are cooler.

[1]When a star **twinkles,** its light appears to go on and off.
[2]**Dust** is powder that is made up of small pieces of sand, earth, dirt, etc.
[3]When something **collapses,** it breaks down suddenly.

C | Work with a partner. Student A will explain why Don Thomas talks about the colors of the stars. Then Student B will explain why stars in the sky appear to twinkle. Use your own words as much as possible.

A | Look at the illustration on this page and read the caption. Then complete each statement with a word from exercise **A** on page 124.

1. For most of us, it is still _____ to think that astronauts traveled to the moon.

2. From Earth, a space station _____ to be a star moving across the night sky.

3. Space stations are in orbit above the earth's _____, where there is no air.

4. People in space need air to breathe, so they bring oxygen and another _____ called nitrogen to space stations.

5. The earth's _____ keeps space stations in their orbits in the same way it keeps the moon in its orbit.

6. Astronauts went to the U.S. space station *Skylab* only three times in 1973 and 1974. _____, cosmonauts[1] went to the *Mir* space station many times over a twelve-year period, mostly in the 1990s.

7. The *Mir* space station had everything the cosmonauts needed— _____ a shower and space toilets!

8. The *Mir* program began in 1986, and it _____ for 15 years.

9. The *Mir* program ended several years _____—in 2001.

10. People from many countries now work on the International Space Station. In the future, space stations will probably _____ even more international as more and more countries participate.

B | **Prior Knowledge.** Take turns asking and answering the questions with a partner. Use the information in this unit and your own ideas.

1. Why is the **atmosphere** important to life on Earth?
2. How long **ago** did the first person go into space?
3. What kind of person wants to **become** an astronaut?
4. Why does the moon **appear** larger when it's low in the sky?
5. How does the earth's **gravity** affect you every day?

[1]A **cosmonaut** is a Russian astronaut.

The Mir space station had a modular design. Workers built the station by adding parts, or modules, to the station once it was in space. Here, cosmonauts inside the station prepare to add two new modules.

Pronunciation

Contractions with *Will*

track 2-27

We often use contractions with *will* when talking about the future. All of the following contractions are pronounced as one syllable.

Examples:

I'll see you tomorrow.
You'll really like that movie.
She'll tell us about the assignment soon.
Do you know when *he'll* get here?
Just think, next week *we'll* be in Hawaii!
After the plane takes off, *they'll* bring us something to drink.

track 2-28 **A** | Listen and repeat each contraction and sentence.

1. I'll   I'll be home by eight thirty.
2. You'll   I know you'll enjoy this book.
3. He'll   He'll call you when he gets to Geneva.
4. She'll   She'll finish the project by the end of the week.
5. They'll   They'll have to wait in line to buy their tickets.
6. We'll   We'll come and visit you as soon as we can.

B | Work with a partner. Take turns saying the sentences.

1. He'll start high school next year.
2. Do you know when they'll arrive?
3. We'll meet them at the airport at five o'clock.
4. She'll stay with her friends in Toronto.
5. You'll see your family in December, right?
6. I'll have the spaghetti next time we eat at this restaurant.

Before Listening

Predicting Content. You will hear a doctor's presentation about the health effects of space travel. With a partner, decide which topic the doctor will probably NOT talk about. Circle your answer.

❑ Astronauts often don't get enough sleep.
❑ Astronauts wear special spacesuits to protect their bodies.
❑ Astronauts need to get a lot of exercise in space.
❑ Astronauts have special jobs to do while they're in space.

An *Apollo* spacesuit on display in Washington, D.C., USA.

Listening: A Presentation by a Medical Doctor

An airplane lets astronauts experience zero gravity for around 30 seconds.

track 2-29 **A** | **Checking Predictions.** Look back at your answer from the Before Listening section on page 126. Then listen and check (✔) each topic you hear about in the presentation.

track 2-29 **B** | **Listening for Main Ideas.** Read the statements and answer choices. Then listen again and choose the correct word or phrase to complete each statement.

1. Spacesuits give astronauts air and _____.
   a. cold temperatures
   b. light
   c. air pressure

2. The astronauts will eat _____ small meals every day on the space station.
   a. three
   b. four
   c. five

3. To get more sleep, the astronauts can _____.
   a. cover windows
   b. take medicine
   c. drink warm tea

4. Astronauts need to get a lot of exercise so that they don't become _____.
   a. heavy and slow
   b. thin and weak
   c. tired and bored

track 2-29 **C** | **Making Inferences.** Read the statements. Then listen again and circle **T** for *true* or **F** for *false*. The answers are not in the speakers' exact words. You need to think about what you hear. *(See page 205 of the Independent Student Handbook for more information on making inferences.)*

1. Dr. Carter is presenting to children for the first time.   **T**   **F**
2. Dr. Carter knows about life in space from his own experience.   **T**   **F**
3. Dr. Carter doesn't like the food in the space station very much.   **T**   **F**
4. One hour of exercise each day is enough to stay healthy in zero gravity.   **T**   **F**

After Listening

A | **Collaboration.** With a partner, create a schedule for one day in the life of an astronaut on the International Space Station. Use the information from the presentation. Remember that astronauts need time each day for both work and leisure.

B | **Critical Thinking.** Form a group with another pair of students and compare your schedules from exercise **A**. Which schedule do you think is better for keeping the astronauts healthy? Which schedule has the astronauts doing more work?

Grammar

> **Future Time: *Will* and *Be Going To***
>
> We use *will* and *be going to* with the base form of a verb to talk about the future.
>> People **will walk** on the moon again in the future.
>> The professor **is going to give** us a quiz tomorrow.
>
> We often use contractions when we use *will* and *be going to*.
>> **I'll / You'll / He'll meet** my brother Nathan at the airport in Boston.
>> **I'm / You're / He's going to write** a report on early astronomers.
>
> To talk about future plans, we usually use *be going to*.
>> After this class, **I'm going to walk** to the library. Would you like to join me?
>> **They're going to eat** dinner at Sanborn's. Then, **they're going to take** a taxi home.

A | Read the conversation and <u>underline</u> *will* and *be going to*. Then practice the conversation with a partner.

Raymond:	How's your presentation going, Kiki?
Kiki:	Fine, but I want to change my topic a little.
Raymond:	How are you going to change it?
Kiki:	Well, I'm still going to talk about life on the space station.
Raymond:	Uh-huh.
Kiki:	But I'll add information about future research on the station.
Raymond:	That sounds interesting. What kind of research are they going to do?
Kiki:	Oh, research on human health, space science, and engineering.
Raymond:	But aren't they researching those things now?
Kiki:	Sure, but the research projects will be even more international in the future.
Raymond:	So astronauts from different countries will work together more?
Kiki:	Exactly!

B | With your partner, take turns asking and answering the questions.

1. When do you think people will walk on the moon again?
2. Where do you think people will travel in space?
3. What are you going to do after this class?
4. What are you probably going to eat for dinner tonight?
5. Who will probably call you on the telephone during the next 24 hours?
6. Where are you probably going to go the next time you travel?

C | Read and listen to a magazine interview with a space scientist. Then underline *will* and *be going to*.

The Future of Space Exploration

Interviewer: Dr. Takei, when do you think humans *will* live on Mars?

Dr. Takei: That's an interesting question. Mars is a cold planet. If astronauts go to Mars, they'll need spacesuits to stay warm. And even though Mars has some atmosphere, it's not like the air on Earth. Those spacesuits will need to provide oxygen and air pressure, too.

Interviewer: I see, but I've read articles about this. They say we can make Mars more like Earth.

Dr. Takei: Yes, that's probably true. There is ice on Mars, and the atmosphere is mostly carbon dioxide. That's a greenhouse gas, and if you add a few things to it, it's going to begin to warm the planet.

Interviewer: Global warming on Mars?

Dr. Takei: Yes, that's the idea—global warming to melt the ice on Mars. However, oxygen is still going to be a problem. Some scientists think that future astronauts will bring plants to Mars to make oxygen—simple plants at first, but over time, even trees could grow!

Interviewer: That's amazing! But what's your opinion? Will any of this really happen?

Dr. Takei: In my opinion, it won't happen during our lives, or any time soon. Space exploration is expensive, and right now, countries don't have the money. It also takes a lot of time. It could take 1000 years to make Mars more like Earth!

D | **Critical Thinking.** Form a group with two or three other students. Discuss the questions.

1. The picture below shows the process of making Mars more like Earth. In the interview, Dr. Takei says that this process is probably possible. What reasons does he give?
2. Do you think this will probably happen? Why, or why not?
3. In your opinion, is making Mars more like Earth a good idea? Explain.

Language Function

Making Predictions

We often use *be going to* and *will* to make predictions, or talk about things we think will happen in the future.

*People **are going to** travel to Mars someday, but they **won't** be able to live there.*
*In 20 years, **we will** know much more about space than we know now.*

A | Complete each sentence with your own predictions about the future.

1. In 15 years, cars will <u>run on hydrogen instead of gasoline.</u>

2. In 20 years, the space station will _____

3. Someday, people are going to _____

4. In the future, computers are going to _____

5. Fifty years from now, electricity will _____

6. In my lifetime, I'm probably going to _____

B | Work with a partner. Read the information in the Student to Student box. Then take turns saying your predictions from exercise **A** and asking for your partner's opinion about them.

> In 15 years, cars will run on hydrogen instead of gasoline. Do you agree?

Student to Student: Asking for Another Person's Opinion

Asking for a person's opinion is a good way to find out more about that person. It's also a way to keep a conversation going. Here are some expressions you can use to ask for someone's opinion.

What do you think?   *Do you agree?*   *What's your opinion?*   *How about you?*

I don't think people will ever live on the moon. **Do you agree?**

What do you think *about the space program?*

I want to learn more about this topic. **How about you?**

View of Mars from the Viking mission's robotic lander

Clouds of frozen water drift over the surface of Mars.

Talking about the Future

A | Look at the timeline that shows John's plans for the future. Then complete the sentences below with the correct verb tenses.

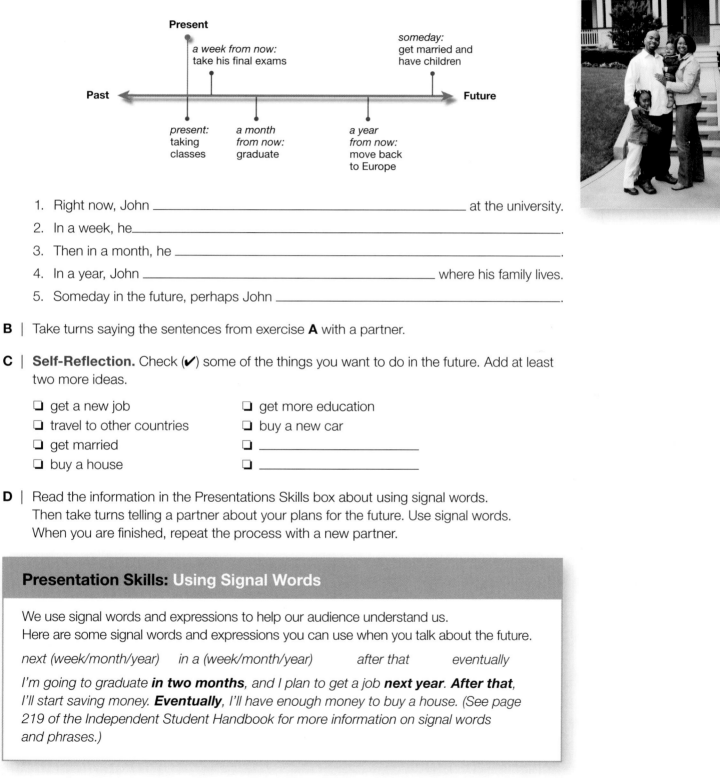

Present

a week from now:
take his final exams

someday:
get married and
have children

Past ← → **Future**

present:
taking
classes

*a month
from now:*
graduate

*a year
from now:*
move back
to Europe

1. Right now, John _____ at the university.

2. In a week, he _____.

3. Then in a month, he _____.

4. In a year, John _____ where his family lives.

5. Someday in the future, perhaps John _____.

B | Take turns saying the sentences from exercise **A** with a partner.

C | **Self-Reflection.** Check (✔) some of the things you want to do in the future. Add at least two more ideas.

- ❏ get a new job
- ❏ travel to other countries
- ❏ get married
- ❏ buy a house

- ❏ get more education
- ❏ buy a new car
- ❏ _____
- ❏ _____

D | Read the information in the Presentations Skills box about using signal words. Then take turns telling a partner about your plans for the future. Use signal words. When you are finished, repeat the process with a new partner.

Presentation Skills: Using Signal Words

We use signal words and expressions to help our audience understand us.
Here are some signal words and expressions you can use when you talk about the future.

next (week/month/year)   in a (week/month/year)   after that   eventually

*I'm going to graduate **in two months**, and I plan to get a job **next year**. **After that**, I'll start saving money. **Eventually**, I'll have enough money to buy a house. (See page 219 of the Independent Student Handbook for more information on signal words and phrases.)*

EXPLORATION OF THE

Before Viewing

A | Critical Thinking. In Lesson A of this unit, you learned about manned space exploration, in which human beings travel to space. With a partner, list two advantages (good things) about manned space exploration and two possible disadvantages (problems).

Manned Space Exploration	
Advantages	**Disadvantages**
We can learn more about space.	It's very expensive.

track 2-31 **B | Using a Dictionary.** Read and listen to the information. Then use your dictionary to help you with the <u>underlined</u> words.

The last people to walk on the moon were the crew of *Apollo 17* in 1972. By that time, however, unmanned space exploration of the <u>planets</u> in our <u>solar system</u> was already taking place.

Sending <u>satellites</u> and <u>probes</u>[1] into space is safer and less expensive than sending people. Probes have been sent to the sun, to other planets, and to their moons. Mars alone has been studied by a <u>dozen</u> space probes. The probes either fly by or orbit a planet, and they send pictures and other valuable information back to Earth.

In 1971, *Mariner 9* became the first satellite to orbit another planet: Mars. Here, it is pictured near the Mars moon Phobos.

[1]A **probe** is a scientific instrument used for collecting information.

SOLAR SYSTEM

While Viewing

A | Look at the illustration showing the relative sizes of the planets. Then watch the video and check (✔) each planet when you hear its name.

- ❑ Earth
- ❑ Jupiter
- ❑ Mars
- ❑ Mercury
- ❑ Neptune
- ❑ Pluto (dwarf planet)
- ❑ Saturn
- ❑ Uranus
- ❑ Venus

B | Read the information below. Then watch the video again and match the name of each celestial body[1] to the probe or probes that studied it. You will use some of the probe names more than once.

Celestial Bodies:
1. The Sun _____
2. Mercury _____
3. Venus _____
4. Jupiter (two probes) _____ _____
5. Jupiter's moons _____
6. Saturn (two probes) _____ _____
7. Uranus _____
8. Neptune _____

Probes:
a. *Magellan*
b. *Ulysses*
c. *Pioneer 10* and/or *Pioneer 11*
d. *Galileo*
e. *Mariner 10*
f. *Voyager 1* and/or *Voyager 2*

After Viewing

Critical Thinking. In Lesson B of this unit, you will learn about telescopes and people who study space, but never leave the earth. In a small group, discuss the questions.

1. Why is the night sky so amazing to human beings?
2. What do you think scientists will discover about outer space in the future?

[1]A **celestial body** is a planet, moon, star, or other large object in space.

track 2-32 **A | Meaning from Context.** Read and listen to the information. Notice the words in **blue**. These are words you will hear and use in Lesson B.

Telescopes of the Past

As far as we know, Galileo was the first astronomer to **observe** the moon, planets, and stars through a telescope. In the seventeenth century, telescopes were just glass lenses[1] inside tubes made of wood. The lenses were shaped by hand to make things appear larger. Soon, however, people wanted bigger telescopes to be able to see farther into space. Large glass lenses were heavy and didn't work well in a telescope, so in 1668, Isaac Newton **invented** something new: a telescope that used a mirror to **reflect** light. Soon, reflecting telescopes became the first choice for astronomers.

This observatory sits on top of Hawaii's Mauna Kea volcano.

Two of Galileo's telescopes are at a museum in Florence, Italy. The oval-shaped frame holds a 1.5-inch (38 millimeter) glass lens made in 1609.

Telescopes of the Present

As telescopes became larger, it became **necessary** to put them inside some kind of building. Observatories, buildings with telescopes inside for doing research, were built as early as the eighteenth century. With these larger telescopes, astronomers **discovered** planets that Galileo never knew about— Uranus and Neptune.

Three of today's largest observatories stand on top of Mauna Kea in Hawaii. At nearly 14,000 feet (4300 meters), Mauna Kea is above 40 percent of the earth's atmosphere. The Keck Observatory is **among** the observatories on Mauna Kea, and the mirrors in its two reflecting telescopes are 33 feet (10 meters) across! Their **size** allows astronomers to see far into space.

Telescopes of the Future

The Hubble Space Telescope was not the first telescope in space, but it is large, and it is **completely** outside the earth's atmosphere. Hubble can **reach** farther into space and **view** more kinds of objects in space than any telescope before it. Work on newer, larger telescopes is also happening here on Earth. The Large Synoptic Survey Telescope will be able to view a wide area of space instead of the narrow area of older telescopes. And the Giant Magellan Telescope will be able to collect four times as much light as the telescopes on Mauna Kea.

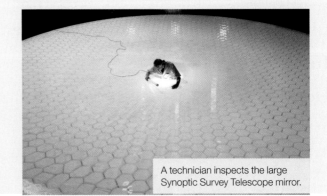

A technician inspects the large Synoptic Survey Telescope mirror.

[1]A **lens** is a curved piece of glass or plastic used in cameras, telescopes, eyeglasses, etc.

B | Write each word in blue from page 134 next to its definition.

1. _____ (adj.) needed in order for something else to happen
2. _____ (prep.) part of a group
3. _____ (v.) thought of and made something new
4. _____ (v.) to watch carefully in order to learn something
5. _____ (adv.) as much as possible, one hundred percent
6. _____ (v.) learned about or became aware of something
7. _____ (v.) to arrive at a place, a level, or an amount
8. _____ (v.) to send back from a surface
9. _____ (v.) to look at or see something
10. _____ (n.) how large or small something is

C | Read each statement. Choose the correct word or phrase.

1. Earth is about the same (**view/size**) as Venus, but Jupiter is a much larger planet.
2. Earth's atmosphere (**reflects/reaches**) some sunlight back into space.
3. A large telescope is nice, but it's not (**necessary/completely**) for viewing the moon.
4. In 2009, scientists (**invented/discovered**) a very large ring around Saturn. Our eyes can't see the ring, but the Spitzer Telescope can use special light to view it.
5. Saturn is (**among/view**) the largest planets in the solar system.

D | With a partner, take turns asking and answering the questions from the quiz below. Then check your answers at the bottom of the page.

ASTRONOMY QUIZ

1. What did Galileo **observe** on the moon?
   a. ice   b. mountains   c. astronauts
2. Who **discovered** the planet Uranus?
   a. Isaac Newton   b. William Herschel   c. Edwin Hubble
3. What did Hans Wolter **invent**?
   a. the X-ray telescope b. the reflecting telescope   c. the Giant Magellan Telescope
4. Why is Mauna Kea **among** the best places in the world to **view** space?
   a. It's very warm.   b. It's very high.   c. It's very wet.

ANSWERS: 1.b, 2.b, 3.a, 4.b

Before Listening

Listening for Time Expressions

When we listen to a talk, it's helpful to notice time expressions. These words and phrases help us to follow a speaker's ideas. Time expressions can be used in more than one way, but here are some common ways they are used.

- At the beginning of a sentence: **First**, *I'll talk about life on the space station*.
  first   *second*   *next*   *finally*

- Before a dependent clause: *Astronauts don't go into space* **until** *they are well-trained*.
  after   *before*   *as soon as*   *until*

- Before a noun to show time order: *This is the* **last** *part of the tour*.
  first   *second*   *next*   *last*

- Before a noun as a preposition: *You can ask questions* **during** *the tour*.
  after   *before*   *during*

A | Listen to part of a talk by a tour guide. Check (✔) the time expressions you hear. *(track 2-33)*

❏ after	❏ as soon as	❏ before	❏ during	❏ finally
❏ first	❏ last	❏ next	❏ second	❏ until

B | With a partner, choose the best time expression to complete each sentence. Then take turns reading the sentences aloud.

1. Galileo studied medicine (first/before) he studied mathematics.
2. You can enter the museum (as soon as/during) you pay and get your ticket.
3. The (finally/last) thing we'll see on the tour is the gift shop.
4. You can raise your hand (then/during) the talk to ask a question.
5. First, she'll give us a tour. (After/Next) that, we'll look at the exhibit by ourselves.
6. (Before/Finally), we'll see the telescope and you can ask questions.

The indoor walkway to the Hayden Planetarium at the American Museum of Natural History, New York, USA.

Albert Einstein with the staff at the Yerkes Observatory in Williams Bay, Wisconsin in the United States. The observatory belongs to the University of Chicago, USA.

Listening: A Talk by a Tour Guide

track 2-34 **A** | **Listening for Main Ideas.** Read the statements and answer choices below. Then listen to the entire talk and choose the correct answer to complete each statement.

1. The Yerkes telescope is special because it's the _____ refracting telescope in the world.
   a. oldest
   b. largest
   c. lightest

2. To look at different parts of the sky, the _____ moves around in a circle.
   a. telescope
   b. scientist
   c. room

3. Scientists used the Yerkes telescope to discover the _____ of the Milky Way galaxy.
   a. age
   b. size
   c. shape

A galaxy is an extremely large group of stars and planets. This galaxy is called a spiral galaxy because of its shape.

track 2-34 **B** | **Note-Taking.** Listen again. Complete the notes.

Age of Yerkes Observatory: from the 18_____
Telescope types: 1. Reflecting (use: _____)
                        2. Refracting (use: lenses)
Size of lenses in Yerkes telescope: _____ inches
Observatory in 1892: 1. in the _____
                     2. on a hill

After Listening

Critical Thinking. Form a group with two or three other students. Discuss the questions.

1. Do you enjoy guided tours such as this tour of the observatory? Explain.
2. Why does the observatory have no elevator? Do you think modern observatories have elevators? Explain.
3. Do you think the Yerkes Observatory is in a good location? Explain.

Grammar

Future Time: The Present Continuous and The Simple Present Forms

In addition to *will* and *be going to*, we often use the present continuous forms to talk about future plans.

> We **are taking** a tour of the observatory on Saturday.
> The professor **is giving** a lecture on Jupiter's moons next week.

We can also use the simple present form to talk about scheduled events in the future.

> My brother's train **arrives** at 10:00 a.m. tomorrow
> The lecture **begins** at 1:20 p.m. in Room 348.

A | Fill in each blank with the present continuous or simple present form of the verb in parentheses. In some sentences, both forms are possible.

1. My friends _____ are taking _____ (take) a vacation next month.

2. The plane _____ (leave) at 7:45 a.m.

3. The professor _____ (give) us a quiz next week.

4. They _____ (get) married in September.

5. Let's hurry! The movie _____ (start) at eight o'clock.

6. My next class _____ (begin) at ten thirty.

B | **Using a Dictionary.** Read and listen to the article. Use a dictionary to help you with any new words. This information will help you with the exercises that follow.

track 2-35

A guest at Kulala Lodge looks at a starry night sky, Sossuvlei, Namib-Naukluft Park, Namibia.

The Dark-Sky Movement

Most of the world's people now live in or near cities, where doing most things at night is as easy as doing them during the day. Seeing the stars at night, however, is not easy to do in a city. Streetlights and lights from businesses and advertisers shine into the night sky, and only the brightest stars can be seen.

The dark-sky movement wants to change this. They argue that seeing the night sky is important for everyone—not only for astronomers. They say that outdoor lighting affects human health and wildlife, and they recommend simple things such as streetlights that only let light shine down at the street, not up at the sky.

C | Read and listen to the conversation. <u>Underline</u> each sentence that uses the present continuous or simple present form to refer to the future.

track 2-36

> **Yoshi:** Hi, Tim. What are you reading?
>
> **Tim:** It's information about a star party.
>
> **Yoshi:** A star party? Is that a party with a lot of movie stars or something?
>
> **Tim:** No, Yoshi. At star parties, people get together to look at the night sky.
>
> **Yoshi:** Do you need to go to a party to do that?
>
> **Tim:** Well, they're going to a national park. It's far from any cities.
>
> **Yoshi:** I see—so there are no city lights nearby.
>
> **Tim:** Exactly. People say it's a lot of fun. Do you want to go?
>
> **Yoshi:** Maybe. When?
>
> **Tim:** The bus leaves at five o'clock on Friday afternoon, and it gets to the park around seven thirty.
>
> **Yoshi:** What time does the bus get back here?
>
> **Tim:** It gets back pretty late—around midnight. What do you think?
>
> **Yoshi:** It sounds like fun. Let's go!

Children in New York City use small telescopes to view the night sky. Bright city lights, however, make it difficult to see the stars.

D | Practice the conversation from exercise **C** with a partner. Then switch roles and practice it again.

Critical Thinking Focus: Discussing Pros and Cons

Considering the different sides of an issue is an important part of critical thinking. Situations are usually not completely good or completely bad, and discussing the pros and cons—the good points and bad points—is a good way to explore a topic and understand it better.

Critical Thinking. Form a group with two or three other students. Discuss the pros and cons of city lights and the dark-sky movement. Talk about the ideas in the chart below and your own ideas.

City Lights		Dark Skies	
Pros	**Cons**	**Pros**	**Cons**
-good for business -safety	-people can't sleep -affects plants and animals	-people can see stars -more natural	-hard to make changes (to lights, people's ideas)

EXPLORING SPACE | **139**

Your group is going to choose a destination and plan a trip to an astronomical site. Then your group will give an informal presentation of your plan.

A | Read the information about three possible destinations for your trip.

Palomar Observatory Tour

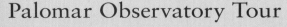

Located near San Diego, California in the United States, the Palomar Observatory offers a six-hour astronomy tour for $65. It includes a tour of the observatory, the museum, gift shop, and the 200-inch Hale reflecting telescope. With the help of observatory guides, visitors can look through several telescopes at the night sky over Palomar Mountain.

Hortobágy National Park

Hortobágy is a certified dark-sky park. Located in eastern Hungary, the park features Europe's largest area of natural grassland. Visitors can ride in an open train through the park to see animals such as grey cattle, water buffalo, sheep, and horses. There are nature trails for hiking and for observing the stars at night. The entrance fee to the park is $3.

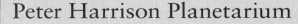

Peter Harrison Planetarium

The planetarium is part of the Royal Observatory complex. It's located on a hill in Greenwich Park, London in the U.K. Visitors can choose from several shows, including one about comets[1] and an exciting show for children called *Space Safari*. Shows take place indoors, so bad weather is never a problem. Tickets are $10 for adults and $6 for children.

B | **Discussion.** Form a group with two or three other students. As a group, decide which astronomical site you want to visit. You should consider the pros and cons of each site, the cost of travel, and the things your group is most interested in.

C | **Planning a Presentation.** Decide which group member(s) will talk about each topic below. Then practice your presentation.

- your group's decision and the reasons for it
- how you will travel to the site
- what you will do at the site

D | **Presentation.** Get together with another group. Tell them about your group's plans. Everyone in your group should do some of the talking.

[1]A **comet** is an object that travels around the sun and looks like a bright star.

Art and Music

Think and Discuss

1. Do you think the building in this photo is beautiful?
Why, or why not?

2. How important are art and music to you? Explain.

Some people think that the outside of the Experience Music Project building in Seattle, Washington, USA, is beautiful, but others do not.

Look at the photos and read the captions. Then discuss the questions.

1. What different kinds of art do you see in the photos?
2. Which of these art forms is done in only one culture?
3. Which of these art forms do you enjoy most? Explain.

A mural by the Mexican artist, Diego Rivera, Detroit, Michigan, USA

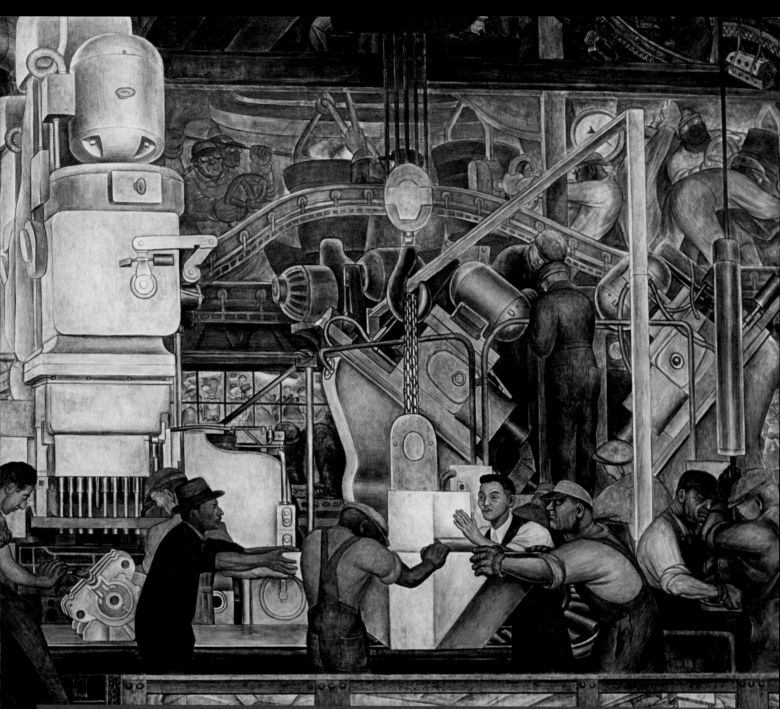

Art and Music in Our Lives

Even at an early age, most people enjoy art. This child is using colored chalk to **draw** pictures on a sidewalk.

This stone **sculpture** of the Egyptian queen Nefertiti was never finished, yet the artist's skill is easy to see.

Topeng dancers such as this man in Bali, Indonesia, **dance** to the **music** of *gamelan* orchestras.

A | **Using a Dictionary.** Listen and check (✔) the words you already know. Use a dictionary to help you with any new words. These are words you will hear and use in Lesson A.

track 3-2

- ❏ conscious of (phrase)
- ❏ constantly (adv.)
- ❏ copies (n.)
- ❏ forever (adv.)
- ❏ huge (adj.)
- ❏ public (adj.)
- ❏ repeat (v.)
- ❏ sculptures (n.)
- ❏ solid (adj.)
- ❏ temporary (adj.)

B | Write each word or phrase from exercise **A** next to its definition.

1. _____ works of art made by shaping stone, wood, or other materials
2. _____ for everybody's use; not private
3. _____ lasting only a short time
4. _____ very large
5. _____ to do something again, to happen again
6. _____ hard or firm
7. _____ for all time
8. _____ things made to look exactly like the original thing
9. _____ noticing or realizing that something is happening
10. _____ happening over a period of time without stopping

C | **Discussion.** With a partner, discuss the questions.

1. What kind of art do you like: **sculptures**, paintings, photographs, or something else?
2. Do you like to see art in **public** places? Explain.
3. In your opinion, is there anything that lasts **forever**? Explain.
4. What is happening in this room that you are **conscious of** right now?
5. Why do you think the **sculptures** in the photo below are underwater?

The artist used real people as models for these unusual sculptures. The model for this sculpture is actually a carpenter from Mexico. The sculptures make a good home for fish and other sea life. They're also a tourist attraction.

track 3-3 Fill in each blank with a word from exercise **A** on page 144. Then listen and check your answers.

Artist Profile: Jason deCaires Taylor

Background: Taylor grew up in Asia and Europe. As a child, he often swam among Malaysia's coral reefs—places where small sea animals and plants grow on rocks or on other (1) _____ objects on the ocean floor. Reefs are important for many kinds of ocean life, but they are in trouble because of fishing and climate change.

Recent Project: These days, Taylor still likes to swim, and he is (2) _____ the need to help ocean reefs and ocean life. His recent art project does exactly that.

The Silent Evolution is a group of (3) _____. Taylor used real people as models when he was making them. In a way, all the sculptures are (4) _____ of people, and they look just like them. The sculptures are in a (5) _____ place, but they are not easy to see. They are on the ocean floor near Cancún, Mexico. There are more than 400 of them, and together, they form one (6) _____ piece of art. It's especially interesting because the artist did not (7) _____ any of the sculptures—each one is a sculpture of a different person.

A beaked coralfish swims through a colorful coral reef, Kapalai Island, Sabah, Malaysia.

The Future: Taylor's artwork is (8) _____ changing. Sea animals and plants make their homes on the sculptures just as they do on natural reefs, and in time, a new reef will form. That means the sculptures are (9) _____, and if you want to see them, you need to do it soon. Taylor hopes the new reef that forms over the sculptures will last (10) _____, or at least far into the future.

Before Listening

Taking Notes While Listening

Note-taking is a very important academic skill. When you take notes, don't try to write down everything you hear. Think about why you are taking notes. Think about the information you need and why you need it. This helps you identify important ideas to write down.

Your notes help you remember and review information after a talk. *(See page 206 of the Independent Student Handbook for more information on note-taking.)*

Using a Dictionary. Write answers to the questions. Use a dictionary to help you with the underlined words. These are words you will hear and use in the Listening section.

1. What can you use to <u>erase</u> <u>marks</u> on a piece of paper? _____

2. Where can you find a lot of <u>sand</u>? _____

3. What do people use <u>chalk</u> for? _____

Listening: A PowerPoint Presentation

🎧 track 3-4 **A | Note-Taking.** Look at the slides and read the incomplete notes below. Then listen to the presentation and complete as many of the notes as you can.

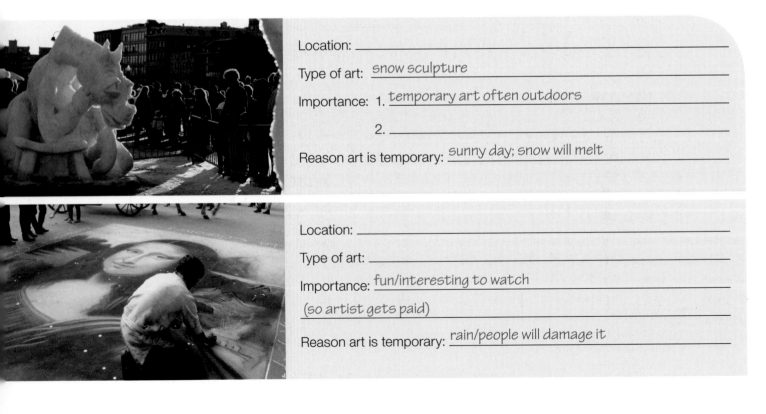

Location: _____

Type of art: _snow sculpture_ _____

Importance: 1. _temporary art often outdoors_

2. _____

Reason art is temporary: _sunny day; snow will melt_

Location: _____

Type of art: _____

Importance: _fun/interesting to watch_

(so artist gets paid)

Reason art is temporary: _rain/people will damage it_

Location: _____

Type of art: _____

Difference from other temporary art: _Artist works alone (doesn't bring_
people together)

Artist Name: _Jim Denevan_

Time to finish a piece: _____

Reason art is temporary: _____

track 3-4 **B** | Listen again and check your notes. Complete any notes you missed the first time.

After Listening

A | **Discussion.** Form a group with two or three other students. Discuss the questions.

1. Which piece of art from the slide show is the most beautiful or interesting to you? Explain.
2. Which piece of art do you think will probably last the longest? Explain.
3. What kinds of temporary art have you seen? Was the art outdoors? Did it bring people together?

B | **Critical Thinking.** Read the information. Then discuss the questions below with your group.

The Art of Julian Beever

Julian Beever creates large 3-D[1] chalk art on streets and sidewalks in the U.K. Beever's art looks so real that you might think you're going to fall into a pool of water or bump into a huge bottle of soda. He became famous when people started sending photographs of his artwork to their friends by email. Now you can buy a book with 75 full-color photographs of Beever's work.

[1]If an object is **3-D** (three-dimensional), it is not flat; it has length, width, and depth.

1. Modern technology can make temporary art last longer, but is a photograph as good as the real thing? Explain.
2. Where can you find pictures of Julian Beever's artwork?
3. Where can you find the title of the book mentioned above?

Grammar

Modals of Possibility and Probability

We use *might (not)*, *may (not)*, and *could* to talk about possibilities or things that are possibly true.

> *Jason is usually here. He* **might be** *sick today.*
> *He* **might not be** *well enough to come to class.*
> *I* **may be** *able to lend you some money.*
> *On the other hand, I* **may not have** *enough. Let me look in my wallet.*
> *Let's try to get to the winter festival early. Finding a parking space* **could be** *difficult.*

We use *must* to talk about things that are probably true.

> *That painting* **must cost** *a lot of money. It's by a famous artist.*

We use *must not* or *can't* to talk about things that are probably not true.

> *You* **must not be** *interested in the lecture. You look half asleep.*
> *That* **can't be** *one of his paintings. The style is very different.*

🎧 track 3-5 **A** | Read and listen to the conversations. Then <u>underline</u> the modals of possibility and probability.

Conversation 1:

Amy: Hmm. Wanda isn't answering her phone.

Bill: She didn't answer my email yesterday, either.

Amy: She must be out of town. She usually answers her phone.

Bill: Right—she could be in Osaka.

Conversation 2:

Reggie: Who is the man over there near the door?

Jenna: He might be Ann's father, but I'm not sure.

Reggie: No, he can't be Ann's father. He's too young.

Jenna: We could go over there and ask him.

Reggie: Yes, but he might not want to talk to us now. It looks like he's leaving.

👥 **B** | Practice the conversations with a partner. Then switch roles and practice them again.

This painting is called *Garden Party*.
The artist is an elephant named Tao.

Language Function

Speculating about a Situation

When we speculate about something, we make a guess based on things we know. Modals of possibility and probability are one way to speculate. We can also use the adverbs *perhaps* and *maybe*.

Examples:

Situation: It's Saturday. I'm at an art fair, but my friend Cindy isn't here, and she loves art.

Speculation: *Cindy **might be** with her nephew today, or **perhaps** she's at her sister's house. She **can't** be at work because her office is closed on Saturdays.*

A | Read and listen to the article. Circle the correct word or phrase. Then listen and check your answers.

Are These Elephants Really Artists?

You might think the paintings are beautiful, or you (1) (**must/might**) not, but you have to admit they're unusual. They're elephant paintings, and some of them cost thousands of dollars. Elephant art began at zoos in the United States. Zookeepers there saw an elephant named Ruby using a stick to make marks in the dirt. They bought paints and brushes for her, and soon she was painting. In a book about Ruby, author Dick George says she loved to paint, and she even chose the colors.

In Thailand, the Thai Elephant Conservation Center (TECC) now teaches elephants to paint. They think it (2) (**can't/might**) be good for them. The animals learn to hold the paintbrush, and trainers help them to move their trunks and paint pictures. Some paintings show real things such as flowers, trees, and even elephants, but according to the TECC, the elephants don't understand the pictures. They just follow the instructions of their trainers.

However, some people think there (3) (**could/can't**) be more to it[1] than that. Different elephants have their own painting styles, and their paintings become more detailed over time. And to people who buy the paintings, some elephants are better painters than others. For example, an elephant named Ramona (4) (**must not/may**) be the most famous elephant in Bali. Many people buy her paintings, and she seems to have an artist's personality. Ramona likes to work with dark colors. She also stops and looks at a painting carefully before choosing the next color, and she only paints when she wants to paint.

[1]When there is **more to** something, there is more that needs to be explained.

B | Form a group with two or three other students. Read the facts and try to explain them. Use information from the article, your own ideas, and the expressions from the boxes on pages 148 and 149.

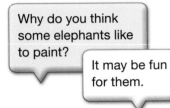

Why do you think some elephants like to paint?

It may be fun for them.

- Some elephants like to paint.
- Some people will pay a lot of money for elephant paintings.
- The TECC in Thailand teaches its elephants to paint.
- Different elephants have different styles of painting.
- Elephants' painting styles change over time and become more detailed.
- Ramona chooses her own colors and prefers dark colors.

C | **Critical Thinking.** Discuss the questions with your group.

1. Why do you think human beings paint or create other kinds of art?
2. Do you like the paintings on pages 148 and 149? Why, or why not?
3. What other animals do you think could create art? Explain.

D | Read the information about three artists. With your group, think of questions about each artist and his or her work. Then use *perhaps* and *maybe* to speculate about the answers.

Why does Jennifer Maestre use colored pencils in her work?

Perhaps she uses colored pencils because she loves color.

Or maybe she uses them because they are cheap.

Artist 1

Bruce Hall is a well-known photographer, and he is legally blind.[1] He can see some shapes and colors, but only from a few inches away. He especially enjoys underwater photography, but he takes pictures on land, too. He plans to put some of his best photographs into a book.

Artist 2

Jennifer Maestre is an American sculptor. Many artists use colored pencils to make drawings, but Maestre makes sculptures out of colored pencils. It takes hundreds of pencils to make each sculpture.

Artist 3

Many artists paint beautiful pictures of birds, fish, and other animals, but Guido Daniele paints them on people's hands. It takes several hours to create one hand painting, but the result is amazing. Daniele makes the animals look almost real.

[1]**Blind** means unable to see. A person who is **legally blind** is blind according to the law, but may be able to see some things.

Discussing Ideas about Photographs

A | Look at the photo. Then practice the conversation with a partner. Then switch roles and practice it again.

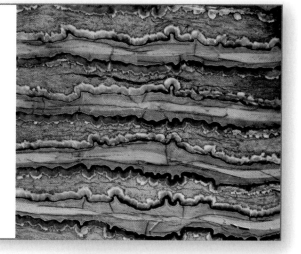

Maggie:	What do you think it is?
Pete:	I don't know, but it might be a piece of art.
Maggie:	I think it must be something from nature.
Pete:	Yes, it could be something natural.
Maggie:	Maybe it's some kind of stone.
Pete:	It does look like a stone.
Maggie:	Or, it may be a piece of wood. It can't be a plant or an animal.
Pete:	You're right. It's probably stone or wood.

B | Look at the two photos on the right. Then have a conversation about each photo with your partner. Use language from the boxes on pages 148 and 149 to speculate about each photo.

C | **Collaboration.** With your partner, choose one of the photos from exercise **B**. Then complete and practice the conversation.

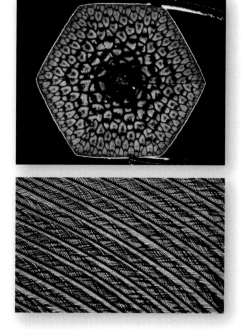

Student A:	What do you think it is?
Student B:	Well, it could _____.
Student A:	Yes, or perhaps it's _____.
Student B:	That's an interesting idea!
Student A:	It must not _____ because _____.
Student B:	You're right. It's probably _____.

Presentation Skills: Speaking at an Appropriate Speed

When you speak to a group of people or role-play a conversation, it's important not to speak too quickly. Of course, you don't want to speak too slowly, either. But for most people, speaking a little more slowly than they speak in a conversation will help the audience to understand.

D | **Role-Playing.** Form a group with another pair of students. Take turns role-playing your conversations from exercise **C**. Be sure to use an appropriate speed while you speak.

Urban Art

This graffiti is on a wall in Athens, Greece.

Before Viewing

A | **Discussion.** Look at the photos and read the captions on this page and on page 153. Then discuss the questions with a partner.

1. Do you see graffiti where you live? If so, where do you usually see it?
2. Do you think graffiti is beautiful? Interesting? Ugly? Explain.

B | **Meaning from Context.** Read the information about the video. Notice the underlined words. These are words you will hear in the video.

Urban Art

This video is called *Urban Art*. It's about art that you find in big cities. In the video, we see a graffiti artist named Nick Posada. He used to paint outdoors—on walls in public places. Like most graffiti artists, Posada's work was not underlined(commissioned). In other words, nobody paid him to create a piece of art. Instead, Posada's work was underlined(spontaneous). It expressed Posada's feelings and ideas in the moment.

Now, however, Posada's art is in an art underlined(gallery) in Washington, D.C. The gallery owner is Chris Murray. He says that people enjoy seeing graffiti because the art is fresh and underlined(inventive). This could mean that graffiti is becoming a more underlined(respected) art form. If art collectors see graffiti in an art gallery instead of in the street, they might enjoy it more.

C | Work with a partner. Fill in each blank in the chart with an underlined word from exercise **B**.

Traditional Art	Graffiti
• We usually see it in an art _____ or a museum.	• The artists don't get paid, and the art is _____, not planned.
• It's often _____ by a wealthy person or the government.	• Graffiti artists are often _____; they create new, exciting art forms.
• Traditional artists are often _____; many people appreciate their work.	

D | Critical Thinking. Discuss the questions with your partner.

1. According to a well-known saying, "Beauty is in the eye of the beholder." The *beholder* is the person who sees something. What do you think the saying means?
2. How might people use this saying to talk about graffiti?

While Viewing

A | Read each statement. Then watch the video and complete the chart with your own opinions.

	Agree	Disagree	Not Sure
1. The outdoor graffiti in the video is beautiful.			
2. Nick Posada knows a lot about art.			
3. Chris Murray wants to make money from Posada's graffiti.			
4. The video presents both good and bad sides of graffiti.			

B | Discussion. With a partner, discuss your answers from exercise **A**.

C | Watch the video again and circle each underlined word in exercise **B** on page 152 when you hear it. You will hear one of the words in a different form.

After Viewing

Critical Thinking. Look at the photos and read the captions. Then discuss the questions with a partner.

1. How does the art in each photo make you feel?
2. What do you think Nick Posada might say about the art in each photo?
3. How is graffiti similar to pop art? How is it different?

Pop art such as this painting by the American artist Andy Warhol reflects popular culture.

Gallery owner Chris Murray thinks graffiti is a new kind of pop art.

A | **Using a Dictionary.** Listen and check (✔) the words you already know. Use a dictionary to help you with any new words. These are words you will hear and use in Lesson B.

track 3-7

❏ afford (v.)	❏ appeal (v.)	❏ interpret (v.)	❏ lyrics (n.)	❏ simple (adj.)
❏ album (n.)	❏ award (n.)	❏ lively (adj.)	❏ perform (v.)	❏ song (n.)

B | **Meaning from Context.** Read the sentences. Notice the words in blue. Circle the correct word or phrase.

1. We saved our money for a long time, and now we can **afford** to buy a piano. We (have/don't have) enough money.
2. The show was fun and the music was **lively**, so everyone wanted to (leave/dance).
3. It's a **simple** piece of music, so it was (easy/hard) for my son to learn.
4. It's good music, but I can't understand the **lyrics**. Can you understand the (words/music)?
5. She's going to **perform** at the Tango Club. You'll need to buy a (CD/ticket) if you want to hear her.
6. You can download just one **song**. That costs (more/less) than downloading the whole **album**.
7. The trumpet can be a loud instrument, but its sound **appeals** to me. I really (like/dislike) it.
8. He **interprets** popular songs in an interesting way. He plays them (just like the original songs/in his own way).
9. They're playing at a classical music competition. There are several **awards** for the (best/worst) musicians.

C | Listen and check your answers from exercise **B**.

track 3-8

D | **Discussion.** Form a group with two or three other students. Look at the photos and discuss the questions.

1. What musical instruments are the people playing?
2. What style of music do you think each person is playing?
3. Do you think these musicians are **performing** or just practicing? Explain.
4. Which person or people could be trying to win an **award**? Explain.

a.   b.   c.

USING VOCABULARY

A | Read the conversations. Fill in each blank with a word from the box. There are two extra words.

afford	appeal	lively	simple
album	interpret	lyrics	song

David: Listen . . . Do you know the name of this (1) _____?

Helena: It's called, *What A Wonderful World*.

David: I like it. I think I'll buy it online.

Helena: You should buy the whole (2) _____. There are a lot of good songs on it.

Mitch: This music is really (3) _____ —it makes me want to get up and dance!

Joaquin: Well, in my opinion, they're playing it too fast.

Mitch: That's the way these musicians (4) _____ the song. It's just their style.

Joaquin: Yes, but it doesn't (5) _____ to me. I prefer calmer music.

Lila: I love this song! Let's sing it together.

Julie: I can't. I don't know the (6) _____.

Lila: That's OK. You can read them right here.

Julie: The words are pretty small, but I can see them. OK, let's sing!

B | Listen and check your answers from exercise **A**.

C | Practice the conversations from exercise **A** with a partner. Then switch roles and practice them again.

D | Read the article. Circle the correct word.

The Ukulele: The Sound of Hawaii

In the 1800s, small musical instruments similar to the guitar arrived in Hawaii with immigrants from Portugal. Hawaiians made changes to those instruments, and now the ukulele is an important part of Hawaiian culture.

The ukulele (1) (**affords/appeals**) to many people because it isn't expensive and it's fairly easy to play. Many parents can (2) (**afford/appeal**) to buy ukuleles, so schoolchildren in Hawaii learn to play traditional Hawaiian (3) (**songs/albums**) on the ukulele in their music classes.

Hawaiian children play ukuleles at the 30th Annual Ukulele Festival, Hawaii, USA.

Ukuleles are small, (4) (**lively/simple**) instruments with a body made of wood or plastic and only four strings,[1] but musicians use these instruments to (5) (**perform/afford**) many styles of music.

[1]**Strings** are the thin wires on musical instruments such as guitars and violins.

Before Listening

Understanding Visuals. Look at the photo and read the caption. Then discuss the questions with a partner.

1. What information do you know about the man in the photo?
   ❏ age   ❏ job   ❏ nationality   ❏ other _____
2. What does the man's facial expression tell you?
3. Would you like to hear this man's music? Why or why not?

Listening: A Radio Program

track 3-10 **A** | **Critical Thinking.** Read the choices. Then listen to the radio program. Choose the speaker's main purpose.

   a. to entertain the audience with a funny story
   b. to inform the audience about a musician
   c. to persuade the audience to buy an album
   d. to teach the audience about Hawaiian culture

track 3-10 **B** | **Note-Taking.** Listen again. Complete the notes.

Hawaiian musician Jake Shimabukuro has brought new popularity to the ukulele.

Title of Shimabukuro's new album: (1) _____,
_____, & Ukulele

1999: Na Hoku Hanohano Award; worked with
(2) _____ other musicians

Songs have no lyrics because Shimabukuro isn't
(3) _____.

New album is unusual because Shimabukuro doesn't
(4) _____.

After Listening

Critical Thinking. Form a group with two or three other students. Discuss the questions.

1. Jake Shimabukuro often plays popular songs by well-known musicians such as Michael Jackson and George Harrison. Would you rather hear a musician perform songs you already know, or hear new music? Explain.
2. Why do you think Shimabukuro continues to play the ukulele instead of playing a more popular instrument such as a guitar? Explain.

Pronunciation

Linking Final Consonants to Vowel Sounds

When we say a sentence, we usually don't pronounce each word separately. We connect one word to the next. This is called *linking*. Compare these sentences.

Separate words: *This – is – Rebecca. She – has – eight – ukuleles – at – home.*

Linked words: *This is Rebecca. She has eight ukuleles at home.*

One common type of linking connects the final consonant sound in one word to a vowel sound at the beginning of the next word.

Examples:

afford any   good example   book about   move over

Note: Vowel sounds include /a/, /o/, /iy/, /u/, and other sounds we make with an open mouth.

Consonant sounds include /k/, /t/, /m/, /l/, /s/, /b/, and other sounds that are not vowels.

A | Draw a line to connect the words that are linked, and cross out the words that are not linked. Then listen and check your answers.

1. ten artists
2. ~~violin music~~
3. favorite song
4. beautiful evening
5. they're outdoors

6. Portuguese immigrants
7. good album
8. rolled under
9. interesting lyrics
10. gave it

B | Practice saying the linked words with a partner.

C | Read and listen to an excerpt from a radio show. Notice how the speaker uses linking.

> He has performed his music since 1998, and in 1999, he won an award called the Na Hoku Hanohano Award for his work with two other musicians. Soon after that, Shimabukuro left the trio and began his solo career. He has become very popular on the Internet, where you can download his songs, or if you can't afford music downloads, you can watch videos of his performances for free.

D | Practice saying the sentences from exercise **C** with a partner. Use linking to connect final consonant sounds to vowel sounds.

Grammar

Modals of Necessity

We use these modals and related expressions with the base form of a verb to talk about things that are necessary or required.

> Students **must** register for classes by September 9th.
> We **have to** buy our tickets before the concert.
> Musicians **need to** take care of their instruments.

When we use these modals and related expressions to talk about things that aren't necessary, we use *don't have to* or *don't need to*.

> We **don't have to** hand in our papers today. They're not due until next week.
> It's warm outside, so we **don't need to** wear our coats.

A | Read each sentence. Circle the correct modal or expression.

1. In very cold weather, people (need to/don't need to) wear coats.
2. Most people (have to/don't need to) study hard to get good grades.
3. You usually (must/don't have to) buy a ticket to get into a movie theater.
4. Some artists learn to paint by themselves. They (need to/don't need to) go to an art school.
5. We (have to/don't have to) spend money in order to have fun. We can take a walk in the park.
6. You (must/don't need to) lock your apartment door. It isn't safe to leave it unlocked.

B | Complete each sentence with your own ideas. Then say your sentences to a partner.

1. Next month, I must _____.
2. Today, I need to _____.
3. I'm a busy person, but fortunately, I don't have to _____
   because _____.
4. Musicians have to _____.
5. Children don't need to _____.

Student to Student: Responding to Invitations

When people invite you to do something, it's easy to accept their invitation. It's more difficult to refuse invitations, so giving a reason is usually helpful. Here are some ways you can respond to invitations.

Invitation: *Would you like to study together this afternoon?*
Responses: *Sure!* **OR** *Sorry, I need to talk to Professor Watts this afternoon.*

Invitation: *Let's go to the art museum on Saturday.*
Responses: *That's a great idea!* **OR** *I'm afraid I can't./I'm sorry. I can't. I have to drive to Chicago on Saturday.*

C | Look at the photos and read the captions. Then read and listen to the information about a Mexican folk dancer and underline the modals and related expressions of necessity.

track 3-14

My name is Alicia, and I live in the state of Guanajuato in central Mexico. Here in Guanajuato, music and dancing are a big part of life. There are a lot of festivals here, and many kinds of music, but my favorite kind of music is traditional Mexican music—the kind of music my grandparents and great-grandparents listened to.

I'm a folk dancer, and I love to perform at special events. To be a folk dancer, you have to love the culture and the music here. That's the most important thing, but we also need to work hard and practice a lot. We dance in groups, and every person has to know the steps. And you can't buy traditional folk dancing dresses at the store, so we have to make our own. We wear traditional dresses that only come from this part of Mexico.

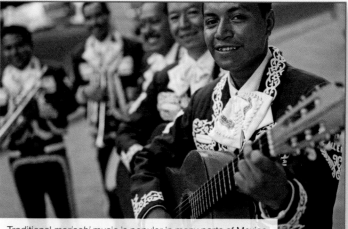

Traditional *mariachi* music is popular in many parts of Mexico.

This folk dancer in Guanajuato, Mexico, performs at festivals and other special events.

D | **Brainstorming.** With a partner, compare the modals and expressions you underlined in exercise **C**. Then brainstorm a list of other things that are probably necessary (or not necessary) for Alicia.

- *She probably has to travel a lot.* _____
- _____
- _____
- _____
- _____

E | **Discussion.** Form a group with another pair of students. Compare your lists from exercise **D**. Then discuss the questions.

1. Do you think it is easy or difficult to be a folk dancer? Explain.
2. In what ways is Alicia's dancing connected with her culture?
3. What other art and music in this unit is a part of the artists' culture? Explain.

You will work in a small group and prepare a presentation about the benefits of art and music education.

A | Self-Reflection. Form a group with two to five other students. Discuss the questions.

1. Which art from this unit is interesting or beautiful to you? Explain why you like it.
2. What kinds of music do you like? When or where do you listen to it?
3. What kind of art and music education (if any) have you had in school? Do you think it's important for people to learn about art and music? Explain.

B | Preparation. Read the following situation and the information in the Critical Thinking Focus box below.

Situation: The schools in your city don't have enough money to pay all of the teachers, so they have to cut some of the schools' programs; for example, foreign languages, sports, art, and music. You think it's very important to keep the art and music classes, so you need to convince[1] the school officials to keep those programs and save money in some other way.

Critical Thinking Focus: Supporting an Argument

When you argue in favor of, or for something, you try to convince your audience to agree with your ideas, or argument. Explaining the benefits of something is one way to make a strong argument.

C | Preparing an Argument. Read the topics and questions in the chart below. For each topic, make a list of benefits of art and music education to support your argument. Use the questions in the chart to help you get started.

Topic 1: Cultural Understanding	Topic 2: Career Preparation	Topic 3: Form of Communication
1. How do art and music help us understand other cultures? 2. How do art and music connect us with our own culture? 3. Other ideas?	1. What skills do people learn when they study art and music? 2. What careers require those skills, or require ability in art and music? 3. Other ideas?	1. How can people use art and music to communicate? 2. What can people feel when they look at art or listen to music? 3. Other ideas?

D | Planning a Presentation. Plan and practice the presentation of your group's argument. Make sure that every group member does some of the talking. *(See page 211 of the Independent Student Handbook for more information on doing group projects and presentations.)*

E | Presentation. Present your argument to the rest of the class. Imagine that you are talking to school officials. Try to convince them to agree with your argument.

[1]When you **convince** someone, you make them believe that something is true or necessary.

Our Relationship with Nature

Think and Discuss

1. Look at the photo. What is this man doing?
2. Is this something you might like to do? Explain.
3. What do you think you will learn about in this unit?

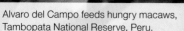
Alvaro del Campo feeds hungry macaws,
Tambopata National Reserve, Peru.

Exploring the Theme:
Our Relationship with Nature

Look at the photos and read the captions. Then discuss the questions.

1. What do you see on these pages that represents the natural world?
2. Which of the photos on these pages show a good relationship between people and nature? Which photos show a bad relationship? Explain.
3. What can people do in order to have a positive effect on the natural world?

Sharing Land with Animals

When people and animals have to share the same land, it sometimes causes conflicts, or problems. This polar bear is looking through a cabin window in Svalbard, Norway.

Hunting and Fishing

These Senegalese fishermen are pulling in nets filled with fish. People fish and hunt animals for food. Fishing is the main reason there are fewer large fish in the oceans today than in the past.

Scientific Research

Biologists are scientists who study living things. The information biologists collect can help the animals they study. This biologist is studying Macaroni penguins on Bird Island, South Georgia.

The top of the volcano Santa Maria appears through the clouds in the western highlands of Guatemala.

A | **Using a Dictionary.** Listen and check (✔) the words you already know. Use a dictionary to help you with any new words. These are words you will hear and use in Lesson A.

track 3-15

- ❑ ahead (adv.)
- ❑ depend (v.)
- ❑ hunt (v.)
- ❑ raise (v.)
- ❑ relationship (n.)
- ❑ respect (n.)
- ❑ responsibility (n.)
- ❑ share (v.)
- ❑ value (v.)
- ❑ within (prep.)

B | **Meaning from Context.** Read the two articles below. Fill in each blank with a word from the box above it. There is one extra word in each box. Then listen and check your answers.

track 3-16

ahead	depend	raise	relationship	share

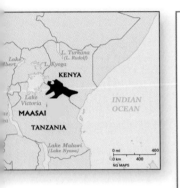

The Maasai People and Cattle[1]

The Maasai people of East Africa have a special (1) _____ with one kind of animal. They (2) _____ on cattle for meat and milk, which make up most of the Maasai diet. In order to (3) _____ cattle in a dry climate, the Maasai people (4) _____ land. Each family has its own animals, but they move the cattle over long distances and onto different families' land in order to find enough grass for the cattle to eat.

[1]**Cattle** are the large animals that beef comes from.

ahead	respect	value	within

The Sami People and Reindeer

Like the Maasai, the Sami people of northern Europe (5) _____ one animal more than any other. In this difficult climate, reindeer give the Sami people food, clothing, and other useful items. Nowadays, some Sami people raise reindeer on farms, but many Sami people still travel long distances with their animals. This gives them a detailed knowledge of the land and a great (6) _____ for nature. No one knows exactly what is (7) _____ for the Sami people because climate change makes the future of the Arctic uncertain.

A | **Self-Reflection.** Discuss the questions with a partner.

1. When people think of your country or culture, what animal do they think of?
2. Why is that animal important to people in your country or culture?

B | **Meaning from Context.** Read the article. Fill in each blank with the correct form of a word from the box. There is one extra word. Then listen and check your answers.

hunted	raise	responsibility	within

The Australian Aborigines and Australian Animals

The Aborigines of Australia have a different kind of relationship with animals. Australia has many kinds of animals, and all of them are part of the Aborigines' traditional culture. In the past, they (1) _____ some of the animals for food. Other animals appeared in stories or in very old paintings on rocks.

For the Aborigines, everything in nature is connected, and human beings have a special role (2) _____ the natural world. One group of Aborigines believes it is their (3) _____ to make sure Australia's kangaroos are doing well.

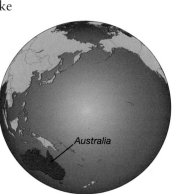
Australia

An Aboriginal painting of a kangaroo, Kakadu National Park, Australia

C | **Critical Thinking.** Form a group with two or three other students. Discuss the questions.

1. In what ways do the Sami and Maasai people have a similar **relationship** with animals?
2. How is the Australian Aborigines' **relationship** with animals different from the Maasai and Sami people's **relationship** with animals?
3. Do you think it is the **responsibility** of human beings to take care of the world's animals? Explain.

Before Listening

A | Using a Dictionary. Read the article and the photo captions. Use your dictionary to help you with the underlined words.

An adult harp seal surfaces at a breathing hole.

An Inuit hunter in Nunavut, Canada, waits on the ice near a seal's breathing hole.

The Inuit People and the Harp Seal

It's winter in the Arctic, and for many Inuit people in Canada, Greenland, and Alaska in the United States, it's time to hunt the harp seal. They hunt the seals for their meat, oil, and skins, and they use guns to kill the animals, or they hit the seals on the head with a tool called a *hakapik*.

For the Inuit, the seal hunt is a very old tradition, and they know there are large numbers of harp seals in the Arctic. Other people, however, question the ethics of the seal hunt. In Europe, for example, it is now illegal to trade any seal products. People who are in favor of this new law think the seal hunt is wrong because of the ways hunters kill the animals.

Critical Thinking Focus: Making Comparisons

In academic work, students often need to make comparisons between two or more things, people, or ideas to show that they understand a topic.

To make a comparison, first list what you know about the things you want to compare. Then, study this information carefully to notice how the things are similar and how they are different.

B | Critical Thinking. Look back at the articles on page 164–165. Then discuss the questions with a partner.

1. Which culture lives in a similar climate to the Inuit people: The Sami, the Maasai, or the Australian Aborigines? Explain.
2. How is the Australian Aborigines' use of animals similar to the Inuit people's use of animals? Explain.

C | Self-Reflection. Discuss the questions with your partner.

1. Is it legal or illegal to hunt wild[1] animals in your country? Explain.
2. How do you feel about people hunting wild animals for food? Explain.

[1]**Wild** animals live in nature. People do not take care of them.

Listening: A Lecture

🎧 track 3-18 **A | Listening for Main Ideas.** Read the statements. Then listen to a part of a lecture from an ethics class and circle **T** for *true* or **F** for *false*.

1.	The new law is popular with people in Europe.	**T**	**F**
2.	The Inuit people raise wheat as a crop.	**T**	**F**
3.	Only Inuit people can hunt seals.	**T**	**F**
4.	The Inuit people want to change the law.	**T**	**F**

🎧 track 3-19 **Identifying Opinions**

Speakers often give personal opinions in addition to facts and other information. This happens in academic contexts as well as in everyday life. Sometimes speakers use special expressions to give their opinions, such as *I think* and *personally* and the other expressions you learned in Unit 5 on page 88. At other times, they change the way that they speak. Here are some ways that speakers express their opinions. Listening for these things can help you identify speakers' opinions.

Extra Emphasis
Speakers may say certain words more loudly than normal.
I do NOT want to WATCH this!   *He gave an EXCELLENT presentation!*

Special Language
Speakers may use positive language to support an idea.
*These **beautiful** animals have the **amazing** ability to see in the dark.* (The speaker admires the animals.)

Speakers may use negative language to criticize an idea.
*Seal meat sounds **disgusting**, and the way people kill seals is **awful**!* (The speaker is against seal hunting.)

🎧 track 3-18 **B | Identifying Opinions.** Read the questions. Then listen to the lecture from exercise **A** again and answer the questions.

1. What is the first student's opinion about the seal hunt? How does he express his opinion?
2. What is the third student's opinion about killing animals? How does he express his opinion?

👥 **C | Discussion.** With a partner, compare and discuss your answers from exercise **B**.

After Listening

👥 **Discussion.** Form a group with two or three other students. Discuss the questions.

1. Do you think the law against trading seal products in Europe is a good law? Why, or why not?
2. Why do the Inuit people think it should be legal for them to sell seal products in Europe? Do you agree with their reasons? Explain.

Grammar

The Comparative and Superlative Forms of Adjectives

We use the comparative form to talk about differences between two people or things. With most one-syllable or two-syllable adjectives, we form the comparative with adjective + *-er* (+ *than*).

> Polar bears are **larger than** black bears. They also live in a **colder** climate.

With adjectives that have more than two syllables, we form the comparative with *more* or *less*.

> Brett is **more responsible than** his brother. He's **less interesting**, though.

We use the superlative to talk about extremes among three or more people or things. With most one or two-syllable adjectives, we form the superlative with *the* + *-est*.

> Mount Everest is **the highest** mountain in the world.

With adjectives that have more than two syllables, we form the superlative with *the most* or *the least*.

> Miranda is **the most intelligent** child in the class, but she is the least **friendly**.

A | With a partner, take turns saying the sentences below with the comparative or superlative form of the adjective in parentheses.

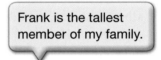

> Frank is the tallest member of my family.

1. Frank is (tall) member of my family.
2. Fishing is (dangerous) job in my country.
3. Your cookies are (delicious) than my cookies.
4. This view is (beautiful) than the view from my hotel room.
5. Your apartment is (clean) apartment in the building.
6. I think cattle are (smart) than horses.

Spelling Changes and Irregular Forms of the Comparative and Superlative

There are a few extra rules for spelling comparative and superlative adjectives correctly.

- With words ending in *e*, just add *-r* or *-st*:   *safe-safer*   *large-largest*
- With words ending in *y*, change the *y* to *i*:   *lazy-lazier*   *happy-happiest*
- With words ending in consonant-vowel-consonant, double the final consonant:
     hot-hotter   *thin-thinnest*

Some common adjectives have irregular comparative and superlative forms.

> *good–better–best*   *bad–worse–worst*   *far–farther–farthest*

B | With a partner, complete each sentence with the comparative or superlative form of the adjective in parentheses. Then practice saying the sentences.

1. My house is _____*farther*_____ (far) from here than your house is.

2. African elephants have _____ (big) ears than Asian elephants have.

3. The monkeys at the zoo are _____ (noisy) than monkeys in the wild.

4. This rose is _____ (pretty) flower in my garden.

5. The _____ (bad) grade I got in any of my classes this semester was a C.

6. My apartment is _____ (small) than your apartment.

Language Function: Making Comparisons

Track 3-20 **A** | Look at the photos and read the captions. Then read and listen to the information about two studies of black bears. Notice the similarities and differences between the two studies.

Black Bear Research: Two Places and Two Methods

North American black bears are shy animals. They are fearful by nature, and will usually run away if they see or hear people. Because of this, it can be difficult for scientists to learn about these animals.

In order to study black bears, researchers in the state of New Jersey, USA, catch bears in traps.[1] Then they sedate the bears with drugs, so they go to sleep and cannot move for a short time. Researchers then measure and weigh the bear, remove a tooth to find out the bear's age, and take blood to test for diseases. From these studies, researchers want to find out how many bears live in New Jersey, how long they live, and how many babies, or cubs, they produce.

A researcher from the New Jersey Department of Environmental Protection measures a sedated black bear.

Several hundred miles to the west, another black bear study is taking place in Minnesota, USA. There, Dr. Lynn Rogers and his team study bears that are completely awake. The bears know the researchers' voices and they are not afraid of the team. They still run away from other people, but with the help of a few grapes or nuts to keep the bears busy, Dr. Rogers can touch the animals to check their hearts, look at their teeth, and change the radio or GPS[3] equipment that the bears wear around their necks. He and his team can also walk or sit with the bears for hours and make videos to learn about the bears' everyday lives.

Dr. Lynn Rogers of the Wildlife[2] Research Institute in Minnesota observes a black bear that is wearing a radio collar.

In both places, the main goal is the same—to make sure there is a healthy population of wild black bears. In contrast, the research methods and the kinds of information researchers are able to collect are quite different.

[1] A **trap** catches and holds an animal that walks into it.

[2] **Wildlife** refers to the animals and other things that live in the wild.

[3] **GPS** (Global Positioning System) equipment allows researchers to follow the bears' movements with satellite technology.

Dr. Lynn Rogers with a black bear cub

B | **Collaboration.** Work with a partner. Look at the types of information in the box below. Decide which bear study can collect each type of information. Use the article on page 169 and your own ideas.

- number of bears in an area
- number of cubs each year
- bears' favorite foods
- how mother bears teach cubs
- how cubs play together

- a bear's age
- a bear's health
- how bears react[1] to danger
- a bear's location
- how bears react to other bears

[1]To **react** is to feel or do something because of something else.

C | **Using a Graphic Organizer.** With your partner, write each type of information from exercise **B** in the correct part of the Venn diagram below. *(See page 214 of the Independent Student Handbook for more information on using Venn diagrams.)*

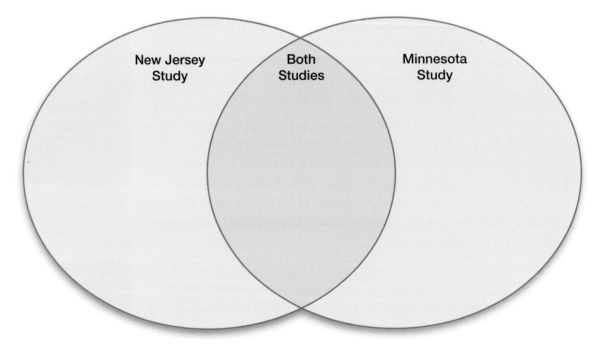

New Jersey Study   Both Studies   Minnesota Study

D | **Critical Thinking.** With your partner, use your Venn diagram from exercise **C** to help you discuss the questions.

1. Which study do you think produces more information?
2. Which study do you think is kinder to the bears/better for the bears?
3. Which study do you think is more expensive?
4. Which study do you think is more useful to science?
5. Which study do you think is more useful to bear hunters?

E | Form a group with another pair of students. Discuss the questions and your answers from exercise **D**.

Comparing Three Natural Attractions

A | **Self-Reflection.** Discuss the questions with a partner.

1. How important is spending time in nature to you? Very important, somewhat important, or not very important? Explain.
2. Check (✔) the outdoor activities that you enjoy and add two more ideas of your own. Explain your choices to your partner.

   ❏ walking in a park or public garden   ❏ sitting near a river, lake, or ocean

   ❏ watching animals outdoors or at a zoo   ❏ other outdoor activities

   _____

   _____

B | Read the three advertisements for tours of natural attractions in South America.

IGUAZÚ FALLS	**COLCA CANYON**	**GALÁPAGOS ISLANDS**

IGUAZÚ FALLS

- Three days and two nights
- Visit the world's largest waterfall.
- Travel by plane from Buenos Aires to the Iguazú Falls.
- Go hiking in the national park and take beautiful photos from the observation areas.
- Enjoy a boat ride on the river below the falls.
- Stay in a luxury hotel.
- Cost: $750 per person

COLCA CANYON

- Two days and one night
- Travel by bus to the Pampas Cañahuas and see wild animals.
- See the amazing Colca Canyon, where it's possible to watch the Andean condor—the largest bird in the world.
- Stay in a small hotel in a village.
- Cost: $300 per person

GALÁPAGOS ISLANDS

- Four days and three nights
- Travel by boat to three islands where wild animals such as penguins, sea birds, and tortoises are common.
- Enjoy sunset walks on the famous Galápagos beaches.
- Stay in budget hotels on the islands and eat in the local restaurants (not included in the cost).
- Cost: $1200 per person

C | With your partner, decide which attraction you would like to visit together. Compare the attractions using the comparative and superlative form of the adjectives in the box and your own ideas. Say as many sentences as you can.

amazing	expensive	interesting	short
beautiful	good	long	unusual

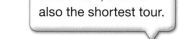

> The tour of the Colca Canyon is less expensive than the other two tours.

> That's true, but it's also the shortest tour.

Horses

A herd of wild horses in the western United States

Before Viewing

A | **Prior Knowledge.** In Lesson A of this unit, you learned about some of the relationships between people and animals. This video is about the relationship between people and horses. With a partner, discuss the questions.

How are horses important to people around the world? How were they important in the past? Consider these areas of life:

sports/recreation   food/farming   art/movies/books   transportation

B | **Using a Dictionary.** Match each word to its definition. Use a dictionary to help you.

1. prey (v.) _____
2. adapt (v.) _____
3. predator (n.) _____
4. die out (v.) _____
5. breed (n.) _____

a. to change in order to be successful in a new situation
b. to become less and less common and eventually disappear
c. to hunt and eat other animals
d. to produce animals with certain qualities in a controlled way
e. an animal that hunts and eats other animals

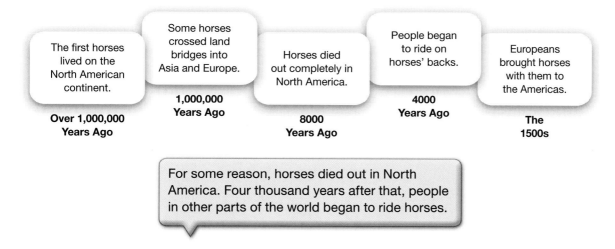

C | Understanding Visuals. Work with a partner. Take turns talking about important events in the history of horses. Use the information in the chart below and your own words to connect the ideas. Then switch roles.

The first horses lived on the North American continent.	Some horses crossed land bridges into Asia and Europe.	Horses died out completely in North America.	People began to ride on horses' backs.	Europeans brought horses with them to the Americas.
Over 1,000,000 Years Ago	**1,000,000 Years Ago**	**8000 Years Ago**	**4000 Years Ago**	**The 1500s**

For some reason, horses died out in North America. Four thousand years after that, people in other parts of the world began to ride horses.

While Viewing

A | Read the statements. Then watch the video and number the statements 1 to 4 in the order you hear about them.

_____ People began to breed horses for different jobs.

_____ Horses are in an animal family with donkeys and zebras.

_____ People measure a horse's size in "hands."

_____ Horses eat grass and use their speed to run from predators.

B | Watch the video again and draw a line from each type of horse to its picture below.

racehorse	draft horse	pony

<14 hands   14-19 hands   >19 hands

After Viewing

Critical Thinking. Form a group with two or three other students. Discuss the questions.

1. In the video, you heard, "Thousands of years before humans invented cars and airplanes, it was the horse who allowed us to go faster, go farther, and explore the world." What do you think this statement means? Explain.
2. What other forms of transportation did people use before cars and airplanes?

 *(pony image: <14 hands; racehorse image: 14-19 hands; draft horse image: >19 hands)*

🎧 **A** | **Using a Dictionary.** Listen and check (✔) the words you already know. Use a dictionary to help you with any new words. These are words you will hear and use in Lesson B.

track 3-21

❏ aggressive (adj.) ❏ avoid (v.) ❏ is worth (phrase) ❏ reserve (n.) ❏ scenery (n.)
❏ attack.(v.) ❏ conflict (n.) ❏ limited (adj.) ❏ save (v.) ❏ wildlife (n.)

🎧 **B** | **Meaning from Context.** Look at the photos and read the captions. Circle the correct word or phrase to complete each conversation below. Then listen and check your answers.

track 3-22

A national park in Uganda is home to this mountain gorilla. Biologists come here to study the gorillas. Tourists come to see them as well.

It's not easy to hike into the hot, wet tropical rain forest. For these tourists, the chance to watch mountain gorillas is worth the long hike.

Marcy: Why did you decide to take this tour?

Hope: Well, I think gorillas and other kinds of (1) (**wildlife/scenery**) are really interesting.

Marcy: I agree, and the (2) (**conflict/scenery**) here is beautiful, too.

Hope: Yeah, all in all, this tour certainly (3) (**is worth/avoids**) the cost.

Dan: I'm scared. The gorillas are so big! Do they ever (4) (**save/attack**) humans?

Okello: Almost never. Gorillas are not (5) (**aggressive/limited**). In fact, they usually try to (6) (**attack/avoid**) trouble. You don't often see a gorilla getting into a (7) (**conflict/wildlife**) with another animal.

Dan: Oh, really? Don't the male gorillas fight each other?

Okello: No. They usually just show their strength, and the other males go away. Anyway, the tour groups don't get too close to the gorillas, so we'll be fine.

Leandro: This part of the national park is a nature (8) (**reserve/save**), right?

Vanessa: That's right. It's illegal to hunt here, so the animals are pretty safe.

Leandro: Do you think that's going to (9) (**be worth/save**) the mountain gorillas?

Vanessa: Maybe. There aren't many gorillas left, but the park helps to protect them.

Leandro: The area of the park is (10) (**scenery/limited**), though. The gorillas can't go very far.

Vanessa: That's true, and I think it's the gorillas' biggest problem these days.

👥 **C** | With a partner, practice the conversations from exercise **B**. Then switch roles and practice them again.

A | Fill in each blank with a word from exercise **A** on page 174.

1. Uganda's government created the national park. One reason was to
_____ the mountain gorillas since there are so few left.

2. The gorillas don't have much land. It's a _____ amount of land.

3. The land in the national park could be excellent for farming. For that reason, the land
_____ a lot of money.

4. There is a _____ between different groups of people over how to
use the park's land. Some people want to keep the nature _____
for the animals. Other people want to use the land differently.

5. The government wants more tourism, and tourists come to see the gorillas
and other _____ such as chimpanzees. The beautiful
_____ is another thing tourists want to see.

6. Mountain gorillas are shy. Most of the time, they _____ human
beings, but the tour guides can usually find them.

7. People on the gorilla-watching tours don't need to worry. The gorillas aren't dangerous,
and they don't _____ tourists.

8. Even though the gorillas are quite large, they aren't _____
animals. They're actually quiet, gentle animals most of the time.

B | **Discussion.** Form a group with two or three other students. Discuss the questions.

1. Do you think a gorilla-watching tour is something you might enjoy? Explain.
2. Do you think it's important to save the mountain gorillas? Explain.

C | **Critical Thinking.** Read the information. Then tell your group members which facts are
surprising or interesting to you.

Mountain Gorilla Facts

- There are fewer than 800 mountain gorillas in the world. They live
  in four national parks in the area where Uganda, Rwanda, and the
  Democratic Republic of the Congo meet.

- Mountain gorillas live in family groups with as many as 40 gorillas.

- Adult male gorillas can weigh over 400 pounds (180 kilograms).
  Female gorillas become mothers at around 10 years old, and have
  one baby every three or four years.

- Mountain gorillas are mainly vegetarians. They eat so many plants
  that they rarely need to drink water.

- The gorilla's only predators are humans and leopards. Losing the
  land where they live is a much larger problem for them.

Before Listening

You are going to hear a conversation about Kariba Town in Zimbabwe, Africa. Look at the photo and read the information.

The Kariba dam on the Zambezi River stands on the border between Zambia and Zimbabwe. It's one of the largest dams in Africa. The dam and the first houses in Kariba Town were built in the late 1950s. At that time, the dam workers needed places to live. Now, Kariba Town is well known for beautiful Lake Kariba and for the wild animals that live nearby.

Listening: A Conversation

🎧 track 3-23 **A** | **Listening for Main Ideas.** Read the four statements. Then listen to the conversation and choose the main idea.

a. Many people now want to leave Kariba Town and let the animals live there.
b. Most people in Kariba Town stay indoors at night because that's when the animals walk around the streets and houses.
c. There are benefits to having animals in and near Kariba Town. However, there are also some conflicts between people and animals there.
d. Tourists visit Kariba Town to see the scenery and wildlife and to go boating and fishing on Lake Kariba.

🎧 track 3-23 **B** | **Listening for Details.** Listen again. Check (✔) the animals the speakers mention.

❏ baboons   ❏ elephants   ❏ giraffes   ❏ gorillas   ❏ leopards   ❏ zebras

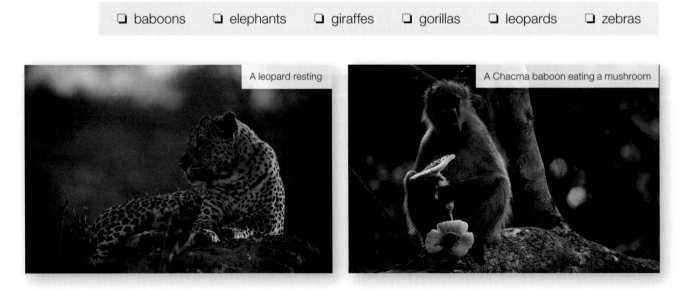

A leopard resting

A Chacma baboon eating a mushroom

After Listening

👥 **Discussion.** With a partner, discuss the questions. Give reasons for your answers.

1. What do you think is the relationship between the speakers in the conversation (e.g., coworkers, friends, etc.)?
2. Is Kariba Town an interesting place to visit? Is it a good place to live?
3. How do you think the speakers feel about the hunting near Kariba Town and Kariba Lake?

Pronunciation

Using Stress for Emphasis

In Lesson A of this unit, you learned that speakers sometimes use extra stress when they give opinions. Speakers may also emphasize certain words to show emotions such as surprise, anger, or happiness, or to help their listeners understand what they are saying.

🎧 track 3-24

Examples:

Showing Emotion: A: *Guess what?! I GOT the JOB!*
                              B: *Oh, that's GREAT!*

To Give Meaning: *The land became a wildlife reserve AFTER it became a national park.* (not before)

🎧 track 3-25   **A** | Read part of the conversation. Then listen and notice the extra emphasis on the underlined words.

Jasmine:	<u>Really</u>? I can't <u>imagine</u> an elephant outside my <u>house</u>—not here in Athens!
Jack:	She's right. There aren't a lot of wild animals in this part of Greece.
Dakarai:	Well, Athens is a very <u>old</u> city, but there <u>was</u> no Kariba Town before the 1950s. The land around Kariba belonged to the animals.
Jasmine:	And then they built the dam.
Dakarai:	Yes, that's right . . . then they built the dam. You know, when the water behind the dam began to rise, people had to save a lot of the animals. They went in boats to get them. Can you <u>imagine</u>? It's not <u>easy</u> to get wild <u>baboons</u> and <u>zebras</u> into a boat!
Jack:	Wow! It's <u>amazing</u> that people did <u>that</u>!

👥 **B** | Form a group with two or three other students. Decide whether each <u>underlined</u> word in exercise **A** shows emotion or emphasizes the speakers' meaning. Then practice the conversation. Then switch roles and practice it again.

Student to Student: Ending a Conversation

To end a conversation, follow these three steps. First, let people know you are going to end the conversation. Second, give a reason for ending it. Third, express your happiness about seeing or talking to the other person.

Well, I need to get going. My son is waiting for me. It was great to see you!

Anyway, I won't keep you. I need to make dinner. It was nice talking to you!

Grammar

Comparisons with *As . . . As*

We use *as* + adjective + *as* to talk about two things that are equal in some way.
> *Ken is **as tall as** his brother.* (Ken and his brother are equally tall.)

We use not *as* + adjective + *as* to talk about two things that are not equal. When we compare unequal things, we say the smaller or lesser thing first.
> *Ponies are **not as large as** horses.* (Ponies aren't equal to horses in size. Ponies are smaller.)

Note: Some common expressions formed with *as . . . as* are:
> *as soon as possible*   *as much as possible*   *as many as possible*

A | With a partner, make comparisons using *as . . . as* and the words and phrases below. Give your own opinions and say complete sentences.

1. baby elephants/baby tigers/cute <u>I don't think baby elephants are as cute as baby tigers.</u>
2. oranges/chocolate/delicious
3. oranges/chocolate/nutritious
4. black bears/baboons/aggressive
5. camels/reindeer/large
6. lions/tigers/beautiful

B | Read the information about two kinds of penguins. With your partner, make as many comparisons as possible using *as . . . as*, the adjectives below, and your own adjectives.

| colorful | heavy | long-lived | numerous | short | tall |

> Rockhopper penguins are not as heavy as Adélie penguins.

Penguin Fact File

Adélie Penguin			Rockhopper Penguin
20" (50 cm)	**Average Height**	20" (50 cm)	
9 lbs.(kg)	**Average Weight**	7 lbs.(kg)	
20 years	**Average Lifespan**	10 years	
4.9 million	**Estimated Population**	3.3 million	

C | Look at the pictures and read the captions. Then read and listen to the article and underline the uses of *as . . . as*.

track **3-26**

Blind Bobcat Finds a Friend

A bobcat named Bear was lucky to be at a sanctuary[1] that takes care of unwanted wildcats. He and the other animals at the sanctuary were not born in the wild, so they couldn't take care of themselves.

Bear had other problems, however. He was almost blind and very unfriendly toward other cats. Because of this, he was always alone. Then, workers at the sanctuary had an idea: Why not introduce him to Nairobi, a caracal, who was just as unfriendly as Bear?

At first, a fence separated the two animals, but Bear knew "Robi" was there. He surprised everyone by acting friendly toward the caracal. Robi was not as friendly as Bear, but after a few weeks, the caracal seemed more comfortable with the other cat, so workers at the sanctuary opened the fence.

Now, Robi and Bear are best friends. Bear stays as close as possible to Robi and follows him around. If the bobcat loses Robi, he chirps[2] until the caracal comes back. "Bear is so reliant[3] on Robi," says Cheryl Tuller, director of the sanctuary, "Robi takes that as his job."

Nairobi the caracal (left) sits next to his best friend Bear the bobcat at the WildCat Haven Sanctuary in Oregon, USA.

Bear the blind bobcat follows Robi's lead. The fence behind the cats separates them from other animals at the sanctuary.

[1] An animal **sanctuary** is a place where people take care of sick or unwanted animals.
[2] To **chirp** means to make a sound like a bird.
[3] If someone is **reliant**, they depend on someone or something.

D | **Critical Thinking.** With a partner, discuss each statement and circle **T** for *true* or **F** for *false*. Use the information in the article and your own ideas.

1. When workers introduced the cats, Bear was friendlier than Robi.   **T**   **F**
2. With Robi's help, Bear is now as active as any cat at the sanctuary.   **T**   **F**
3. Now, Bear is probably happier than Robi.   **T**   **F**

E | **Discussion.** Form a group with another pair of students. Discuss the questions.

1. What parts of the article are interesting or surprising to you? Explain.
2. Do you think other wildcats at the sanctuary have such close friendships? Why, or why not?
3. Have you heard other stories about unusual animal friendships? Explain.
4. Is a wildcat sanctuary a place you might like to visit? Why, or why not?

You are going to choose a topic for a short presentation. Think about details to include, and then practice your presentation before you present to the whole class. Your teacher will tell you how long your presentation should be.

A | **Brainstorming.** Use the question below to brainstorm ideas for your presentation. Write a list of your ideas in your notebook. How is the natural world important to you?

B | **Using a Graphic Organizer.** Look at your list of ideas from exercise **A**. Choose the ideas that you want to use in your presentation. Then follow the steps below. *(See pages 214-215 of the Independent Student Handbook for more information on using Graphic Organizers.)*

- Choose a topic from your notes. Put a check (✔) next to it.
- Choose three or four main ideas to support your topic. Circle them.
- In your notebook, draw a "spider map" similar to the one below.
- Write your topic in the center of your spider map.
- Write three to four main ideas at the end of the lines, or "arms."
- Write a few details for each main idea.

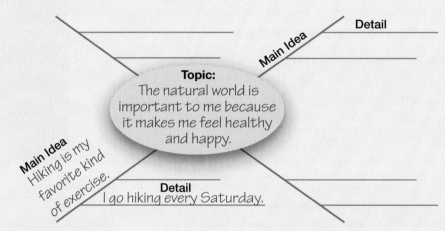

Presentation Skills: Ending a Presentation

At the end of a presentation, you need to give a strong conclusion. Your conclusion reminds your audience about the most important ideas from your presentation. It also tells your audience why they should care about the topic of your talk. For example, a presentation about a nearby lake might conclude in this way:

Lake Ripley is a home for wildlife as well as a popular place for people to have fun. As long as we take care of the lake, people will be able to enjoy it for a long, long time.

C | **Planning a Presentation.** Use your spider map from exercise **B** and follow these steps.

- Decide which of your ideas you will talk about first, second, and so on, and make notes for your talk. Think of a strong conclusion for your presentation.
- You may want to look back at page 60 in Unit 3 for information about speaking from notes.

D | **Practicing Your Presentation.** Work with a partner. Take turns practicing your presentations and making helpful suggestions for improvement. You may want to use a Presentation Checklist to help you. *(See page 218 of the Independent Student Handbook for information on Presentation Checklists.)*

E | **Presentation.** Give your presentation to the class.

How We Communicate

Think and Discuss

1. Look at the photo. What do you think these men are talking about?
2. Do you think they know each other well? Explain.
3. What kinds of topics do you think you will discuss in this unit?

Two men talking, Komotini, Greece

Exploring the Theme:
How We Communicate

Look at the photos and read the captions. Then discuss the questions.

1. What kinds of communication do you see on these pages?
2. In human history, what kinds of communication are the oldest? The newest?
3. What kinds of communication do you use every day? How do you use them?

Non-Verbal Communication

Non-verbal communication includes hand gestures, facial expressions, eye contact, and other ways we communicate without words.

A 560-acre complex of satellite dishes, Menwith Hill, England

Verbal Communication

Verbal communication is all about words and speech. We use verbal communication when we speak.

Written Communication

Written communication uses letters and other symbols to represent spoken words.

Technology for Communication

Modern technology has given us many devices for communication such as radios, telephones, computers, and satellite TVs.

A | **Using a Dictionary.** Listen and check (✔) the words you already know. Use a dictionary to help you with any new words. These are words you will hear and use in Lesson A.

track 3-27

❑ access (v.)	❑ connect (v.)	❑ device (n.)	❑ message (n.)	❑ speed (n.)
❑ basic (adj.)	❑ contact (v.)	❑ involved (adj.)	❑ represent (v.)	❑ unfortunately (adv.)

B | Write each word from exercise **A** next to its definition.

1. _____ taking part in something
2. _____ how fast something moves or happens
3. _____ to join or form a relationship with something or someone
4. _____ to stand for or to mean another thing
5. _____ a piece of equipment invented for a certain purpose
6. _____ a piece of information that someone sends
7. _____ simplest or most important
8. _____ to telephone someone or send them a message or letter
9. _____ to find or get something
10. _____ sadly or unluckily, used to express regret about what you are saying

C | **Meaning from Context.** Circle the correct word in blue to complete each sentence. Then listen and check your answers.

track 3-28

1. Non-verbal communication is more (basic/involved) than speaking a language. Babies, for example, are able to communicate with their parents by crying or smiling.
2. I'm not feeling well, so I need to (contact/connect) my boss and tell her I can't work today.
3. An MP3 player is a popular (basic/device) for playing music.
4. It's easy to (represent/access) some kinds of information on the Internet.
5. Most computers are, (speed/unfortunately), quite expensive.
6. Many parts of the mouth are (access/involved) in speaking.
7. I tried to go online, but I couldn't (connect/unfortunately) to the Internet.
8. Anna didn't answer her phone, so I left a (contact/message) for her.
9. For many people, the dollar sign ($) (accesses/represents) money.
10. Information travels at a high (message/speed) from one computer to another computer.

A | Look at the photos and read the information. Then discuss the questions below with a partner.

There are many ways to **contact** people these days. The telephone is often **involved**, either for calling someone or sending a text **message**.

Life moves at a slower **speed** in rural areas. These men are taking the time to enjoy a conversation. **Unfortunately**, many people in big cities may not have time to speak with their neighbors.

For these boys, shaking hands with the other players is a **basic** part of any baseball game. It **represents** a feeling of respect and friendliness.

1. How do you usually **contact** your close friends? Your family members?
2. What are some things that move at a low or slow **speed**? At a high **speed**?
3. What are the **basic** parts of a presentation? What information do you need to include?
4. What does each of these five symbols **represent**?
   a. # b. & c. + d. % e. !
5. What sports or other leisure activities are you **involved** in? Why do you take part in them?

B | Read the article. Fill in each blank with a word from the box. There is one extra word.

access	connect	device	message	represent

National Geographic Emerging Explorer Ken Banks

Each year, National Geographic names several new Emerging Explorers. They receive an award of $10,000. The money supports the work of young people at the beginning of their careers in many fields—biology, engineering, music, and others.

Ken Banks is one of the Emerging Explorers. In places where people can't (1)_____ the Internet, his software[1] lets them send a (2)_____ or other kinds of information with an inexpensive (3)_____: a basic cellular telephone. They just (4)_____ the phone to a computer. Then they can send information from the computer without using the Internet.

[1]Programs used to operate a computer are called **software**.

Pronunciation

Thought Groups

When we speak, we usually do not pronounce each word separately. In Unit 8, you learned that two words can be linked, or joined together. In a similar way, groups of words are often pronounced together as phrases, or *thought groups*.

If you practice using *thought groups*, you can make your pronunciation smoother and improve your listening comprehension.

🎧 track 3-29

Examples:
I'll call you later,/or I'll send you/an email.
My older brother/has always been/my best friend.

🎧 track 3-30 **A** | Read part of a news report. Then listen and notice how the speaker uses thought groups.

> With that software/on your computer,/you just need a device/that connects the computer/to a cell phone. Then the computer/uses the cell phone/to send messages/to a lot of different people./It's pretty cool!/And the Internet/is not involved.

These birds in Hungary have their own ideas about the purpose of a cell phone tower.

👥 🎧 track 3-31 **B** | Listen to the sentences. Notice the thought groups. Then practice saying each sentence with a partner.

1. Professor Jones/is the oldest professor/at the university.
2. I almost never/send a real letter/to anyone.
3. Lily has a phone,/but she doesn't have/a computer.
4. We had a good conversation/about our families.
5. Tom and Marsha/are my only friends/in the city.
6. The assignment/is to read a chapter/and write some questions/ for discussion.

Before Listening

👥 Work with a partner. Read the information and discuss the question below. You are going to listen to a news report about Ken Banks, a man who does work in places where people do not have access to the Internet.

How do you think life might be difficult for people who don't have access to the Internet?

Listening: A News Report

Ken Banks' FrontlineSMS software in use

A | Listening for Main Ideas. Listen to the news report. Choose the correct word or phrase to complete each statement.

track 3-32

1. Ken Banks does a lot of work in _____.
   a. Asia   b. Africa   c. Europe
2. The United Nations has said that being able to access the Internet is a basic human _____.
   a. need   b. right   c. wish
3. Ken Banks worked on a project at the _____ National Park.
   a. Borjomi   b. Lauca   c. Kruger

B | Making Inferences. Read the statements. Then listen again and circle **T** for *true* or **F** for *false*. The answers are not in the speakers' exact words. You need to think about what you hear.

track 3-32

1. The UN says that countries should limit people's use of the Internet.   **T**   **F**
2. Ken Banks invented software because he saw a need for it.   **T**   **F**
3. Everyone uses Banks' software in the same way.   **T**   **F**
4. Banks' software can be used in poor countries.   **T**   **F**

After Listening

A | Critical Thinking. Discuss the questions with a partner.

1. Can you access the Internet easily? Explain.
2. If you can access the Internet, how do you use it in your daily life? Explain.
3. Rank the following ways people use the Internet from most important (1) to least important (6).

   _____ chat online with friends   _____ look up facts and information

   _____ do online banking or pay bills   _____ shop online for clothes, music, etc.

   _____ read or hear the news   _____ create a business or personal Web site

B | Join another pair of students. Compare your rankings from exercise **A**. If your rankings are different, explain your decisions.

Grammar

The Present Perfect Tense

We form the present perfect tense with *have* or *has* + the past participle of a verb.
> I **have talked** to Melinda three times this week.

We use the present perfect tense to talk about:

- actions that began in the past and continue until now.
  > We **have lived** on Mountain Street since 2004.

- actions that have happened several times already.
  > Matthew **has bought** three different smartphones this year.

- actions that happened at some time in the past and are connected with the present.
  > I **haven't read** that book, so I can't tell you anything about it.

Regular Past Participles			
walked	talked	closed	finished
called	allowed	traveled	improved

Irregular Past Participles				
been	eaten	left	had	given
gone	slept	fallen	read	seen

With a partner, use the words and phrases to say complete sentences. Use the present perfect tense of the underlined verbs.

1. The Morgans/<u>travel</u> to Europe/four times.
2. Celine/not <u>visit</u> her family in Romania/since 2009.
3. Randal/<u>cook</u>/a delicious meal. Can you join us for dinner?
4. I/not <u>see</u>/the new action movie. Let's go see it tonight!
5. He/<u>call</u> me/twice today.
6. They/<u>know</u> each other/for a long time.

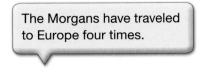

The Morgans have traveled to Europe four times.

Language Function

Talking about Duration: The Present Perfect Tense with *For* and *Since*

We use the present perfect tense with *for* to talk about how long a situation has existed. *For* is usually followed by a length of time.
> I started this job at the age of 20. I <u>have had</u> this job **for seven years**.

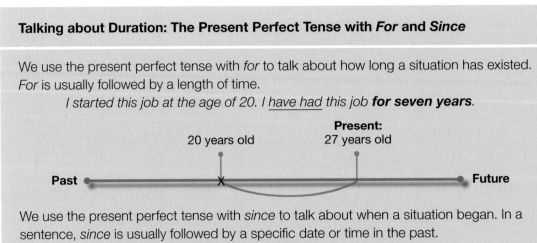

We use the present perfect tense with *since* to talk about when a situation began. In a sentence, *since* is usually followed by a specific date or time in the past.
> I <u>have worked</u> here **since January, 2009**.
> Molly and Brianna <u>have been</u> best friends since **high school**.

A | Read the conversation. Fill in each blank with *for* or *since*. Then listen and check your answers.

Early telephone

Layla: Hi, David. I don't think I've seen your car before.

David: It's an old one. I've had it (1) _____ 2002.

Layla: It looks good. I've only had my car (2) _____ two years, and it already looks old.

David: By the way, have you seen Alice recently?

Layla: No, I haven't seen her (3) _____ several weeks.

David: Me neither. I sent her an email, but it bounced[1] back.

Layla: Oh, she changed her email address. She's had a new one (4) _____ February, I think.

David: Really? Could you give me her new email address?

Layla: Sure, no problem.

[1]If an email **bounces back**, it is returned because the address is incorrect.

Radio-telephone

B | Practice the conversation from exercise **A** with a partner. Then switch roles and practice it again.

C | **Collaboration.** Work with your partner. Read the list of important events and inventors in the history of communication. Then plot each event on the timeline below.

1829	Braille system of printing and reading for people who are blind (Louis Braille)
1910	Movies with sound (Thomas Edison)
1896	Early form of radio (Guglielmo Marconi)
1980s	Personal computers (various inventors)
1979	Cellular telephone (Martin Cooper)
1927	Television (Philo Taylor Farnsworth)
1876	Telephone and microphone (Alexander Graham Bell)
1991	World Wide Web (Tim Berners-Lee)

Cellular telephone

Internet video calling

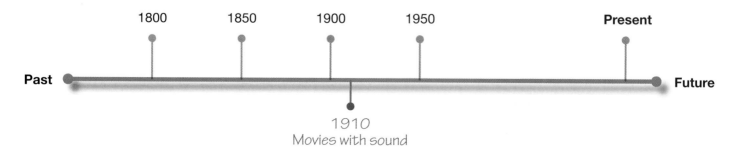

1910
Movies with sound

D | Complete each conversation. Use information from the timeline in exercise **C**.

Ken: How long has Braille printing been around?

Miguel: A long time! It's been around since (1) _____.

Scott: How long has the telephone existed?

Rocio: It has (2) _____ for (3) _____ years.

Megan: How old is television?

Sandra: It's pretty old! There's been TV (4) _____ 1927.

Marta: How long have we had cellular telephones?

Li: We have (5) _____ cellular telephones since (6) _____.

E | Practice the conversations from exercise **D** with a partner. Then switch roles and practice them again.

F | With your partner, have more conversations about the timeline in exercise **C**.

> How long have we had microphones?

> We've had them since 1876.

G | **Discussion.** Form a group with another pair of students. Discuss the questions.

1. What information from exercise **C** was interesting or surprising to you? Explain.
2. Which technology for communication is the most important to you? Explain.
3. How many different telephone numbers have you had in your life?
4. Have you made any phone calls today? If so, whom did you call?
5. Have you checked your email today? If so, how many times?
6. Which of your friends do you talk to the most? How long have you known him or her?

A shop in Zacatecas, Mexico, gives travelers a place to access the Internet.

Talking about the Recent Past

A | Match each question to its answer.

1. Have you seen my cell phone? _____b_____
2. Where will the meeting be? _____
3. Have you gone to the theater lately? _____
4. Is that a good book? _____
5. Why are you so tired? _____
6. Have you eaten tacos before? _____

a. I don't know. I haven't read it yet.
b. Yes, I saw it on the table.
c. Only once.
d. They haven't told us yet.
e. No, I prefer a good movie.
f. I haven't slept well in days!

B | Practice saying the questions and answers from exercise **A** with a partner.

C | Read and listen to the conversation. Notice the verb tenses the speakers use. Then practice the conversation with your partner. Switch roles and practice it again.

track 3-34

Lionel:	Have you written a letter to anyone recently?
Candice:	Yes, I wrote a letter to my grandmother last week.
Lionel:	A real letter—on paper?
Candice:	Yes, my grandma doesn't use email.
Lionel:	Oh, I see.
Candice:	Have you used a videophone system recently?
Lionel:	Yes, I talked with my brother last night. He's in Germany.

D | Read the list of ways to communicate. Add two of your own ideas.

- call someone on the phone
- use a videophone system
- send a text message
- have a face-to-face conversation

- use polite expressions, e.g., "thank you"
- make facial expressions
- _____
- _____

E | With a partner, ask and answer questions about ways to communicate using the present perfect. Use the list of ways to communicate from exercise **D**. Use the conversation from exercise **C** as a model.

Touching the Stars

Before Viewing

A | Critical Thinking. Form a group with two or three other students. Read the information below. Then discuss the questions.

In Lesson A of this unit, you discussed several different ways to communicate. Many of these ways require us to see (e.g., reading a text message) or to hear (e.g., talking on the telephone).

1. What kinds of communication challenges do you think a person who is blind might face? A person who is deaf?[1]
2. What are some ways you know about for people who are blind and people who are deaf to communicate?

track 3-35 **B | Using the Present Perfect Tense.** Read the information and fill in each blank with the present perfect form of the verb in parentheses. Then listen and check your answers.

The Hubble Space Telescope (1) _has been_ (be) in orbit since 1990, and people around the world (2) _____ (enjoy) the beautiful images that the telescope (3) _____ (send) back to Earth. One group of people, however, (4) _____ (have) no opportunity to enjoy Hubble's discoveries—until recently. The National Aeronautics and Space Administration (NASA) (5) _____ (create) a special book for people who are blind. It allows them to "see" images from Hubble and other telescopes with their fingers.

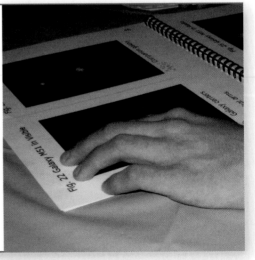

[1] A person who is **deaf** has difficulty hearing or cannot hear at all.

While Viewing

A | Read the statements. Then watch the video and circle the correct information.

1. The students (have the same level of vision/have different levels of vision loss).
2. The students are helping NASA to (sell/change) the book.
3. The book has sheets of (plastic/paper) over the images.

B | Watch the video again and choose the correct answer to each question.

1. Where is the school? _____
2. How do the students read the book? _____
3. How does the book show details of images? _____
4. What was wrong with the early version of the book? _____
5. One girl holds up a photo. What does it remind her of? _____

a. too many dots and ridges
b. onion rings
c. Colorado
d. with their fingers
e. as raised dots and ridges

After Viewing

Critical Thinking. Form a group with two or three other students. Discuss the questions.

What do you know, or what can you imagine about the lives of people who are deaf or blind? For example:

- How do people who are deaf communicate with other people? How do they hear music?
- How do people who are blind find their way around?
- How are the lives of people who are deaf or blind the same as the lives of people with hearing and vision? How are they different?

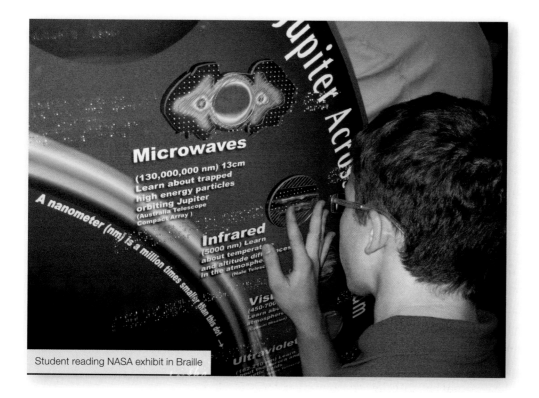

Student reading NASA exhibit in Braille

🎧 **A** | **Meaning from Context.** Look at the graphic and read the caption. Then read and listen
track 3-36   to the article. Notice the words in **blue**. These are words you will hear and use in Lesson B.

Communications Satellites: How Many Is Too Many?

In one way or another, you probably use a satellite every day.
If you watch TV, check the weather, or make a long-distance phone
call, a satellite is involved. Satellites have changed the way we
communicate, and they've also changed the space around Earth.

Back in the 1970s, former NASA scientist Donald Kessler **realized**
that with thousands of satellites in orbit around the earth, a **collision**
between two or more satellites was **probable**. He also knew that after
such a collision, hundreds of small pieces of **metal** would be in orbit
instead of two large satellites. Those pieces could cause even more
collisions, and so on until the space around the earth was full of metal
pieces. No satellite or spacecraft would be able to travel safely in space.

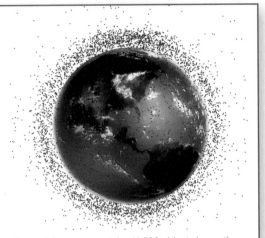

The red dots represent the 11,500 objects larger than
4 inches (10 centimeters) across in a low orbit around
the earth. Another 10,000 objects are smaller or in a
higher orbit.

Then on February 10, 2009, a large communications satellite actually
did collide with another satellite and added about 2000 pieces of space **garbage** to the cloud of
objects in orbit. The **response** to the collision was an international conference to discuss ways to
reduce the number of objects in orbit.

In 2007, the UN had already given some **sensible** advice to the world's space agencies. In order
to **prevent** collisions, for example, countries should not use old satellites for missile[1] target practice.[2]

At the conference, scientists discussed ways to **get rid of** old satellites and metal pieces, such
as a collector satellite to catch space garbage and bring it down into the earth's atmosphere
to burn up. Such a solution, however, may be a long way away. Until then, space garbage will
remain a danger to travel in space and communication on Earth.

[1]A **missile** is a large weapon on a rocket.
[2]In **target practice**, people try to improve their skills by shooting guns or other weapons at something.

B | Write each word or phrase in **blue** from exercise **A** next to its definition.

1. _____ (n.) the act of objects or people crashing into each other
2. _____ (n.) waste material, trash
3. _____ (n.) a reply or reaction to something
4. _____ (n.) a hard material such as iron, steel, gold, or silver
5. _____ (v.) became aware of something or understood it
6. _____ (adj.) good, based on reasons rather than emotions
7. _____ (phrase) to throw away
8. _____ (adj.) likely to happen
9. _____ (v.) to make sure that something does not happen
10. _____ (v.) to make less or smaller

A | Using a Dictionary. Use your dictionary to find other forms of the vocabulary words.

Noun	Verb	Adjective	Adverb
collision		X	X
metal	X		X
prevention	prevent		X
	X	probable	
response			X
	realize	X	X

B | Fill in each blank with a word from the box. There is one extra word.

| garbage | prevent | probable | realize | reduce | response | sensible |

1. We need to _____ our phone bill! We're paying way too much!
2. The driver in the red car tried to stop, but he couldn't _____ the collision. Fortunately, no one was hurt.
3. If you only need the Internet occasionally, using an Internet café is a _____ choice.
4. Smoking cigarettes is the _____ cause of some illnesses.
5. Her business has lost a lot of money recently. When will she _____ that she has a bad business partner?
6. I asked Bob a question, but I couldn't hear his _____.

C | Discussion. With a partner, discuss the questions.

1. What things in your classroom are made of **metal**?
2. Have you ever seen a **collision**? Who or what collided? What happened?
3. How do you **get rid of** the **garbage** where you live? What happens to the **garbage** after that?
4. How can people **reduce** the amount of **garbage** they throw away?

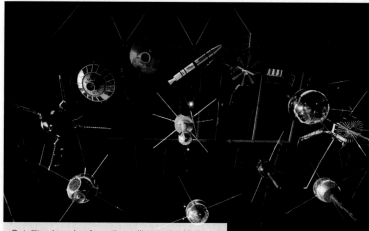

Satellites hanging from the ceiling at the National Air and Space Museum in Chantilly, Virginia

Before Listening

👥 **Discussion.** Look at the photos and read the captions. Then discuss the questions with a partner.

A woman uses a cell phone at a train station in Avignon, France.

Deciding how to get rid of old cell phones and batteries is not always easy.

1. Do you use a cell phone? If so, how and where do you use it?
2. Have you ever needed to get rid of an old telephone, computer, or other electronic device? If so, how did you get rid of it?
3. What things do people usually send away for recycling[1] instead of just throwing them away?

Listening: A Telephone Conversation

🎧 track 3-37 **A | Note-Taking.** Listen to the telephone conversation. Write short answers to the questions.

1. What happened when Todd's plane landed? _____
   _____

2. What did Todd see on the plane before the movie? _____
   _____

3. What does Todd say about the Web site? _____
   _____

🎧 track 3-37 **B | Listening for Details.** Listen again. Choose the correct word or phrase to complete each sentence.

1. Todd's plane landed in _____.
   a. Cincinnati   b. Chicago   c. Cleveland
2. On the plane, Todd saw a commercial from a _____.
   a. computer company   b. comedy network   c. cell phone service
3. Todd says the _____ in old electronics can be worth a lot of money.
   a. chemicals   b. metal   c. glass
4. Some companies allow people to _____ their old electronic devices.
   a. return   b. keep   c. buy

Student to Student: Having a Telephone Conversation

Here are some expressions you can use when making or answering a telephone call.

Calling: *Hi, this is/it's (your name).*
Could I please speak to (name)?
Could I leave her/him a message?

Answering a call: *Hello?*
This is she/he.
Who is calling?
Would you like to leave a message?

---

[1]When you **recycle** materials such as paper or glass, you process them in order to use the materials again.

After Listening

A woman in New Delhi, India, recycles circuit boards from old electronics.

Critical Thinking Focus: Drawing Conclusions

When we draw conclusions, we put together pieces of information and decide what else is likely to be true based on that information. For example, if our coworker walks into the office out of breath and wearing wet clothes, we might conclude that it is raining outside and he or she ran to get inside.

ack 3-38

A | **Preparation.** Read and listen to the information below.

Low-Tech Recycling of Electronics	High-Tech Recycling of Electronics
Where? Ghana, Nigeria, India, China	**Where?** Ontario, Canada
How? People take apart electronic garbage by hand. They may also burn some of the garbage. Dangerous chemicals go into the air or onto the ground. Most of the electronic garbage comes from Europe, the United States, and other wealthy parts of the world.	**How?** A high-tech recycling company uses machines to separate different materials such as metal, glass, and plastic. Objects such as batteries[2] with dangerous chemicals inside are removed by hand. Ontario has strong laws to protect the environment and charges a fee to recycle old electronics. That money makes the recycling company possible.
Why? In the United States and other places, people either can't or don't want to send old electronic devices to landfills.[1] Instead, they send them to recycling companies. Many recycling companies then send the garbage to other countries.	**Why?** A large amount of electronic garbage is produced nearby in the United States, and Canadian laws require recycling of electronics.

[1]A **landfill** is a large area where communities take their garbage and cover it with earth.
[2]**Batteries** are small objects that provide electricity to things such as radios.

B | **Critical Thinking.** Form a group with two or three other students. Follow the steps.

1. Find information in exercise **A** to answer these questions.
   - Where does electronic garbage come from?
   - Where does it go?
   - Is there a cost for recycling electronics?
   - What environmental damage does recycling cause?
2. What conclusions can you draw from the information you have?

Grammar

The Present Perfect Tense with *Ever*, *Already*, and *Yet*

The present perfect tense is often used with the signal words, *ever, already,* and *yet.* These words add extra information to questions and statements.

We use *ever* in <u>questions</u> with the present perfect to emphasize "anytime before now."
> Have you **ever** made a phone call to Central Asia?

We use *already* in <u>questions and affirmative statements</u> to emphasize that something happened before now or happened very soon or early.
> Toby has **already** read the newspaper. Would you like to read it now?
> Have you **already** had lunch?
> *X* We haven't **already** done our grocery shopping.

We use *yet* in <u>questions and negative statements</u> to talk about or ask about something that we expected to happen before now.
> Has your father arrived **yet**? I'm looking forward to meeting him.
> He has not arrived **yet**, but he will be here soon.
> *X* Amber and Mina have finished the assignment **yet**.

A | **Collaboration.** With a partner, choose the correct signal words to complete each conversation. Then practice the conversations. Switch roles and practice them again.

> **Carla:** I'm surprised. The meeting hasn't started (1) (already/yet).
>
> **Lee:** The director isn't here (2) (yet/ever), so we're waiting for her.

> **Juan:** Has your son (3) (ever/yet) studied a foreign language?
>
> **Amy:** Yes, he studied Japanese in high school.

> **Ali:** Have you (4) (already/ever) given your presentation?
>
> **Oscar:** No, I haven't given it (5) (yet/already).

> **Fatima:** I'm worried about Celia. She's in London by herself.
>
> **Rosa:** Has she (6) (yet/ever) been there before?

B | Fill in each blank with *ever*, *already*, or *yet*. There may be more than one correct answer. Then practice the conversation with your partner. Switch roles and practice it again.

> **Emily:** I can't believe it! The airline lost my suitcase.
>
> **Mia:** Oh, no! Have you called the airline (1) _____?
>
> **Emily:** No, not (2) _____. I'll call in a few minutes.
>
> **Mia:** Has this (3) _____ happened to you before?
>
> **Emily:** No, never! I've been lucky, I guess.
>
> **Mia:** Maybe you should use a different airline next time.
>
> **Emily:** It's too late! I've (4) _____ bought my ticket for Istanbul.
>
> **Mia:** Oh, well. I think you'll have a great trip.
>
> **Emily:** Have you (5) _____ been to Istanbul?
>
> **Mia:** No, but I hear it's wonderful.

C | Form a group with another pair of students. Follow the instructions.

1. Choose a person to be the secretary for the group. The secretary will write down your group's ideas. *(See page 211 of the Independent Student Handbook for more information on doing group projects.)*

2. With your group members, make a list of things you think everyone should do in their lifetime. Brainstorm as many things as possible; for example: *go to Paris, learn to play a musical instrument.*

3. Place your list where all the group members can see it. Then take turns asking and answering questions using items from your list and the present perfect tense.

> Have you ever gone to Paris?

> Yes, I have. It's beautiful!

> No, I haven't, but I want to.

D | **Critical Thinking.** Look at the photos. With your group members, draw some conclusions about the people in the photos. Use the present perfect tense.

> He's wearing work clothes, so I think he has just finished work.

> He looks young. I think he has only had the job for a few months.

You are going to give a group presentation about one form of communication. At the end of your presentation, you will invite and answer questions from the audience.

Presentation Skills: Inviting and Answering Questions from the Audience

After you conclude a presentation, there is often time to invite and answer questions from the audience. Here are some ways to invite questions.

Are there any questions?   *I have time for a few questions.*   *Does anyone have a question?*

Sometimes, an audience member might ask about something you've already discussed in your presentation. However, it's important not to say, *"As I said in my presentation . . ."* That could make the audience member feel bad or uncomfortable. Instead, just answer the question clearly.

At other times, an audience member might ask a question that you don't know the answer to. You should not pretend to know the answer. Instead, you can use these expressions.

I'm sorry, that's not something I know about.   *I'll need to find out and get back to you.*
I'm afraid I don't know the answer to that question.   *Perhaps someone in the audience knows?*

A | Form a group with two other students and choose a topic for your presentation from the box below.

books	letters	radio	telephone calls
email	newspapers	social networking sites	television

B | **Planning a Presentation.** Follow the steps.

1. As a group, brainstorm several advantages and disadvantages of the form of communication you chose for your topic. You can use a T-chart like the one below to help you organize your ideas.

Disadvantages	Advantages

2. Discuss the reasons why you do or don't use that form of communication as well as your personal experiences with it.
3. Assign one part of the presentation to each group member: Introduction and advantages; Disadvantages; Summary of personal experiences and conclusion.
4. Practice your presentation.

C | **Presentation.** Give your presentation to the class. At the end of the presentation, invite and answer questions from the audience.

Overview

The *Independent Student Handbook* is a resource that you can use at different points and in different ways during this course. You may want to read the entire handbook at the beginning of the class as an introduction to the skills and strategies you will develop and practice throughout the book. Reading it at the beginning will provide you with another tool to understand the material.

Use the *Independent Student Handbook* throughout the course in the following ways:

Additional Instruction: You can use the *Independent Student Handbook* to provide a little more instruction on a particular skill that you are practicing in the units. In addition to putting all the skills instruction in one place, the *Independent Student Handbook* includes additional suggestions and strategies. For example, if you find you're having trouble following academic lectures, you can refer to the Improving Your Listening Skills section to review signal phrases that help you to understand the speaker's flow of ideas.

Independent Work: You can use the *Independent Student Handbook* to help you when you are working on your own. For example, if you want to improve your vocabulary, you can follow some of the suggestions in the Building Your Vocabulary section.

Source of Specific Tools: A third way to use the *Independent Student Handbook* is as a source of specific tools such as outlines, graphic organizers, and checklists. For example, if you are preparing a presentation, you might want to use the Research Checklist as you research your topic. Then, you might want to complete the Presentation Outline to organize your information. Finally, you might want to use the Presentation Checklist to help you be a more effective speaker.

Table of Contents

Formal Listening Skills

Predicting

Speakers giving formal talks or lectures usually begin by introducing themselves and then introducing their topic. Listen carefully to the introduction of the topic, and try to anticipate what you will hear.

Strategies:

- Use visual information including titles on the board, on slides, or in a PowerPoint presentation.
- Think about what you already know about the topic.
- Ask questions that you think the speaker might answer.
- Listen for specific phrases.

Identifying the Topic:

Today, I'm going to talk about . . .
Our topic today is . . .
Let's look at . . .
Tonight we're talking about...

Understanding the Structure of the Presentation

An organized speaker will use certain expressions to alert you to the important information that will follow. Notice the signal words and phrases that tell you how the presentation is organized and the relationship between the main ideas.

Introduction

A good introduction should include a thesis statement, which identifies the topic and gives an idea of how the lecture or presentation will be organized.

Introduction (Topic + Organization):

I'll be talking about . . .   *My topic is . . .*
There are basically two groups . . .   *There are three reasons . . .*
Several factors contribute to this . . . *There are five steps in this process . . .*

Body

In the body of the lecture, the speaker will usually expand upon the topic presented in the introduction. The speaker will use phrases that tell you the order of events or subtopics and their relationship to each other. For example, the speaker may discuss several examples or reasons.

Following the Flow of Ideas in the Body:

The first/next/final (point) is . . .   *First/next/finally, let's look at . . .*
Another reason is . . .   *However, . . .*
As a result, . . .   *For example, . . .*

Conclusion

In a conclusion, the speaker often summarizes what has already been said and may discuss what it means or make predictions or suggestions. For example, if a speaker is talking about an environmental problem, he or she may end by suggesting what might happen if we don't solve the problem, or he or she might add his or her own opinion. Sometimes speakers ask a question in the conclusion to get the audience to think more about the topic.

Restating/Concluding:

As you can see, . . .
In summary, . . .
At the end, . . .

In conclusion, . . .
To sum up, . . .

Listening for Main Ideas

It's important to tell the difference between a speaker's main ideas and the supporting details. In school, a professor often will test a student's understanding of the main ideas more than of specific details. Often a speaker has one main idea, just like a writer does, and several examples and details that support the main idea.

Strategies:

- Listen for a statement of a main idea at the end of the introduction.
- Listen for rhetorical questions, or questions that the speaker asks, and then for the answers. Often the answer is the statement of the main idea.
- Notice ideas that are repeated or rephrased.

Repetition/Rephrasing:

I'll say this again . . .
What you need to know is . . .
Let me say it in another way . . .

So again, let me repeat . . .
The most important point is . . .

Listening for Details (Examples)

A speaker will often provide examples that support a main idea. A good example can help you understand and remember the main idea better.

Strategies:

- Listen for specific phrases that introduce an example.
- Notice if an example comes after a general statement the speaker has given or is leading into a general statement.
- If there are several examples, decide if they all support the same idea or are different parts of the idea.

Giving Examples:

The first example is . . .
Here's an example of what I mean . . .
For instance, . . .

Let me give you an example . . .
For example, . . .
. . . such as . . .

Listening for Details (Reasons and Results)

Speakers often give reasons or list causes and/or effects to support their ideas.

Strategies:

- Notice nouns that might signal causes/reasons (e.g., *factors, influences, causes, reasons*) or effects/results (e.g., *effects, results, outcomes, consequences*).
- Notice verbs that might signal causes/reasons (e.g., *contribute to, affect, influence, determine, produce, result in*) or effects/results (often these are passive, e.g., *is affected by*).
- Listen for specific phrases that introduce reasons/causes and effects/results.

Giving Causes or Reasons:

The first reason is . . .　　　　　　*This is due to . . .*
This is because . . .　　　　　　　*This is very important because . . .*

Giving Effects or Results:

As a result, . . .　　　　　　　　*One consequence is . . .*
Consequently, . . .　　　　　　　*Therefore, . . .*
Another effect is . . .

Understanding Meaning from Context

Speakers may use words that are new to you, or you may not understand exactly what they've said. In these situations, you can guess at the meaning of a particular word or fill in the gaps of what you've understood by using the context or situation itself.

Strategies:

- Don't panic. You don't always understand every word of what a speaker says in your first language either.
- Use context clues to fill in the blanks. What did you understand just before or just after the missing part? What did the speaker probably say?
- Listen for words and phrases that signal a definition or explanation.

Giving Definitions:

. . . which means . . .　　　　　　*In other words, . . .*
What that means is . . .　　　　　*Another way to say that is . . .*
Or . . .　　　　　　　　　　　　*That is . . .*

Recognizing a Speaker's Bias

Speakers often have an opinion about the topic they are discussing. It's important for you to understand if they are objective or subjective about the topic. Being subjective means having a bias or a strong feeling about something. Objective speakers do not express an opinion.

Strategies:

- Notice words such as adjectives, adverbs, and modals that the speaker uses (e.g., *ideal, horribly, should, shouldn't*).
- Listen to the speaker's voice. Does he or she sound excited, happy, or bored?
- When presenting another point of view on the topic, is that other point of view given much less time and attention by the speaker?
- Listen for words that signal opinions.

Opinions:
I think . . .
In my opinion, . . .
Personally, I . . .

Making Inferences

Sometimes a speaker doesn't state information or opinions directly but instead, suggests them indirectly. When you draw a conclusion about something that is not directly stated, you make an inference. For example, if the speaker says he or she grew up in Spain, you might infer that he or she speaks Spanish. When you make inferences, you may be very sure about your conclusions, or you may be less sure. It's important to use information the speaker states directly to support your inferences.

Strategies:

- Note information that provides support for your inference. For example, you might note that the speaker lived in Spain.
- Note information that does not support your inference. For example, the speaker says she was born in Spain (maybe she speaks Spanish) but moved away when she was two (maybe she doesn't speak Spanish). Which evidence is stronger—the evidence for or against your inference?
- If you're less than certain about your inference, use words to soften your language such as modals, adverbs, and quantifiers.

She probably speaks Spanish, and she may also prefer Spanish food. Many people from Spain are familiar with bullfighting.

Summarizing or Condensing

When taking notes, you should write down only the most important ideas of the lecture. To take good notes quickly:

- Write down only the key words. You don't need complete sentences.

  ~~In~~ Okinawa, ~~people have~~ very low rates ~~of~~ cancer and heart disease compared to Americans. One ~~of the~~ reasons ~~for this is~~ Ikigai, ~~a Japanese word which translates to~~ "reason for living."

- Use abbreviations (short forms) and symbols when possible.

  info = information   dr = doctor   w/ = with   < = less than/= fewer than   > = more than

  b/c = because   /→ = leads to/causes   1/4 = one-fourth

Recognizing Organization

When you listen to a speaker, you practice the skill of noticing that speaker's organization. As you get in the habit of recognizing the organizational structure, you can use it to structure your notes in a similar way. Review the signal words and phrases from the Improving Your Listening Skills section.

Some basic organizational structures (and where they are often used):

- Narrative (often used in history or literature)
- Process (almost any field, but especially in the sciences)
- Cause and Effect (history, psychology, sociology)
- Classification (any field, including art, music, literature, sciences, history)
- Problem and Solution

Using Graphic Organizers

Graphic organizers can be very useful tools if you want to rewrite your notes. Once you've identified the speaker's organizational structure, you can choose the best graphic organizer to show the ideas. See the Resources section starting on page 214 in this handbook for more information.

Distinguishing between Relevant and Irrelevant Information

Remember that not everything a speaker says is important. A lecturer or presenter will usually signal important information you should take notes on.

This is important . . .   *Let me say again . . .*
The one thing you want to remember . . .   *Write this down . . .*

Instructors and other lecturers may also signal when to stop taking notes.

Signals to Stop Taking Notes:

You don't have to write all this down. . . .   *This information is in your book. . . .*
You can find this in your handout. . . .   *This won't be on your test. . . .*

In a similar way, they may let you know when they are going to discuss something off-topic.

Understanding Sidetracks:

That reminds me . . .   *By the way, . . .*
This is off the subject, but . . .   *As an aside, . . .*
On a different topic, . . .

Recognizing a Return to a Previous Topic

When a speaker makes a sidetrack and talks about something that is not directly related to the main topic, he or she will often signal a return to a previous topic.

Returning to a Previous Topic:

So, just to restate . . .
Back to . . .
Getting back to what we were saying . . .
To return to what we were talking about earlier . . .
OK, so to get back on topic . . .
To continue . . .

Using Notes Effectively

It's important to not only take good notes, but to use them in the most effective or helpful way.

Strategies:

- Go over your notes after class to review and to add information you might have forgotten to write down.
- Compare notes with a classmate or study group to make sure you have all the important information.
- Review your notes before the next class so you will understand and remember the new information better.

Independent Vocabulary Learning Tips

Keep a Vocabulary Journal

- If a new word is useful, write it in a special notebook. Also write a short definition (in English if possible) and the sentence or situation where you found the word (its context). Write a sentence that uses the word.
- Carry your vocabulary notebook with you at all times. Review the words whenever you have a free minute.
- Choose vocabulary words that will be useful to you. Some words are rarely used.

Experiment with New Vocabulary

- Think about new vocabulary in different ways. For example, look at all the words in your vocabulary journal, and make a list of only the verbs. Or list the words according to the number of syllables (one-syllable words, two-syllable words, and so on).
- Use new vocabulary to write a poem, a story, or an email message to a friend.
- Use an online dictionary to listen to the pronunciation of new words. If possible, make a list of words that rhyme. Brainstorm words that relate to a single topic that begin with the same sound (*student, study, school, skills, strategies, studious*).

Use New Words As Often As Possible

- You will not know a new vocabulary word after hearing or reading it once. You need to remember the word several times before it enters your long-term memory.
- The way you use an English word—in which situations and with what other words—might be different from a similar word in your first language. If you use your new vocabulary often, you're more likely to discover the correct way to use it.

Use Vocabulary Organizers

- Label pictures.

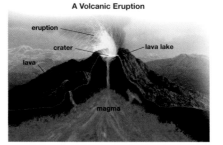

- Make word maps.

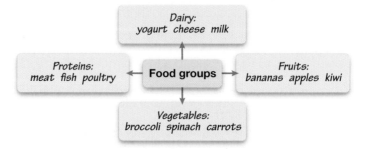

- Make personal flashcards. Write the words you want to learn on one side. Write the definition and/or an example sentence on the other.

Prefixes and Suffixes

Use prefixes and suffixes to guess the meaning of unfamiliar words and to expand your vocabulary. Prefixes usually change the meaning of a word somewhat. Suffixes usually change the part of speech.

Prefix	Meaning	Example
a-	completely	awake
bi-	two	bilingual, bicycle
dis-	not, negation, removal	disappear, disease
pre-	before	preserve, predict
mis-	bad, badly, incorrectly	misunderstand, misjudge
re-	again	research
un-	not, the opposite of	unhappy, unusual

The following are derivational suffixes that change the part of speech of the base word.

Suffix	Part of Speech	Example
-able	adjective	available
-al	adjective	mental, controversial
-ary	noun	summary
-ent/-ant	adjective	different, significant
-ful	adjective	beautiful, successful
-ed	adjective	endangered, interested
-ical	adjective	logical, psychological
-ize	verb	summarize, memorize
-ment	noun	attachment
-tion	noun	information
-ous	adjective	dangerous

Dictionary Skills

The dictionary listing for a word usually provides the following helpful information:

Synonyms
A *synonym* is a word that means the same thing (e.g., *help—assist*). Use synonyms to expand your vocabulary.

Word Families
Word families are the words that have the same stem or base word but have different prefixes or suffixes.

Different Meanings of the Same Word
Many words have several meanings and several parts of speech. The example sentences for a word in a dictionary entry can help you figure out which meaning you need.

Collocations
Dictionary entries often provide *collocations*, or words that are often used with the target word.

Everyday Communication

Summary of Useful Phrases for Everyday Communication

It's important to practice speaking English every day with your teacher, your classmates, and anyone else you can find. This chart lists phrases you can use to perform each communication task—from more formal phrases to less formal.

Getting Clarification:
I'm not sure what you mean.
What did the professor mean by that?
Did you catch what the professor said about that?
Do you mean . . . ?
I don't understand.
Could you say that again . . . ?
What's that . . . ?

Expressing Thanks and Appreciation:
Thank you.
Thank you for . . . (e.g., doing something).
I appreciate it.
I really appreciate your . . . (e.g., help).
Thanks.

Agreeing:
That's true.
Absolutely.
I agree.
Definitely.
Right!

Showing Interest:
Oh, . . . ?
Oh, that's too bad.
Good for you.
Really?

Disagreeing:
I'm afraid I disagree.
That's a good point, but I don't agree.
I see what you mean, but I think that . . .
Are you sure about that?
I don't know . . .
Maybe . . .

Refusing:
Thank you, but (I have other plans/I'm busy tonight/I'd rather not/etc.).
I wish I could, but (I don't have a car/I have a class at that time/etc.).
I'm sorry, I can't.
Maybe some other time.

Inviting:
Would you like to study together this afternoon?
Do you have time before your next class?
Let's go to the art museum on Saturday.
What are you doing now?

Signal Words for the Future:
next (week/month/year)
in a (week/month/year)
after that
eventually

Showing Surprise:
That's unbelievable/incredible.
You're kidding!
Wow!
Really?
Seriously?

Congratulating:
That sounds great!
Congratulations!
I'm so happy for you.
Well done!
Good for you!
Way to go!

Making Suggestions:
I recommend/suggest . . .
Why don't I/you/we . . . ?
Let's . . .

Expressing Sympathy:
Oh, no, I'm sorry to hear that.
That's really too bad.

Making Suggestions (continued): *Maybe you could . . .* *Why don't you . . . ?* *I recommend . . .* *I suggest that you . . .* *Let's . . .*	**Asking for Repetition:** *I'm sorry?* *I didn't catch what you said.* *I'm sorry, I missed that. What did you say?* *Could you repeat that, please?*
Expressing Likes and Dislikes: *I like . . .* *I love . . .* *I can't stand . . .* *I hate . . .*	**Asking Sensitive Questions:** *I hope this isn't too personal, but . . . ?* *Do you mind if I ask . . . ?* *Would you mind telling me . . . ?* *Can I ask . . . ?*
Clarifying: *What I mean is . . .* *Let me explain . . .*	**Interrupting:** *Can/Could/May I stop you for a second?* *Can/Could/May I interrupt?*
Asking for Opinions: *What do you think?* *Do you agree?* *What's your opinion?* *How about you?*	**Giving Opinions:** *I think . . .* *In my opinion . . .* *For/To me . . .* *Personally, I . . .*

Doing Group Projects

You will often have to work with a group on activities and projects. It can be helpful to assign group members certain roles. These roles should change every time you do a new activity. Here is a description of some common roles.

Group Leader—Makes sure the assignment is done correctly and all group members participate. Ask questions: *What do you think? Does anyone have another idea?*

Secretary—Takes notes on the group's ideas (including a plan for sharing the work).

Manager—During the planning and practice phases, the manager makes sure the presentation can be given within the time limit. If possible, practice the presentation from beginning to end, and time it.

Expert—Understands the topic well; asks and answers audience questions after the presentation. Make a list of possible questions ahead of time to be prepared.

Coach—Reminds group members to perform their assigned roles in the group work.

Note that group members have one of these roles in addition to their contribution to the presentation content and delivery.

Classroom Presentation Skills

Library Research

If you can go to a public library or school library, start there. You don't have to read whole books. Parts of books, magazines, newspapers, and even videos are all possible sources of information. A librarian can help you find both print and online sources of information.

Online Research

The Internet is an easy source of a lot of information, but it has to be looked at carefully. Many Web sites are commercial and may have incomplete, inaccurate, or biased information.

Finding Reliable Sources

Strategies:

- Your sources of information need to be reliable. Think about the author and the publisher. Ask yourself, "What is their point of view? Can I trust this information?"

- Your sources need to be well respected. For example, an article from a journal of medical news will probably be more respected than an article from a popular magazine.

- Start with Web sites with *.edu* or *.org* endings. Those are usually educational or non-commercial Web sites. Many *.com* Web sites also have good information, for example www.nationalgeographic.com or www.britannica.com.

Finding Information that is Appropriate for Your Topic

- Look for up-to-date information, especially in fields that change often such as technology or business. For Internet sources, look for recent updates to the Web sites.

- Most of the time, you'll need to find more than one source of information. Find sources that are long enough to contain some good information, but not so long that you won't have time to read them.

- Think about the source's audience. If it's written for computer programmers, for example, you might not be able to understand it. If it's written for university students who need to buy a new computer, it's more likely to be understandable.

Speaking Clearly and Comprehensibly

It's important that your audience actually understands what you are saying for your presentation to be effective.

Strategies:

- Practice your presentation many times in front of at least one other person, and ask him or her for feedback.

- Make sure you know the correct pronunciation of every word—especially the ones you will say more than once. Look them up online, or ask your instructor for the correct pronunciation.

- Try to use thought groups. Keep these words together: long subjects, verbs and objects, clauses, prepositional phrases. Remember to pause slightly at all punctuation and between thought groups.

- Speak loudly enough so that everyone can hear.

- Stop occasionally to ask your audience if they can hear you and follow what you are saying.

Demonstrating Knowledge of Content

You should know more about your topic than you actually say in your presentation. Your audience may have questions, or you may need to explain something in more detail than you planned. Knowing a lot about your topic will allow you to present well and feel more confident.

Strategies:

- Practice, practice, practice.
- Don't read your notes.
- Say more than is on your visuals.
- Tell your audience what the visuals mean.

Phrases to Talk about Visuals:

This graph/diagram shows/explains . . .
The line/box represents . . .
The main point is that . . .
You can see . . .
From this we can see . . .

Engaging the Audience

Presenting is an important skill. If your audience isn't interested in what you have to say, then your message is lost.

Strategies:

- Introduce yourself.
- Make eye contact. Look around at different people in the audience.
- Use good posture. *Posture* means how you hold your body. When you speak in front of the class, you should stand up straight on both feet. Hold your hands together in front of your waist if you aren't holding notes. This shows that you are confident and well prepared.
- Pause to check understanding. When you present ideas, it's important to find out if your audience understands you. Look at the faces of people in the audience. Do they look confused? Use the expressions from the box below to check understanding.

Phrases to Check for Understanding:

Do you know what I mean?
Is that clear?
Does that make sense?
Do you have any questions?
Do you understand?

Understanding and Using Visuals: Graphic Organizers

T-Chart

Purpose: Compare or contrast two things, or list aspects of two things. We often write good things (pros/benefits) on one side and bad things or problems (cons/drawbacks) on the other. This can help people make choices.

Climate Change in Greenland

Benefits (good things)	Drawbacks (bad things)
1. _____	1. _Possible for oil to get into the ocean._
2. _____	2. _____

Venn Diagram

Purpose: Show differences and similarities between two things, sometimes three. The outer sections show differences.

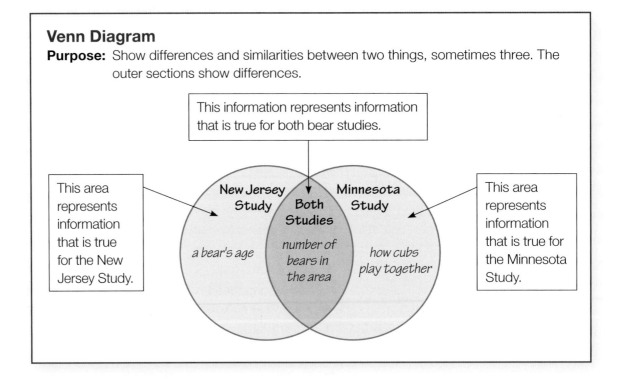

This information represents information that is true for both bear studies.

This area represents information that is true for the New Jersey Study.

This area represents information that is true for the Minnesota Study.

New Jersey Study — *a bear's age*

Both Studies — *number of bears in the area*

Minnesota Study — *how cubs play together*

Grids and Charts

Purpose: Organize information about several things. Grids and charts can show information in different groups, different time periods, different processes, or different qualities.

Noun	Verb	Adjective
exploration	explore	exploratory
	communicate	
	help	
		creative

Spider Map

Purpose: Help organize ideas for a presentation or writing assignment.

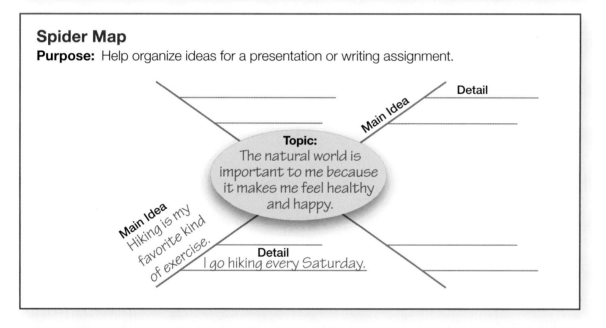

Time line

Purpose: Show the order of events and when they happened in time. Timelines start with the oldest point on the left. Timelines are frequently used to show important events in someone's life or in a larger historical context.

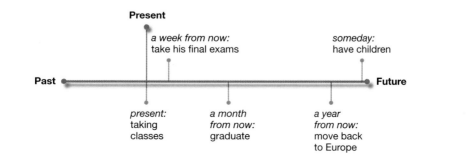

Reading Maps, Graphs, and Diagrams

Maps are used to show geographical information.

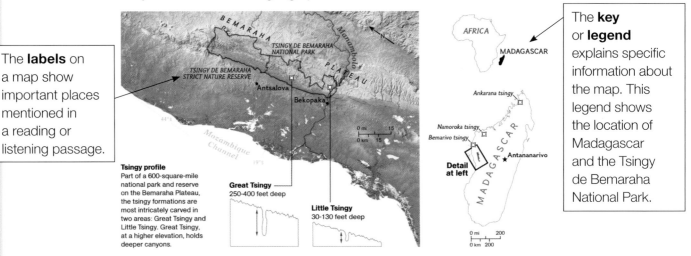

The **labels** on a map show important places mentioned in a reading or listening passage.

Tsingy profile
Part of a 600-square-mile national park and reserve on the Bemaraha Plateau, the tsingy formations are most intricately carved in two areas: Great Tsingy and Little Tsingy. Great Tsingy, at a higher elevation, holds deeper canyons.

Great Tsingy
250-400 feet deep

Little Tsingy
30-130 feet deep

The **key** or **legend** explains specific information about the map. This legend shows the location of Madagascar and the Tsingy de Bemaraha National Park.

Bar and **line graphs** use axes to show the relationship between two or more things.

Bar graphs compare amounts and numbers.

Daily Servings of Fruit

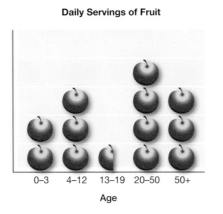

Age: 0–3 4–12 13–19 20–50 50+

Line graphs show a change over time.

The **y axis** shows the amount of sugar people eat in pounds

Sugar Use

Pounds of Sugar — 0, 20, 40, 60, 80, 100, 120, 140, 160
Year — 1950, 1960, 1970, 1980, 1990, 2000

The **x axis** shows the year.

Pie charts show percents of a whole, or something that is made up of several parts.

This section shows that 26 percent of the people in Mexico work more than 48 hours a week.

Mexico

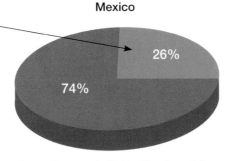

26%

74%

Source: Table 3.4, in *Working Time Around the World* (ILO and Routledge 2007), pp. 46–51.

Diagrams are a helpful way to show how a process or system works.

The earth's atmosphere

Heat

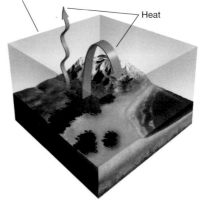

Presentation Outline

When you are planning a presentation, you may find it helpful to use an outline. If it is a group presentation, the outline can provide an easy way to divide the content. For example, someone could do the introduction, another student the first main idea in the body, and so on.

1. **Introduction**

   Topic: _____

   Hook/attention getter: _____

   Thesis statement: _____

   _____

2. **Body**

   First step/example/reason: _____

   Supporting details: _____

   _____

   _____

   Second step/example/reason: _____

   Supporting details: _____

   _____

   _____

   Third step/example/reason:_____

   Supporting details: _____

   _____

   _____

3. **Conclusion**

   Major points to summarize: _____

   _____

   Any implications/suggestions/predictions: _____

   _____

   Closing comment/summary: _____

   _____

Research Checklist

☐ Do I have three to five sources for information in general—and especially for information I'm using without a specific citation?

☐ Am I correctly citing information when it comes from just one or two sources?

☐ Have I noted all sources properly, including page numbers?

☐ When I am not citing a source directly, am I using adequate paraphrasing (a combination of synonyms, different word forms, and/or different grammatical structure)?

☐ Are my sources reliable?

Presentation Checklist

☐ Have I practiced several times?

☐ Did I get feedback from a peer?

☐ Have I timed the presentation?

☐ Do I introduce myself?

☐ Do I maintain eye contact?

☐ Do I explain my visuals?

☐ Do I pause sometimes and check for understanding?

☐ Do I use correct pronunciation?

☐ Am I using appropriate volume so that everyone can hear?

☐ Do I have good posture?

Pair and Group Work Checklist

☐ Do I make eye contact with others?

☐ Do I pay attention when someone else is talking?

☐ Do I make encouraging sounds or comments?

☐ Do I ask for clarification when I don't understand something?

☐ Do I check for understanding?

☐ Do I clarify what I mean?

☐ Do I express agreement and disagreement politely?

☐ Do I make suggestions when helpful?

☐ Do I participate as much as my classmates?

☐ Do I ask my classmates for their ideas?

Summary of Signal Phrases

Identifying the Topic:
Today, I'm going to talk about . . .
Our topic today is . . .
Let's look at . . .
Tonight we are going to talk about . . .

Introduction (Topic + Organization):
I'll be talking about . . .
My topic is . . .
There are basically two groups . . .
There are three reasons . . .
Several factors contribute to this . . .
There are five steps in this process . . .

Following the Flow of Ideas:
The first/next/final (point) is . . .
Another reason is . . .
However, . . .
As a result, . . .
For example, . . .

Restating/Concluding:
As you can see, . . .
In conclusion, . . .
In summary, . . .
To sum up, . . .

Repetition/Rephrasing:
I'll say this again . . .
So again, let me repeat . . .
What you need to know is . . .
The most important thing to know is . . .
Let me say it in another way . . .

Giving Examples:
The first example is . . .
Let me give you an example . . .
Here's an example of what I mean . . .

Giving Causes or Reasons:
The first reason is . . .
This is due to . . .
This is because . . .

Giving Effects or Results:
As a result, . . .
One consequence is . . .
Consequently, . . .
Therefore, . . .
Another effect is . . .

Giving Definitions:
. . . which means . . .
In other words, . . .
What that means is . . .
Another way to say that is . . .
Or . . .
That is . . .

Opinions:
I think . . .
In my opinion, . . .
Personally, I . . .
If you ask me . . .
I feel . . .

Signal to Stop Taking Notes:
You don't have to write all this down . . .
This information is in your book . . .
You can find this in your handout . . .
This won't be on your test . . .

Returning to a Previous Topic:
So, just to restate . . .
Back to . . .
Getting back to what we were saying . . .
*To return to what we were talking about
    earlier . . .*
OK, so to get back on topic . . .
To continue . . .

Understanding Sidetracks:
That reminds me . . .
By the way . . .
This is off the subject, but . . .
As an aside . . .
On a different topic . . .

Phrases to Check for Understanding:
Do you know what I mean?
Is that clear?
Does that make sense?
Do you have any questions?
Do you understand?

VOCABULARY INDEX

*These words are on the Academic Word List (AWL). The AWL is a list of the 570 highest-frequency academic word families that regularly appear in academic texts. The AWL was compiled by researcher Averil Coxhead based on her analysis of a 3.5 million word corpus (Coxhead, 2000).

Critical Thinking

analyzing information, 1, 2–3, 15, 18, 21, 22–23, 33, 35, 41, 42–43, 61, 62–63, 67, 72, 73, 75, 76, 81, 82–83, 87, 92, 101, 102–103, 107, 113, 121, 122–123, 133, 141, 142–143, 153, 161, 162–163, 170, 173, 181, 182–183, 192, 193

applying prior knowledge, 12, 32, 56, 66, 76, 86, 116, 125, 172

assessing conversations, 97

brainstorming and, 40, 100, 120, 159, 180, 200

checking predictions, 27, 113, 127

considering pros and cons, 139

describing foods, 99

determining interesting information, 91, 100, 175

distinguishing between main ideas and details, 99

distinguishing between relevant and irrelevant information, 207

drawing conclusions, 197, 199

evaluating alternatives, 2–3, 10, 11, 13, 107, 110, 120, 132, 140

evaluating content, 129

evaluating schedules, 127

evaluating the importance of the past, 47

explaining content, 124

explaining facts, 150

explaining ideas and opinions, 2, 87, 113, 118, 121, 129, 137, 141, 161, 165, 173, 177, 181, 187

explaining plans, 117

explaining processes, 118

explaining reasons, 11, 13, 61, 110, 156

expressing ideas and opinions, 11, 37, 69, 90, 93, 95, 113, 114, 118, 129, 133, 141, 147, 150, 153, 156, 170, 178, 179, 187

forming judgments, 165

identifying main ideas, 6–7

identifying opinions, 167

identifying what makes us laugh, 26, 27

making comparisons, 166, 169–170, 171, 178–179

making inferences, 7, 47, 57, 127, 187, 205

making lists, 71

meaning from context, 4, 14, 24, 34, 44, 54, 64, 74, 84, 94, 124, 134, 152, 164, 165, 174, 184, 194, 204

ordering items on a timeline, 189

organizing ideas for a presentation, 60

organizing notes for a presentation
chart for, 20

predicting content, 6, 36, 52, 113, 126, 161

ranking items, 97, 120, 187

recalling facts, 59

recognizing return to previous topic, 207

recognizing speaker's bias, 205

reflecting on content, 6–7

self-reflection, 7, 17, 25, 31, 60, 65, 77, 85, 87, 97, 112, 131, 160, 165, 166, 171

speculation, 149–150

summarizing, 206

supporting an argument, 160

understanding graphic/visual organizers
charts, 4, 20, 31, 91, 95, 152, 153, 173, 215
diagrams, 80, 216
grids, 215
maps, 2–3, 32, 46, 54, 79, 216
spider map, 180, 215
T-charts, 92, 200, 214
timelines, 51, 131, 189, 215
Venn diagrams, 170, 214

understanding speaker's purpose, 26, 156

using context clues, 106, 107

using new vocabulary, 5, 15, 25, 35, 45, 55, 65, 75, 85, 95, 105, 115, 125, 135, 145, 155, 165, 175, 185, 195

using notes effectively, 207

Grammar

a, an, any and *some,* 78

adverbs of frequency, 18–19

can and *can't,* 89

comparative and superlative forms of adjectives, 168–169

comparisons with *as. . . as,* 178–179

coordinating conjunctions, 108

count and noncount nouns, 69–70

descriptive adjectives, 98–99

prefixes and suffixes, 209

verbs
modals of necessity, 158
modals of possibility and probability, 148
past tense signal words, 58
present continuous and simple present forms, 138
present perfect tense, 188–189
present perfect tense with ev*er, already,* and *yet,* 198–199
simple past tense, 48
simple present vs. present continuous, 9–10
time relationships in simple present tense, 119
Wh- questions in simple past tense, 51
Wh- questions in simple present tense, 38–39
will and *be going to,* 128
yes/no questions in simple past tense, 50
yes/no questions in simple present tense, 29

Language Function. *See also* Grammar; Pronunciation; Speaking

adverbs of frequency, 19

agreeing, 109, 210

asking for opinions, 130, 211

PHOTOS (continued)

74: Janina Dierks/Shutterstock.com, 74: NASA Goddard Space Flight Center (NASA-GSFC), 74: Rita Januskeviciute/Shutterstock.com, 74: Peter Essick/ National Geographic Image Collection, 76: Peter Essick/ National Geographic Image Collection, 77: Peter Essick/ National Geographic Image Collection, 78: ilker canikligil/ iStockphoto.com, 78: cstar55/iStockphoto.com, 80: acilo/ iStockphoto.com, 81: Manoocher/National Geographic Image Collection, 82: Nicole Duplaix/National Geographic Image Collection, 82: Eye Ubiquitous/Glowimages.com, 82: Elena Elisseeva/Shutterstock.com, 82: Gordon Wiltsie/ National Geographic Image Collection, 82: Don Tran/ Shutterstock.com, 82: David Doubilet/National Geographic Image Collection, 82-83: George Steinmetz/ National Geographic Image Collection, 84: Mark Doherty/ Shutterstock.com, 84: Muellek Josef/Shutterstock.com, 84: whethervain/iStockphoto.com, 85: Mark Thiessen/ National Geographic Image Collection, 86: Chico Sanchez/Alamy, 86: Aaron Huey/National Geographic Image Collection, 87: Jakub Pavlinec/Shutterstock.com, 89: Lisa F. Young/Shutterstock.com, 90: Joel Sartore/ National Geographic Image Collection, 91: Gina Martin/ National Geographic Image Collection, 91: phloen/ Shutterstock.com, 91: Maria Dryfhout/Shutterstock.com, 91: Elena Elisseeva/iStockphoto.com, 91: Nataliya_ Ostapenko/Shutterstock.com, 92: Michael Durham/ Minden Pictures, 93: Neil McAllister/Alamy, 93: Michael Durham/Minden Pictures, 94: 4kodiak/iStockphoto.com, 94: Stephen Harrison/Alamy, 94: elena moiseeva/ Shutterstock.com, 95: Catherine Karnow /National Geographic Image Collection, 95: Stephen Alvarez/ National Geographic Image Collection, 96: Stephen Alvarez/National Geographic Image Collection, 97: John Giustina/Riser/Getty Images, 98: RoJo Images,2010/ Shutterstock.com, 98: Christopher Paquette/Istockphoto. com, 98: Justin Guariglia/National Geographic Image Collection, 98: Nayashkova Olga/Shutterstock.com, 100: 54613/Shutterstock.com, 100: Luiz Rocha/ Shutterstock.com, 100: Jordan Tan/Shutterstock.com, 101: Photoshot Photoshot/PhotoLibrary, 102: Raymond Gehman/National Geographic Image Collection, 102: Jason Edwards/National Geographic Image Collection, 102: GJS/Shutterstock.com, 102: Scott S. Warren/ National Geographic Image Collection, 102-103: Alexander Heilner, 104: Chris Hill/National Geographic Image Collection, 104: Chris Hill/National Geographic Image Collection, 104: Chris Hill/National Geographic Image Collection, 105: Kochey, Ken/National Geographic Image Collection, 105: Tino Soriano/National Geographic Image Collection, 107: Rob Melnychuk/Jupiter Images, 107: r.nagy/Shutterstock.com, 108: Vlue/Shutterstock .com, 110: Jason Edwards/National Geographic Image Collection, 110: Pattie Steib/Shutterstock.com, 110: Breadmaker/Shutterstock.com, 111: EdBockStock/ Shutterstock.com, 112: Kordcom Kordcom/Age fotostock/ PhotoLibrary, 112: Hemis/Alamy, 113: Arne Hodalic/ CORBIS, 114: George Steinmetz/National Geographic Image Collection, 114: Skip Brown/National Geographic Image Collection, 115: Ralph Lee Hopkins/National Geographic Image Collection, 116: Steven Stanek, 117: Taylor S. Kennedy/National Geographic Image Collection, 118: gillmar/Shutterstock.com, 118: Phil

Schermeister/National Geographic Image Collection, 118: Jason Edwards/National Geographic Image Collection, 118: Associated Press, 119: Camera Lucida/ Alamy, 120: Bridwell/PhotoEdit, 121: NASA/National Geographic Image Collection, 122: SOVFOTO/National Geographic Image Collection, 122: NASA/National Geographic Image Collection, 122: Pictorial Press Ltd/ Alamy, 122-123: Gianfranco Casano/National Geographic Image Collection, 124: Crippen, Robert L. & Young, John W./National Geographic Image Collection, 124: NASA/ ESA/National Geographic Image Collection, 125: Pierre Mion/National Geographic Image Collection, 126: Greg Dale/National Geographic Image Collection, 127: James A. Sugar/National Geographic Image Collection, 129: Kangah/iStockphoto.com, 129: Morrell, Stephen/ National Geographic Image Collection, 130: NASA/ National Geographic Image Collection, 130: NASA/ National Geographic Image Collection, 131: Justin Horrocks/iStockphoto.com, 132: NASA/JPL/Space Science Institute/National Geographic Image Collection, 132: Ludek Pesek/National Geographic Image Collection, 133: NG MAPS/National Geographic Image Collection, 134: Robert Madden/National Geographic Image Collection, 134: Art Resource, 134: Joe Mcnally/National Geographic Image Collection, 136: George Steinmetz/ National Geographic Image Collection, 136: Yerkes Observatory/National Geographic Image Collection, 137: Wolfgang Kloehr/Shutterstock.com 138: Xfrans Lanting/National Geographic Image Collection, 139: Diane Cook and Len Jenshel/National Geographic Image Collection, 140: Ken Freeman/Shutterstock.com 140: Attila Jandi/Shutterstock.com, 140: John Gaffen/ Alamy, 141: Kathrine Lloyd/National Geographic Image Collection, 142-143: George Steinmetz/National Geographic Image Collection, 143: Joel Sartore/National Geographic Image Collection, 143: Kenneth Garrett/ National Geographic Image Collection, 143: Michael Nichols/National Geographic Image Collection, 144: © 2011 Jason deCaires Taylor/ARS, NY/DACS, London, 145: Tim Laman/National Geographic Image Collection, 146: Sisse Brimberg/National Geographic Image Collection, 146: O. Louis Mazzatenta/National Geographic Image Collection, 147: Brent Stirton/Getty Images, 147: Brent Stirton/Getty Images, 147: Gustavo Cuevas/ EPA/Newscom, 148: Original painting by Tao the elephant available at Novica.com, 149: STR/AFP/Getty Images/ Newscom, 150: Bruce Hall Photography, 150: Solent News/Splash News/Newscom, 150: Tom Dulat/UPPA/ Photoshot/Newscom, 151: Frans Lanting/National Geographic Image Collection, 151: Jim Brandenburg/ National Geographic Image Collection, 151: Frans Lanting/ National Geographic Image Collection, 152: Scott S. Warren/National Geographic Image Collection, 153: Chris Hill/National Geographic Image Collection, 153: SuperStock/Getty Images, 154: Tino Soriano/ National Geographic Image Collection, 154: Emory Kristof/ National Geographic Image Collection, 154: Jodi Cobb/ National Geographic Image Collection, 155: Jodi Cobb/ National Geographic Image Collection, 156: AP Photo/ Ronen Zilberman, 159: Justin Guariglia/National Geographic Image Collection, 159: Raul Touzon/National Geographic Image Collection, 161: Frans Lanting/National Geographic Image Collection, 162: Paul Nicklen /National

Geographic Image Collection, 162: Randy Olson/National Geographic Image Collection, 162: Frans Lanting/National Geographic Image Collection, 162-163: Joe Scherschel// National Geographic Image Collection, 164: brittak/ istockphoto.com, 164: Alison Wright/National Geographic Image Collection, 165: Sam DCruz/Shutterstock.com, 166: Bill Curtsinger/National Geographic Image Collection, 166: Gordon Wiltsie/National Geographic Image Collection, 169: New Jersey Division of Fish and Wildlife, 169: North American Bear Center, 170: North American Bear Center, 171: Michael & Jennifer Lewis/National Geographic Image Collection, 171: Jarno Gonzalez Zarraonandia/Shutterstock.com, 171: javarman/ Shutterstock.com, 172: Melissa Farlow/National Geographic Image Collection, 172: Raul Touzon/National Geographic Image Collection, 174: Gerry Ellis/ Minden Pictures, 174: Michael Nichols/National Geographic Image Collection, 175: Michael Nichols/National Geographic Image Collection, 176: Willis D. Vaughn/National Geographic Image Collection, 176: Beverly Joubert/ National Geographic Image Collection, 176: Beverly Joubert/National Geographic Image Collection, 178: Hallam Creations/Shutterstock.com, 178: Frans Lanting/National Geographic Image Collection, 179: Karine Aigner Photography, 179: Karine Aigner Photography, 181: James P. Blair/National Geographic Image Collection, 182: Peter Essick/National Geographic Image Collection, 182-183: George Steinmetz/National Geographic Image Collection, 183: Tania Zbrodko/ Shutterstock.com, 183: Pete Ryan/National Geographic Image Collection, 183: Steve Winter/National Geographic Image Collection, 184: Joel Sartore/National Geographic Image Collection, 185: zhangyang13576997233/ Shutterstock.com, 185: Bruce Dale/National Geographic Image Collection, 185: Steve Raymer/National Geographic Image Collection, 185: Bedford, James/National Geographic Image Collection, 186: Joe Petersburger/ National Geographic Image Collection, 187: Ken Banks, 189: Elena Ray/Shutterstock.com, 189: Thomas J. Abercrombie/National Geographic Image Collection, 189: Yuri Arcurs/Shutterstock.com, 189: Joel Sartore/ National Geographic Image Collection, 190: Justin Guariglia/National Geographic Image Collection, 191: Brad Killerhttp//killerb10/iStockphoto.com, 192: Richard Nowitz/National Geographic Image Collection, 192: Noreen Grice, You Can Do Astronomy LLC www.youcandoastronomy.com, 193: Noreen Grice, You Can Do Astronomy LLC www.youcandoastronomy .com, 194: Sean Mcnaughton/National Geographic Image Collection, 195: Raul Touzon/National Geographic Image Collection, 196: MikLav/Shutterstock.com, 196: Joel Sartore/National Geographic Image Collection, 197: Peter Essick/National Geographic Image Collection, 198: Scott Hortop/Alamy, 199: James L. Stanfield/National Geographic Image Collection, 199: stefanolunardi/ Shutterstock.com, 199: Joel Sartore/National Geographic Image Collection

MAP AND ILLUSTRATION

2-3: National Geographic Maps; 32: National Geographic Maps, 32: National Geographic Maps; 45: National Geographic Maps; 46: National Geographic Maps; 52: National Geographic Maps; 54: Fernando G. Baptista/ National Geographic Magazine; 75: National Geographic Magazine Maps; 79: Sean McNaughton/National

Geographic Magazine; 92: National Geographic Maps; 115: National Geographic Maps; 116: National Geographic Maps; 164: National Geographic Maps, 164: National Geographic Maps; 165: National Geographic Maps, 208: Bob Kayganich/illustrationonline; 216: National Geographic Maps